DISCARDED

Mediums, Puppets, and the Human Actor in the Theatres of the East

Frontispiece shows Kongô Hisanori, the *iemoto* ('head') of the Kongô School, as the 'Angel' or 'Heavenly Maiden' in the Noh play *Hagoromo* ('Feather Robe'). This performance took place on 8th November 1998 in a Noh Theatre built over a famous hot spring in the city of Matsuyama on the island of Shikoku. Note the strong feather motif on the robe.

MEDIUMS, PUPPETS, AND THE HUMAN ACTOR IN THE THEATRES OF THE EAST

Poh Sim Plowright

Mellen Studies in Puppetry
Volume 4

The Edwin Mellen Press
Lewiston•Queenston•Lampeter

Library of Congress Cataloging-in-Publication Data

Plowright, Poh Sim.
　　Mediums, puppets, and the human actor in the theatres of the East / Poh Sim Plowright.
　　　p. cm. -- (Mellen studies puppetry ; v. 4)
　　Includes bibliographical references and index.
　　ISBN 0-7734-7057-3
　　1. Puppet theater--Asia. 2. Nårå (Dance) I. Title. II. Series.

PN1978.A75 P56 2002
791.5'3'095--dc21

2002025062

```
This is volume 4 in the continuing series
Mellen Studies in Puppetry
Volume 4 ISBN 0-7734-7057-3
MSP Series ISBN 0-7734-8552-X
```

A CIP catalog record for this book is available from the British Library

Front cover photo shows one of the twenty-four birdwomen that support the roof of the Great Buddha Hall, Kai Yuan Temple, Quanzhou. Note the scholar's writing brush.
Photo courtesy of the author.
Back cover photograph of author by Simon Hay
Courtesy of Royal Holloway, University of London

Copyright © 2002 Poh Sim Plowright

All rights reserved. For information contact

　　　　The Edwin Mellen Press　　　The Edwin Mellen Press
　　　　　　　Box 450　　　　　　　　　　　Box 67
　　　　Lewiston, New York　　　　　Queenston, Ontario
　　　　USA 14092-0450　　　　　　　CANADA L0S 1L0

　　　　　　The Edwin Mellen Press, Ltd.
　　　　　　Lampeter, Ceredigion, Wales
　　　　　　UNITED KINGDOM SA48 8LT

Printed in the United States of America

*To Piers, Natasha, Francesca
and Matthew Han Yu with love*

CONTENTS

List of Illustrations   xi
Acknowledgements   xiii
Foreword by Professor C. Andrew Gerstle   xv

Introduction   1

Chapter One
The Art of Manora – An Ancient Tale of Feminine Power   9
Preserved in South-East Asian Theatre
Story and History 10, The Tale and the Occult 11, The Two Princesses 11, Magic and Power 13, Dance and Kingship 16, Two Historical 'Birdwoman' Figures 17, Female Power in South-East Asia 18, The Indirectness of Female Control 19, A Visit to a *Bomoh* 22, *Manora* in Thailand 24, *Manora* Performance: Ritual in Action 26, The Lotus as Symbol 28, Money, Sex and Ritual, 29, Hunting and Cleansing, 31, The Japanese Connection 32, 'Holder of the Strings' 33, *At the Hawk's Well* 35, Notes and References 38

Chapter Two
The Birdwoman and the Puppet King – A Study of   43
Inversion in Chinese Theatre
The Image of the Bird and the Theatre 44, Puppets, Jokes and Exorcism 47, Puppet and Human Theatre in Quanzhou 49, The King 51, The Continuity of Tradition 53, Enter Bertolt Brecht: A Western Misunderstanding 55, The Paradoxes of Chinese Theatre 57, Back to the 'Birdwoman' 58, Notes and References 60

Chapter Three
Puppet Dominance in Chinese Thought and the Art of   63
T'ai Chi Ch'uan
Emperor Qin Shi Huangdi and his Puppet Obsession 63, 'The Thread from Heaven': Control and the Transmission of Power 64, Jean Lévi's *The Chinese Emperor* 65, Puppets and Healing: The Merging of the Medium/Healer, Puppet and Scapegoat 66, The Exorcistic Power of The Dancing Puppet and *T'ai Chi Ch'uan* 69, The Dancing Puppet and Primal Energy 72, *Wu-Hsing*: The Five Elements Theory 73, The Synchronisation of Marshal Tian with Two Key Symbols in Chinese Thought 75, Trigrams and String Images 76, Marionette Movement and Embryonic Behaviour 79, The Power of *T'ai Chi Ch'uan* 79, Notes and References 82

Chapter Four
In Search of Lady Jôruri 85
Lady Jôruri – A Japanese Heroine? 87, The Tale 88, The Yahagi
Connection 91, A 'Map of Life' 92, The Prostitute Element 98,
A Contemporary Account of the Puppeteer's Life 100, The Impact
of Buddhism 105, The Origins of the Story 108, Sex and Healing 110,
Pleasure Houses and their Power 112, The Art of Love and the Context
of Sacrifice 114, The Impact of Confucianism and the Chinese Concept
of Sacrifice 118, The Kabuki and the Puppet World 119, Forgotten
Women 121, Lady Jôruri and the Diaries 124, Female Sacrifice, Puppets
and Society 126, The Puppet Theatre, Healing and Shamanism 129,
The Puppet Theatre, Control and Exorcism 133, Awaji Island, Puppets
and the Art of Survival 138, *Jôruri Ningyô* and its Debt to Lady Jôruri 141,
Notes and References 146

Chapter Five
The Image of the String Puppet, its Indian Origin and 161
Relevance to Zen Buddhism, Noh Drama and Chinese Theatre
Rajasthan and the Indus Valley Civilisation 162, Puppet Culture
as fostered by the Dravidians and Babylonians 163, Puppets in
Ancient Egypt, Babylonia and the Indus Valley Civilisation 163,
Shiva, Parvati and Puppets 164, *Tandava*: Shiva's Dance and
Exorcism 166, String Puppets and the Measuring String: Connections
and Influences 167, Puppets, *Puttalika* or 'Little Son' 170,
The Role of the *Sutradhara* ('Holder of the Strings') 170, The String
Puppet and Zen Buddhism 171, The Unconscious and the 'True Heart' 172,
'Ego-lessness', the Marionette and Swordsmanship 174,
'An Art Tied to the Heart by Strings' 176, 'Move the Heart Ten;
Move the Body Seven' 178, The Theory of *Riken* ('Detached Eye')
and Shiva's 'Third Eye' 179, 'The Feelings of One's Heart
Show in One's Face' 179, Inner Directives for Tuning the Spirit:
'In Shinra the Sun Shines at Midnight' 180, The Secret Strings 181,
Swordsmanship and Noh Acting 183, Zeami and Zen Buddhism 184,
Zeami and Rinzai Zen 185, Kanze Hisao and the String Puppet Image 187,
The Noh Mask and Movement 188, The String Puppet and Chinese
Theatre 191, Puppets and Mortuary Figures 192, Puppets and Early
Chinese Folk Religion 193, Quanzhou and the String Puppet 194,
'Pear Garden Theatre' Movements, Marshal Tian and String Puppets 197,
Notes and References 200

Chapter Six
Western Attitudes to Puppets – Their Allies and Adversaries 207
The Origin of the Term 'Marionette' 208, Savonarola and 'The Burning of the Vanities' 211, Moving Statues and the 'Boxley Rood of Grace' 212, Puppets and their Secular Popularity 215, The Battle of the Puppets 216, Puppets and their Advocates 217, Puppets, the Longing for a Lost Paradise and Heinrich Von Kleist 218, Edward Gordon Craig and the 'Über Marionette' 222, William Butler Yeats and Marionettes 224, Etienne Decroux and his use of the Marionette Image 225, Decroux, Zeami, the Principle of Opposition and the Marionette 226, Notes and References 229

Postscript 233

Bibliography 237

Index 245

List of Illustrations

1. Two female dancers dressed to resemble the mythical bird (*nok isi*) at a *Manora* rehearsal in the Thai village of Plaiyuan.

2. The 'Angel', played by Kongô Hisanori, in a ceremonial costume change on stage (*monogi*) during a performance of the Noh play *Hagoromo*. Matsuyama, Shikoku, Japan, 1998.

3. A performance of Hanji Chikamatsu's Bunraku puppet play *Keisei Awa no Naruto*, Fukura, Awaji Island, Japan, 2000.

4. The puppet god, Xianggong or Marshal Tian, dancing on the *T'ai Chi* symbol and 8 trigrams as part of a rite of exorcism in Singapore, 1999.

5. The same puppet god performing a postlude to a 5 day performance of *Mu Lien Saves His Mother*. Quanzhou, 1994.

6. One of the twenty-four angels at the top of the East Pagoda, Yakushiji Temple, Nara.

7. A puppet-based folk art performance of Kirijô's Noh play *Rashômon*. Nôgô village, Hida prefecture, 13th April 2000.

8. One of the most famous memorial sites in homage to Lady Jôruri in Yahagi.

9. Puppet cases in the National Museum of Ethnology, Osaka.

10. Hsieh Yong Chien demonstrating string-puppet derived movements in Quanzhou, 1994.

11. Map of the Memorial Sites in Yahagi and Okazaki to Lady Jôruri. Courtesy of the estate of Ishida Mosaku.

12. Diagram of *T'ai Chi* symbol and Eight Trigrams (Chapter 3, p. 70).

[Unless otherwise stated, all the photos have been taken by the author.]

Acknowledgements

It is with gratitude that I record the names of individuals and institutions that have made my research abroad possible, particularly, Professor Piet van der Loon, Emeritus Professor of Chinese at Oxford University, whose book *The Theatre and Art Song of South Fukien* paved the way for my particular line of research. Shi Jian Dong of the Cultural section of the Chinese Embassy in London opened many doors to me in Quanzhou, Fujian Province, where the scholar Wu Jie Chiu was generous in sharing his knowledge with me. He and his wife were also immensely hospitable to me during my stay there and Master Puppeteer Huang Yi-que, Wang Jing Xian, Chief of the Quanzhou Puppet troupe, together with puppeteers Xia Rong Feng, Shen Su Ge and Meng Su Ping, tirelessly answered my questions and took me back to the Fukienese community my grandfather left behind at the beginning of the 20th century. Hsieh Yong Chien and Li Lei Bin, both *Li Yuan Xi* ('Pear Garden Theatre') teachers, were also invaluable to my research as were the many individuals who showed me kindness and acted as guides and friends in Quanzhou. I felt as though I had 'come home'.

My research in North Malaysia and Southern Thailand also constituted a homecoming in that some of my work was done at the Department of Drama in the University of Penang, Malaysia, where I received great support from its head – Dr Ismail Abdullah – through whose contacts I was able to live for a while in Kelantan. Dr Surapone Virulak of Chulalongkorn University, Bangkok, was immensely helpful to my research in Nakhon Sri Thammarat, and provided me with two excellent guides, Teerawat Changsan and Suwimon Pathiyut, without whom I would not have been able to visit remote villages to observe performances of *Manora*.

For my Japanese research I'm particularly grateful to Professor Drew Gerstle of SOAS, London, who set me on the right track and to my host in Osaka – Professor Fujita Minoru of Kansai University – who arranged 'Visiting Scholar' status for me, enabling me to make full use of the excellent University Library. I'm also indebted to Takahashi Miho, a postgraduate of the same university who gave me invaluable translation help and to a former postgraduate of mine, Yamase Chiaki, who drew attention to, and translated, the writings of Kanze Hisao. I also received crucial help from Professor Iwasaki Soji, Professor Shingyo Norikazu and from Professor Ike Minoru, who personally took me to the pilgrimage sites set up in homage to Lady Jôruri in Yahagi and Okazaki, Aichi prefecture. I owe an enormous debt of gratitude to Urano Tamiko, former Chief Administrator of the National Museum of Ethnology, who arranged my accommodation and took me to meet the priests of various temples in Nara and Kyoto and to Dr Sasahara Ryoji, of the same museum and an expert in folklore, who pointed me in the direction of folk performances taking place during my stay in Osaka. On Awaji Island, I received much help from Mitsuyo Matsuyama of the Awaji Puppet Theatre and from its director, Masaru Umazume.

I am of course extremely grateful to Royal Holloway, University of London, for allowing me three sabbaticals in which to gather and write up the material for this book, as well as a travel grant, and to the British Academy and the Japan Society for the Promotion of Science for their generous financial assistance. I am also grateful to Simon Trussler and Clive Barker, the Editors of *New Theatre Quarterly*, Cambridge University Press, for permission to reprint two articles originally written for their periodical as chapters in this book.

Last but by no means least, I'm grateful to Ann Ormesher for typing the bibliography, my son, Matthew Han Yu, for his unstinting technical assistance, and to my husband, Piers, without whose support in so many ways, I would not have been able to complete this book.

A Note on Eastern names and spelling: Eastern names have generally been written with surnames first, in accordance with Eastern convention. It has been almost impossible to regularise the romanisation of Chinese words because of the two different systems of transcription. For example, *Xianggong* is sometimes represented as Hsiang Kung, according to sources.

Foreword

Most people have at some time in their lives experienced a magical moment of live theatre, that epiphany-like flash, when we lose ourselves into a communal fantasy and are moved individually by the spiritual power of the moment. Such encounters may be in modern, secular, commercial theatres, or more rarely today in the West, at a festival or religious occasion. Poh Sim Plowright has offered us insights into the role and underlying power of theatre from two distinctive perspectives. The first is that of the vast area of eastern Asia from the Indian/Thai/Malay folk traditions through China and finally to Japan. The second is through a focus on the important role of women – both as protagonist and as medium. Two images from Asian theatre tie the various parts of the book together: the 'puppet' and the 'birdwoman', as both metaphor and medium. Through a journey across time and space, Plowright shows us how central these two images have been in many different Asian societies, and how these images have been received in the West from early in the twentieth century. She analyses the representation of woman as both caring and willing to sacrifice herself for others, but also as being the source of an awesome and mysterious power of creation, a spiritual and sexual force that gives her access as a medium to other worlds. The book is an excellent resource for anyone interested in the portrayal of female spiritual power.

Plowright, through her many years of research into Asian theatre, and her hands-on experience of the living traditions, argues persuasively for the centrality of the puppet (and mask) as the medium between communities and the higher (or lower) spiritual worlds. She further makes a case for the puppet as the most important inspiration for the actor's art. She shows also how theatre was and is integral to community life and how it reflects the most important elements of male/female and family power relations, as well as the community's relationship to spiritual realms and powers. Her work reaffirms how deep is the human instinctual need to use the stage to reach out and touch the spiritual world, even in the face of governments who try to suppress theatre in their domains.

Professor C. Andrew Gerstle
School of Oriental and African Studies
University of London

Introduction

> *Grace appears most purely in that human form which either has no consciousness or an infinite consciousness. That is, in the puppet or in the god.*
> Heinrich von Kleist, 'On the Marionette Theatre', 1810.

In 1994 I went to Quanzhou in the Fujian Province of China to research the connection between the movements of human actors and string puppets, something that had long interested me. My grandfather came from the vicinity of Quanzhou at the beginning of the 20th century so, in a sense, I was on a double quest, one to do with scholarship, the other with family roots. While exploring, I wandered into the huge Buddhist Kai Yuan Temple in the fast disappearing old quarter of the town and, looking up, saw for the first time, the twenty-four carved birdwomen that, interlocked with a complex system of brackets, support the ceiling of the Grand Buddha Hall (see cover photograph). I was immediately fascinated by these striking female figures – so much so that I seemed, for some days, in danger of forgetting the central purpose of my research.

Who were these birdwomen? Why were some of them carrying the traditional four treasures of the scholar (brush, paper, ink and inkstand) and why were they occupying such a prominent position in a temple that housed the oldest altar in China? The priest told me some of what I wanted to know: they were the Buddha's attendants and their job was to play music and sprinkle flowers whenever he preached the sûtras. Later I discovered that they had been made the official emblem of all cultural activity in Quanzhou, but nobody seemed to know any more about them, or if they did, they weren't telling. I was convinced that they were more than decorative designs and that their meaning was more complex than that given by the priest. So I began to dig deeper into the symbolism of these particular birdwomen, exploring the wider meaning of their function which I was later able to relate to other Birdwoman figures in Asia – for example the twenty-four dancing birdwomen that fly from the roof of the East Pagoda of the Yakushiji

(Healing Buddha Temple) in Nara, Japan (see Plate 3) – and, most importantly, uncovering the crucial link for my research and this book.

The Greek root for the word 'symbol' is *symbalein* meaning 'to put together corresponding pieces of an object for the purposes of identification'. In this deep sense the symbolism common to all the birdwomen I have researched in China, Japan, Malaysia and Thailand is one of control and negotiation. All the stories about them involve semi-divine women made captive and forced to strike a hard bargain with their captors to achieve their freedom and almost invariably the birdwomen themselves are connected with warriors and military exploits – an interesting link with the Valkyries in Teutonic mythology. In its most common form the birdwoman tale is of an immortal who loses her wings or feather robe while bathing in a pool to a warrior/husband who imprisons her and with whom she has children. In devising a strategy for freedom and the recovery of her 'wings' she symbolizes a far wider exchange between humans and the spirit world and, in a reversal of roles, sheds light on arduous human struggles to placate and come to terms with the supernatural. Bargaining with higher powers to achieve favours or blessings, as the American anthropologist, Weston La Barre, has pointed out, begins in early childhood and the Birdwoman myth is a powerful expression of this exchange, in which power shifts from captor to captive through sacrifice and exorcism. It is a kind of fight for freedom between two powers, one supernatural and one human, perhaps most perfectly expressed outside the Far East by the Genesis account (Chapter 32, v.26) of Jacob's struggle with the Angel: *I will not let thee go unless thou bless me,* a text powerfully illustrated by Jacob Epstein's great carving (in the Tate Britain, London). And we find exactly this sense of struggle in one of the most frequently performed Japanese Noh plays, *Hagoromo.* In this play, a fisherman holds 'the Angel' to ransom by taking possession of her Feather Robe without which she cannot return to Heaven. A similar tension can be found in the *Manora* (Birdwoman) plays of Thailand and Malaysia which I saw performed on another field trip in 1997, plays which celebrate the ancient magical powers of women and relate the telling of the tale to the needs of local communities, while in the Chinese version of the story, known as *Tien Kun Lun*, a text of which can now be seen in Tokyo's Museum of Calligraphy, we are once again presented with negotiation between captor and captive. Such negotiations usually end in the Birdwoman's escape from a web of 'politics', either at court or at home, at a time when her husband is called away, though in many cases the pair are reunited either on her terms or his. Whatever the terms, such Birdwomen symbolize, like the strikingly carved examples in the Kai Yuan Temple, the power of women to endure, to support, and ultimately to transcend, the societies that imprison them.

China, where I began my research, has no known play directly based on the story of the Birdwoman, as there is in Nakhon Sri Thammarat in Southern Thailand which I will come to shortly, but there are two figures, one fictional, one historical, who represent connections with the story. In the fiction, which takes the form of a well-known Chinese play *Liang Shan Po and Chu Ying Tai*, the heroine (Chu Ying Tai), wanting to sacrifice herself for her dead lover, walks into his grave which miraculously opens, allowing them both to emerge transformed into birds who fly away. The historical figure is the celebrated Yang Kuei Fei, beloved consort of the 8th century Emperor Tang Ming Huang (Xuan Zhong) and referred to by the poet Li Po as the most beautiful trapped 'swallow' in the Emperor's harem. Before he 'entraps' her, the emperor spies on her while she is bathing, just like the hunter figure in the Birdwoman story itself or the Japanese warrior Yoshitsune, peering through the fence at Lady Jôruri, another semi-mythical birdwoman figure and archetypal medium, whose story includes a magical flight to save her dying lover and who provides the material for a key chapter in this book. Yang Kuei Fei, like Lady Jôruri, is forced to sacrifice her life for the supposed good of the nation in the context of war – a sacrifice demanded by Ming Huang's angry soldiers – and the Emperor is so grieved that he sends a magician to contact her spirit on *Peng Lai Shan* (Peng Lai Mountain). The Japanese have placed this mountain at Hôraiji in Aichi Province – another connection with Lady Jôruri who is supposed to have been 'immaculately' conceived there – and the story of the journey to appease Yang Kuei Fei's spirit has been turned into a Noh play, *Yohiki*. Birdwoman imagery, it would seem, with implications of sacrifice and transformation, is deeply embedded in the Chinese subconscious, a context which Bertolt Brecht, in his celebrated analysis of Chinese acting (see Chapter 2) managed to miss.

I said that the Birdwoman, who first looked like a distraction, became the crucial link for my research into the relationship between puppet and human movement in Eastern theatre. This relationship is made particularly clear in the subject of my second chapter, 'The Birdwoman and the Puppet King,' and here again Emperor Tang Ming Huang plays a part. It was this Emperor who founded the famous 'Pear Garden Theatre', probably China's earliest theatre school and one which ran alongside, and drew inspiration from, another type of dramatic presentation, also founded by Emperor Ming Huang, the Imperial Court's puppet theatre. To this court, the story goes, was summoned a young musical prodigy from the town of Quanzhou called Tian. He could play so beautifully on the flute that he was immediately made Chief Imperial Scholar, leader of the 'Pear Garden' actors, and chief string puppeteer. Later he became known as 'Marshal Tian' and a puppet made in his likeness became the theatre's principal puppet. There is some dispute over the historicity of all this which I deal with at length later but what is important here is the connection between the Emperor, his 'lost' concubine and the marionette theatre he championed. It is said that Yang Kuei Fei was strangled by the Emperor's rebellious soldiers with her own silk scarf and left hanging from a tree, like a string puppet dangling from its cross-bar: birdwoman, sacrifice and puppet coalescing into a single image – and here it is interesting to note that there is etymological support for this connection since, in some parts of Fujian province, the word *ang* is used for female mediums (birdwomen are sometimes referred to as female mediums), puppets and sacrifice. When Yang Kuei Fei's grief-stricken lover shortly after abdicated in favour of one of his sons he described himself in a famous poem as another string puppet, deprived of his will by grief and age, his plight seeming reflective of the human condition itself.

The story of Yang Kuei Fei's sacrifice and death was given dramatic expression in the 17th century by playwright Hung Sheng in his play *The Palace of Eternal Youth* in which the Imperial Concubine is portrayed performing the famous 'Dance of the Feather Robe' for the Emperor's pleasure before her death at the hands of his guards. The same dance occurs at the climax of the two Noh plays mentioned above: Zeami Motokiyo's *Hagoromo* or 'The Feather Robe' (a direct adaptation of the stereotypical Birdwoman story) and *Yokihi* (the Japanese name for Yang Kuei Fei). In the latter version, the heroine, like the trapped Angel in *Hagoromo*, performs a 'Feather Robe' dance, in this case for the magician sent by the Emperor, after instructing him to remind her lover of their mutual promise: *in Heaven we shall become birds flying ever wing to wing*. The connection with the Birdwoman story is made.

If female sacrifice is one of the key elements in this widespread tale, another is the idea of intercession and exorcism which was powerfully demonstrated to me as a spectator of *Manora* (Birdwoman Plays) in Nakon Sri Thammarat, Southern Thailand (see Chapter 1). Here was a celebration of feminine magical power which goes back to the ancient South-East Asian practice of a victorious ruler carrying home the wives and dancers of his defeated rivals as booty. Since most of the members of these royal harems were mediums, they were seen as valuable additions to a ruler's aura of divinity and, consequently, to his terrestrial power. The *Manora* form itself is said to have been founded by two royal female trance mediums, regarded as guardians of a life-renewing elixir, so that each performance is seen as a shamanistic and healing ritual while the movements of the dancers who perform this ritual are unmistakably puppet-like and stem, according to local opinion, from the exorcistic nature of the Thai puppet theatre. The close connection between these two forms of theatre even extends to the use of materials since the wood of the yaw tree which normally protects a puppet stage is also used to make the mask of the hunter who follows and 'nooses' the birdwoman in *Manora* performances.

I also connect the theme of the Birdwoman in *Manora* with that in the Noh play *Hagoromo*, and with that of W.B.Yeats's Birdwoman play *At the Hawk's Well* which features a 'Hawk Woman' guarding a well of miraculous water against male intrusion. The Irish poet, who had been closely involved with female medium séances just before writing this Noh-based play, specifically instructed his actors to move like marionettes, and so in a sense unconsciously echoes the theme of this book by joining female mediums to puppets. Yeats was one of several Western theatrical thinkers, culminating in the maverick but brilliant Edward Gordon Craig, who thought that the marionette represented the highest ideal of acting, and thus allied themselves with the great co-founder of the Japanese Noh Theatre, Zeami Motokiyo, and with Chikamatsu Monzaemon, the leading writer for the world's most sophisticated puppet theatre, *Bunraku*, formerly known as *Ningyô Jôruri*. And here we come to the subject of my fourth chapter, who gave her name to this form of theatre and whom I've briefly mentioned: Lady Jôruri. In the research I carried out in Japan in 2000, I was able to confirm the importance of this legendary woman for the people of Yahagi who claim her as a historical figure of great spiritual and moral importance for their community. Historical or not, she represents, like many of the heroines of Noh drama, the tensions between a repressive, male dominated, samurai society and the ego-less and sacrificial role expected of women – puppets if you like – in a brutal and ruthlessly controlled world. No wonder the form of *Bunraku* (*Ningyô Jôruri*) and the highly stylized movements of the puppets in the hands of their masked operators are so constricted (see Plate 3). And no wonder that Lady Jôruri, who sacrifices herself for her hunter/lover and who has connections both with Buddhist sainthood and the world of the courtesan, is one of the most compelling of Eastern 'Birdwomen'.

The training required for a *Bunraku* puppeteer, particularly the one controlling the head and right arm of the puppet – three puppeteers are needed to control a main character – is extremely rigorous as is the discipline required for most Eastern theatrical systems, whether it is Noh, Kabuki, Kathakali, or Balinese

Legong, a discipline that in effect turns the trainees themselves into puppets. The puppet image is also a philosophical concept implying the dependence of humans on a higher power and the image of the string puppet a further refinement of this concept. I have devoted a chapter to this last subject and considered its origin and relevance to Zen Buddhism, Noh Drama and Chinese Theatre, detailing the importance of the string puppet not only in relation to the Birdwoman but also to the art and strategy of controlling movement itself and to the business of negotiating with the supernatural. In this connection, India provides a potent symbol in the God Shiva who is seen as God of the Dance and all Cosmic movement as well as God of Puppets, so that puppet movements are identified with life itself and puppet drama seen as a crucial part of the process of communication with other worlds and powers. In the same context I examine the use in Hindu mythology of the *soota* or 'measuring string' and the important use of the string puppet image in a seminal treatise of Zeami Motokiyo. There are no such treatises on Chinese acting but there is no doubt, as I was able to see for myself in Quanzhou, that it is the example of the ancient string puppet theatre of Southern China that inspires and informs the movements of human actors and I argue in my chapter on 'Puppet Dominance in Chinese Thought and the Art of *T'ai Chi Ch'uan*', itself based on a puppet-like set of movements, that the figure of Marshal Tian, at once patron and puppet, is crucial to the healing and exorcistic powers of the puppet theatre in Fujian province and in other parts of South-East Asia where there is a large Fukienese community.

As a coda to the book, I have included a chapter on the largely ambiguous Western attitudes to the puppet from earliest classical times, through the Christian Church's love/hate affair with the form, to the enthusiasms of later champions like Von Kleist, Craig, Yeats, Shaw and Decroux. Heinrich Von Kleist is particularly interesting in that he saw the ego-less nature of the puppet as something 'paradisal' or, in Zen terms, something that touches the Unconscious — a state crucial for generating pure effective movement in performance. What perhaps links East and West where puppets are concerned is the concept of tension, between good and evil, control and freedom, idealization and sacrifice, sacred and profane, yin and yang. Always there is a pull of opposites, quite literally in the case of 'marionettes' – the word *marionette* itself being ambiguous, perhaps implying a connection with the Virgin, perhaps with the Fool – and always there is a power struggle. In this struggle, the image of the Birdwoman continually returns, a figure at once heroine and victim, goddess and prostitute, intercessor and captive, free to fly but always in danger of entrapment. Those twenty-four flying Angels in the Kai Yuan Temple encapsulate all these tensions, just as their wooden forms and their proximity to an ancient string puppet tradition remind us of the continuing importance of this theatrical genre and its power to change us.

Chapter One: The Art of Manora – an ancient tale of feminine power preserved in South-East Asian Theatre

A hunter sees a beautiful birdwoman bathing in a forest pool; he steals her feather robe and captures her with a noose. The captive is taken by the hunter to his master – a prince – who forces her to be his bride and later to bear his children. While her husband is away on an expedition, she becomes hopelessly enmeshed in a web of court intrigue that threatens her with imminent death. However, she is sufficiently resourceful to recover her stolen feather robe on the pretext of performing a pre-sacrificial dance and this enables her to make her flight to freedom.

Still sung or recited by Japanese fishermen, Swedish hunters, and North American Indians, the story of the 'birdwoman' continues to cast a world-wide spell, and though it cannot be traced to a single source, there is one place in which this tale of female magic and resourcefulness is still performed as a vital theatrical ritual to large and enthralled, participating audiences. This is the province of Nakhon Sri Thammarat – in Pali Sanskrit, *Nagara Sri Dhammaraja* or 'The City of the Sacred Dharma King' – in South Thailand. Situated on the old Malay Buddhist site of *Ligor*, which in the fourteenth century became part of Thailand (known then as Siam), it once shared with the ancient capital *Ayuthaya* the distinction of being one of the two most powerful cities in South-East Asia. Until fairly recently, the North Malaysian states of Kedah, Penang, and Kelantan also celebrated the birdwoman story through theatrical performances. But the increasing Islamic antipathy towards theatre [1] has led to an almost total prohibition of performances in Kelantan and only infrequent ones in Kedah and Penang. The mainly Buddhist Nakhon Sri Thammarat is therefore the one place where the power of this story remains undiminished and its theatrical expression officially sanctioned. Here, the heroine of the story, *Manora* (from the Sanskrit *Manohara*) has given her name (abbreviated to 'Nora'), to the seminal theatrical genre of South Thailand.[2] In the original and most famous version of the story, *Manora* is the captive bride of Prince *Suthon* (from the Sanskrit *Sudhana*) but there are altogether twelve distinct narratives in this theatrical form, which employ a mixture of song, dance, clowning and satire in many variations of the principal story, outlined above, sometimes omitting it altogether. This is both a testimony to its deep familiarity in the consciousness of Thai audiences, and a recognition that its original base needs to be continually widened and modernized to include other tales from Thai literature as well as current popular stories.

Story and History

One of the problems confronting anybody researching the *Manora* theatrical art is that there is far more anecdote than hard evidence concerning its historical origin, function, relevance, organization, and preservation. Responses to direct questions are invariably oblique, and, though always entertaining, cannot be taken as factual and the problem of documenting *Manora* data is further compounded by the fact that those who are steeped in its tradition – 'The Keeper of the Sacred Crown', for instance – either genuinely cannot dissect it or dare not for fear of breaking its magic spell. In the realm of female trance mediumship in which this theatrical art is sited, fiction and inventiveness are paramount: the female medium in a seance, fulfilling her function as story-teller, magician, and healer, is at her most authoritative, commanding the highest respect from the community through her fictive persona; before she became a medium, she was usually an ailing individual, of little consequence in the village. So narrative assumes disproportionate significance – at least as far as Western scholars are concerned – in this society, replacing reverence for demonstrable data, with the transforming power of the story. By this token, the strange story of the *Manora* heroine and her capture by a prince can also (as will be shown later) be read as the history of a South-East Asian power struggle which was dominated by the seizure of royal trance-medium wives as booty.

The Tale and the Occult

There is a further dimension to this rare form of drama, one that exerts a strange power over local people and brings it into the world of magic – the term '*Nora magic*' even being used to describe it. In Southern Thailand, for example, there is an expression *mi ta sua nora*, which describes a person who has fallen under the charm of *nora*, as well as various superstitions like that of *thuk khru*, which suggests succumbing to the curse of a *Nora* leader. The use of these terms points to the existence of an almost indefinable power, with its roots both in the origin of the universally known 'birdwoman' tale and in the peculiar history, organization, and continuation of the *Manora* theatrical genre, which make it undoubtedly one of the world's most potent and occult dramatic forms.

In Northern Malaysia (which was part of Thailand until the beginning of the twentieth century) the *Manora* form is inextricably linked with magic of a general nature, and specifically with 'female' magic. This connection is reinforced by the fact that the Malay word for 'magical power' – *empu* – is itself incorporated in the common term for the female: *perempuan*. There is no doubt that from an etymological viewpoint, even in a strongly Islamic country where women ostensibly take a secondary place and where the *Manora* art is now officially banned, the 'female' is associated with 'magical power'.

The Two Princesses

If we examine the stories concerning the two legendary founders of the *Manora* theatrical form – the Thai princess *Nuensamli* and the Malay princess *Mesi Mala* – there is a strong link between these two royal females as spirit mediums and practitioners of the art of healing.[3] Their journey from ill health to spirit possession and finally to the role of 'healer' is the archetypal induction of neophyte to shamaness. The Thai princess *Nuensamli* was possessed by a god which led to her insanity and exile. A son was born to her who was taught the art of dance by mythical birdwomen called *kinnari*, a clown was magically created from a rock, and a god became a mortal to play the third character in the genre.

This formula of using three male roles played by actors (the last one 'masked' to undertake more than one part), originated from the *Manora* theatrical art form and has dominated Thai drama as well as later masked theatrical genres in South-East Asia.[4] In the Malay 'Kedah' version, the princess *Mesi Mala*[5] contracted a strange illness as a result of spirit possession which led to an obsession with drumming on a coconut shell – the use of a drum[6] being another characteristic feature of the induction of a shamaness, since the drum is the instrument most conducive to trance possession. A group of children followed her in this strange occupation, and they were exiled to an island called Pulau Kecang where they were joined by a clown[7] figure, *Phran Bun,* who first appeared as an Indian bead-seller. He returned to India and brought back from the Buddha to the princess the famous 'crown' – a major element in a *Manora* performance. The princess's return and intervention through dance produced the healing which saved her nation from an epidemic, turned the founder into a source of healing, and began the *Manora* theatrical art form.

It is believed that in a performance the spirit of *Mesi Mala* enters the body of a female dancer in trance and reinforces the healing power of this theatrical genre so deeply rooted in female trance mediumship. From both the literal and figurative perspective, there is perhaps no clearer connection between the rites of female trance mediumship and theatre than those manifested in *Manora:* invocations at the beginning and end of the performance to the original female medium founder, whose presence is visibly attested to by the altered state of the trancer she chooses to enter, serve as a strong framework within which the various stages of the drama unfold. Incense, food, and song-offerings merge with dance and trance-inducing drum-beats to constitute elements at once theatrical and ritualistic. Such is the magical aura surrounding *Manora* in Southern Thailand that non-ritual performances hardly take place.

It is important to realize that the two legendary founders of the *Manora* theatrical art – one Thai, the other Malay and Thai – are more culturally unified than the detail of their separate stories suggests. Nakhon Sri Thammarat (formerly known as *Ligor*), where the *Manora* theatrical genre still thrives, was once part of the old Malay kingdom comprising the countries of Malaya, Siam, and Indonesia, and I will be using two Malay stories drawn from the *Hikayat* (ancient personal histories written for Malay kings to immortalize their kingship) to illuminate the meaning of *Nora* power.

Magic and Power

There is an unmistakable element of magic associated with the organization and continuation of *Manora* theatrical troupes. *Nora* actors will testify that if they have a relative who has been closely connected with this art, their involvement with it is sealed, and *Nora* leaders have the reputation of being able to draw crowds who will obsessively follow their performances from one venue to another. In short, a *Nora* leader not only enjoys supreme authority over his or her actors, but manages to hold them to their vocation. In their own village, leaders are regarded as both doctors and magicians (the unofficial term in Thai for a doctor is *maw*, which also means 'magician'), and the *Nora* leader radiates extraordinary magnetism: physical attractiveness and sexuality seem inseparable from *Nora* magic.

Though *Nora* or 'birdwoman' theatre, combining elements of magic, enchantment, superstition, sexuality, and most importantly healing, is essentially of female derivation, whether we are thinking of the universal 'birdwoman' myth or of its theatrical form, power can be transmitted through the male. The word *Nora* can serve as a title followed by the name of the leader (for example, the currently famous *Nora* Yok, born in 1922, who has been performing *Manora* for over fifty years), and the leader can be either male or female, but must be gifted – like the redoubtable Manee Burinkoat – with charisma, sexuality, and powers of exorcism and healing. A male leader is usually reputed to have seductive power over female spectators, with whom he frequently has affairs, and in the legendary competition for attracting audiences between two former celebrated *Manora* troupe leaders, Nora Wan and Nora Toem (the latter having died in 1970), the defeated rival, Nora Wan, was forced to forfeit wives and daughters to the winner[8] – just as in the ancient South-East Asian power struggle between Siam and Cambodia, which resulted in the sack of Angkor by the Siamese in 1431, many royal Cambodian wives-dancers were forfeited to the Siamese ruler and carried off to Siam as part of the victor's booty. Apart from being spoils of warfare, royal wives-dancers were prized as valuable spirit mediums through whom the victorious king was able to enhance his own magical powers. Underpinning these practices is the ancient Hindu concept of the ruler as a god-king drawing on female chthonic powers of fertility and magic – a belief so strongly adhered to that it had the weight of dogma in the old Malay world of Indonesia, Siam, and Malaya.

The earliest genealogies of the Melaka[9] kings in Malaya have been traced back to the Hindu Chola invaders of India in the eleventh century. Thus, the first known King of Melaka, Raja Iskanda Shah, claiming ancestry from the first Chola ruler of India, established a court system characteristic of Hindu kingdoms in India, and the system by which a ruler was symbolically upheld by characteristics of divinity was eventually adopted by other kings in the Malay Peninsula.[10] Every attempt was made to reinforce the ruler's special access to and protection by supernatural powers, since his subjects were determined to see him as someone specially endowed with magical powers, the king being regarded as the supreme medium through whom his subjects could get in touch with the invisible world. The ubiquitous belief in the power of unseen spirits to influence human affairs brought into prominence the crucial role of female dance trance mediums who had been co-opted into a ruler's harem precisely because of their ability to communicate with spirits and so enhance his magicality. There is no doubt that the capture of the 'birdwoman' (a semi-divine creature) to be the bride of the prince in the classical 'birdwoman' tale was part and parcel of the ancient practice of members of the aristocracy linking themselves to spiritually empowered women whose divinity they could share.[11] Far from being a spectacular detail, the theft of the birdwoman's feather robe and her capture with a noose (a kind of bottled magic) served as a crucial political stratagem to ensure the future ruler's authority over his people – hence the prince's pursuit of his missing wife when she was forced to fly away in the course of the narrative: the future ruler's authority was dependent on, if not equivalent to, the magicality symbolized by his 'birdwoman' spouse.

The central role of the birdwoman's dance in the story, once she regains her feather robe, elevates her performance to a level closer to shamanistic ecstasy than entertainment. It is her ambivalence, simultaneously as super-heroine and shamaness, fictitious and non-fictitious, that gives her a unique strength and attraction, since the dividing line between a real-life seance (which is intrinsically dramatic) and the miraculous narrative world of gods, spirits, and semi-divine flying heroines into which the medium transports his or her audience, is virtually non-existent. Not every shamaness is necessarily a heroine, or vice versa, but the 'birdwoman' heroine and the shamaness share common attributes, including the feather robe and magical flight.[12] Moreover, the 'narrative' passage of the flight of the birdwoman from the corrupt world of political intrigue into that of the supernatural could easily have been borrowed from an 'actual' seance in which the shaman, as story-teller and healer, charts his or her journey from one realm into another. The fact that the original narrators of this tale were reputedly women[13] has led to the story being regarded as a piece of propaganda for women's rights. But the ambience surrounding this tale goes far beyond that of politics, and even to call it an allegory about male usurpation of the female's control of her body and reproductive function is an over-simplified reading: both the story and its theatrical genre are entrenched in magic in a way that defies categorization. So scholarly suggestions that the magical flight of the birdwoman back to her own home illustrates the mating and reproductive patterns of certain migratory birds,[14] or that the circumstances prompting her escape reflect the cruel dilemma of social disorientation suffered by a foreign wife[15] surrounded by her husband's hostile relatives, or that the birdwoman story is simply a *jataka* tale[16] concerning the previous life of Buddha, undervalue its complexity. According to this last interpretation, the Buddha was supposed to have cited this tale as an illustration of how, even in the past, his wife was won only after great effort.[17] Despite the popularity of this theory, the origin of the Southern Thai *Manora* remains obscure and there is little evidence linking it to Indian sources.[18] It is more likely that the origin of this archaic and universally known story is identifiable with the deepest need of the human psyche to explain the mystery and magic of the female in a way that transcends propaganda, allegory, social history, and the polemics of gender. Indeed it is precisely because the tale is so genuinely perplexing, defying all normal conventions and divisions of time, place, culture, narrator and narration, subject and object, that the androgynous world of the medium, where all such boundaries dissolve, provides the story of the 'birdwoman' with its most plausible setting. Hence the close connection between the strongly mediumistic puppet theatre of Southern Thailand – *Nang Talung* – and *Manora:* both belong to the irrational zone of magic where, in the process of communicating with spirits, the dividing line between human and puppet theatres, puppeteers and puppets, trance mediums and the spirits they are invoking, disappears.

Dance and Kingship

As a corollary to the mediumistic implications underlying the dance of the birdwoman, it is important to emphasize the role of dance in the old Malay Hindu kingdom as an intrinsic part of the ritual worship of the god Shiva, widely regarded as the Cosmic Dancer and the King of Actors.[19] So, apart from being visually pleasing and entertaining, these court dances, provided by the sovereign's medium wives, ritually and symbolically aligned him with Shiva and not only reinforced his position as ruler over his people but, most importantly, underscored his invincibility, divinity, and protection by the invisible world.

Kingships in the Malay Peninsula did not begin with the Melaka dynasty established in the fifteenth century, but this period so abounds in records concerning the extraordinary role played by women in controlling and balancing spheres of political dominance at court that it is worth scrutinizing just two examples of these women to see what light they shed on the prevalent 'birdwoman' story so central to the old Malay culture: Tun Kudu and her grand-daughter Tun Fatimah,[20] both referred to by historians as *Seri Kandi* – a class of warrior heroines with extraordinary qualities of leadership similar to those of *Seri Kandi*, the legendary wife of *Arjuna* in the fourth century Hindu epic *Mahabharata* (as also to the Valkyries,[21] the 'birdwoman' warrior figures of Teutonic mythology).

Two Historical 'Birdwoman' Figures

Tun Kudu entered the fierce political arena of the Melaka court in 1446, when Raja Kassim, a half-Tamil prince, murdered his half-brother, ascended the throne, and took her as his wife despite her prior engagement to a warrior. She was a daughter of the House of *Bendahara,* an immensely powerful family who thus provided the 'stranger king' with a much-needed local wife to legitimize his kingship. Though not of royal blood, the *Bendahara* was the King's chief minister and would lead the army in the event of a war. No sooner had Tun Kudu become royal consort than she became the centre of court intrigue: her father was murdered by the king's evil uncle, Tun Ali, who not only assumed the role of the new *Bendahara* but insisted on having the beautiful Tun Kudu as his wife. Realizing the full extent of Tun Ali's ruthlessness and his power to destroy her beloved Melaka, she yielded to his demands. For that she is referred to in the *Hikayat* as *Bungah Bangsa* ('Flower of the People') as well as *Tibang Negara* ('Pillar of the Country').

Tun Fatimah, the grand-daughter of Tun Kudu, was another charismatic figure who dominated the political scene just before the fall of Melaka to the Portuguese in 1511. Like her grandmother, she belonged to the house of *Bendahara*, but she also enjoyed the reputation of being a skilful warrior; and in 1509, disguised as a male warrior, she participated in a battle to drive out the first group of Portuguese traders from the port of Melaka. Sultan Mahmud, the last ruler of Melaka who died in 1530, ordered the complete liquidation of the house of *Bendahara*, with the exception of Tun Fatimah whom he forced to be his wife. In 1511 when the Portuguese returned with Alfonso D'Albuquerque, the Sultan was forced to flee to Kampar in Sumatra. In contrast to her husband, who was weak, scandalous, and incompetent, Tun Fatimah is extolled in the *Hikayat* as a high-spirited warrior whose courage and sacrifice in defending Melaka against her adversaries earned her the title *Semangat Melaka* ('Spirit of Melaka'). Through her children she later extended her power to other parts of the Malay Peninsula. Her remarkable skill as a warrior was both a physical and spiritual asset, distinguishing her as a spiritually empowered female of a high order.

In this connection, a point often glossed over in the West is that there is a spiritual dimension in the East to the deployment of martial arts – which are perceived not only as a means of fighting real enemies but also as a way of opposing the host of invisible spirits inimical to humans. In Chinese theatre, which is also strongly directed at appeasing evil spirits, the flags which a general wears on his shoulders in a similar way represent divisions of both actual and celestial armies engaged in combat against terrestrial and metaphysical enemies. The connection between the staging of Chinese theatre and trance mediumship is very strong, and the fact that martial arts form the basis of Chinese theatre makes them doubly potent against evil spirits, just as *silat* (the Malay term for martial arts) underlies most forms of Malay theatre, and so turns it into an effective offensive against the invisible world.

Female Power In South-East Asia

It is true that there is a difficulty in defining female power in a region like South-East Asia. On the surface, male supremacy is taken for granted, within the larger historical context of ancient male-imposed practices such as chastity belts,[22] footbinding,[23] and vagina tightening – this last still current. Indeed these restrictions on the female were so fearsome – tantamount to mutilations in some instances – that there is an argument for regarding them as male counter-offensives against the presence of a deeply felt and feared female force.[24]

It is certainly true that the real centre of power in the King's court in the old Malay kingdom lay with women like Tun Kudu and Tun Fatimah, the arch-mediators of political influence, deliberately preserving the balance of power between the 'House of *Bendahara*' (the wife-giver) and the King (the wife-receiver). For this reason, a certain magical force, not unmixed with sexuality, became associated with the 'female', outwardly tractable and compliant but inwardly the focus of control and decision-making. There is a Malay proverb which reflects this 'female' characteristic: 'Follow the way of the *padi* stalk; the more it fills, the more it bends.'

The Indirectness of Female Control

It is interesting in this connection that in a country like Malaysia, in which Islamic laws seem to give advantage to the male on issues concerning divorce, inheritance, and the formulation of public policies, at grass roots level, in *kampongs* (or villages), it is *adat* – an Arabic term covering a wide spectrum of age-old customs, proverbs, and mores – which, expressed obliquely if not figuratively, effectively controls and shapes the flow of everyday life in a village and, by extension, the nation. Such is the compelling force of the rule of *adat*, which lies at the heart of Malay life, that there is a saying, *Biar mati anak, jangan mati adat,* meaning 'Better a child die than *adat* perish.' So just as the House of *Bendahara* (the wife-giver to the King) assumed a superior role to that of the sovereign through the mediating agency of the queen (bearer of future kings), and so enforced the power of 'woman' at court, similarly *adat,* obliquely and relying on an inextricable network of animism, magic, and superstition (elements inimical to Islam), found a way of incorporating and circumventing an indomitable religion to assert its own brand of poetic truth. The following verse, guided by *adat* and ritually recalled during marriage and other ceremonial events, reveals subtle but strong female control in a supposedly male-oriented country:

When we receive a man as bridegroom
If he is strong, he should be our champion.
If a fool, he will be ordered about
To invite guests distant and collect guests near;
Clever and we'll invite his counsel;
Learned and we'll ask his prayers,
Rich and we'll use his gold;
If lame, he shall rear chicken,
If blind, he shall pound the mortar,
If deaf, he shall fire the salutes,
When you enter a byre, low;
When you enter a goat's pen, bleat,
When you tread the soil of a country and
live beneath its sky,
Follow the customs of that country.[25]

It may be surprising to many to learn that the majority of divorce cases registered in the *Pejabat Agama Islam*, the 'Religious Department' in Kelantan and Trengganu states, are initiated by women. Polygamous marriages are only common among the wealthy urban or elite rural Malays. And the only divorces which do not invite derision are those which take place when the wife is barren and the husband yearns to have children – but if a menopausal wife is put aside so that her husband can marry another, he is likely to be censured by the community. Women also exercise a certain degree of prerogative in divorce issues and resort to numerous informal procedures to procure a divorce should the husband prove reluctant. According to the writer Wazir Jahan Karim, Islamic divorce laws are not as discriminatory against the female as imagined,[26] and in everyday *kampong* life women assert their power through sexual prowess – the strong implication being that, as with female magic, female sexuality is more potent than its male counterpart. A typical Malay proverb expresses the derivative nature of male power: '*The strength of man lies in woman.*' However, because such a high premium is placed on female sexuality (or more precisely the ways in which it can be deployed), Karim devotes space in her book to enumerating the measures undertaken by women to maintain their sexual prowess. For example, after childbirth, when vaginal muscles tend to slacken or be damaged, many women apparently resort to traditional tonics and herbs (*jamu* and *majun*), which are believed to have the effect of shrinking the uterus, and stomach and tightening the vagina.[27] Within the time-tested scale of village priorities, the wife's ability to resume active sex with her husband takes precedence even over the care of her new offspring. So, not surprisingly, according to Karim, a woman's ability to participate actively in sex is regarded as a far more vital asset than a good complexion or an alluring figure. Hence the idiomatic Malay expression for wife as well as husband is *lawan* – meaning, literally, 'a sparring partner'. This helps to bring into focus the unusual emphasis on active female participation in marital sexual relationships in the context of South-East Asian social and domestic mores, customs, and expectations – in other cultures a characteristic often associated rather with a mistress than a wife. And – ironically in such an outwardly modest society – 'wifely' virtues elsewhere upheld, like decorum and thrift, are pointedly excluded. Indeed, if the wife is particularly adept at love-making, she is not simply known as a *lawan*, but a *melawan*, or 'super *lawan*'. The fact that such an emphatic differentiation exists, and has been transmitted into everyday language, attests to the very real power of women in old and new Malay society.

At first glance it might be difficult to see the heavily-robed women in an Islamic stronghold such as Kota Bharu in Kelantan as the real power-houses of the nation, but as I was able to determine for myself during my visit to North Malaysia in 1997, it is the women who control their husband's pay packets, as well as highly lucrative cottage industries like weaving the intricate fabrics for which Kelantan is renowned.

A Visit to a *Bomoh*

The 'adatization' of Islam, manifested for example, in the inclusion of Qu'ranic verses in animistic charms and spells,[28] has meant that despite the official ban on all ritualistic theatrical performances, which are often indistinguishable from the propitiation of spirits and acts of exorcism, they have been in a sense legitimized, yet still take place on an unofficial basis.

The ambiguous official attitude towards these performances was clearly revealed when I was planning my field trip to North Malaysia in April 1997 to observe *Nora* performances and healing rituals. Although I went through correct official channels, including the Cultural Section of the Malaysian Embassy in London, to get sanction for my research, it was only on arrival in Kota Bharu that I was told categorically that *Nora* performances and exorcisms were banned. However, accompanied by the local cultural officer, I was taken fifteen kilometres outside Kota Bharu to the village of Kemasin to witness a healing exorcism undertaken by a shadow puppet-master who also serves as the village *bomoh*, or witch-doctor. This ritual turned out to be one of the most impressive theatrical feats I witnessed during my entire field trip: no less than a disguised negotiation with the spirit world, capitalizing on the intrinsically dramatic nature of such engagements. Who indeed can upstage an antagonist endowed with charisma borrowed from another world?

The hut of the *bomoh* was in the vicinity of a cemetery, and he and his patient were awaiting our arrival to begin the exorcism. A small area had been prepared for the ritual, and offerings to the spirit world consisting of fruit, flowers, rice, and a pot of incense sticks were laid beside a huge pail of water. The *bomoh* lit the incense, filling the small room with its aroma, and began his incantations in a low, quiet voice. The sick woman sat in front of him and let down her thick and beautiful hair, which he proceeded to stroke with his immensely long, tapering fingers while continuing his incantations and, with his other hand, transferring fruit and flowers into the pail of water. Almost imperceptibly, his voice rose a little as sprigs of multi-coloured leaves were added to the water until, using a piece of yellow cloth which had been slung across his shoulder, he began to flail the patient, imperiously commanding the spirit to leave her body. Sitting barely three feet away, I became powerfully aware of the entrance of a strange presence which, though invisible, was palpably registered in the reactions of the *bomoh:* his voice became increasingly strident and urgent as he struck the spirit in the patient in a more violent manner. There were now two conflicting forces in the room, a visible protagonist and an invisible antagonist, and the two were locked in a fierce negotiation, through the real *silat* (martial art) which was originally used to ward off evil spirits. As the volume of the protagonist's voice rose, he called for a branch of the *semeru* tree which is believed to have special powers over evil spirits, and began to throw rice at the patient, initially gently and then more violently. The *semeru* branch was then used to strike the ground in accompaniment to his voice, which rose to an unbearable pitch of authority. Grains of rice were flying everywhere, but the two combatants had reached a stalemate. Unperturbed, the *bomoh* resumed stroking the hair of his patient, who had remained slumped and inert throughout the entire operation. The seance had ended, but would continue on another day, and the wife of the *bomoh* assisted the patient to the adjoining bathroom where she had to wash herself with the consecrated water from the pail. In a few minutes she appeared with wet hair, looking more reassured. The *bomoh* seemed confident that he would eventually be able to persuade the spirit afflicting her to leave her in peace.

The next day I met the same *bomoh* and his wife at the Gelangang Seni, which is the cultural centre for tourists in the heart of Kota Bharu. He was wearing western trousers and a batik shirt and swinging his car keys from those same long tapering fingers. On the agenda for that afternoon were *silat* displays, spinning top contests, and relaxing games like *chongkla* (a board game involving the use of marbles), presided over by his wife. The compère began to greet a large group of tourists in various languages, and before I knew what was happening I was pulled onto the stage to try my hand at drumming. This was part of the official drive to promote tourism, but the atmosphere of relaxation was beguiling:

only what was shown within this cultural complex had been authorized, but it was difficult to distinguish what was truly traditional theatre from the censored fragments of shadow puppet theatre we were permitted to see.

Political interference – either through strict laws forbidding local residents from being involved in their own theatre, or compelling traditional theatrical troupe leaders to obtain licences two weeks before the staging of their shows – strikes at the heart of a form of theatre that cannot really be governed by 'human' time. Since nearly all traditional theatrical performances are shaman-based, and are consequently staged to prevent an epidemic or in response to cues from the spirit world, they cannot be subjected to the whims of an official with the power to grant or withhold a licence. As though to forestall any further questions from me about the curious position of the Gelangang Seni in promoting theatre officially banned by the powerful Islamic party in control of Kelantan, I was told that its venue was sited on land owned by the Federal Government, and came directly under the control of the Ministry of Arts, Culture, and Tourism, based in the capital. Such casuistry was beyond me, but I noted with interest that on an evening devoted to a shadow puppet performance, and widely advertised among tourists, the huge open-air auditorium in front of the stage (clearly not built according to strict religious prescriptions) was packed with local residents fully absorbed in this ancient form of theatre. To suit the convenience of tourists, the performance ended well before midnight rather than awaiting the traditional waning of the moon, an old superstition which held that by a process of sympathetic magic evil spirits would then be compelled to leave. But for tourism, such an event would not have been permitted; because of it, the sanctioned or 'sanitized' form seemed a travesty of the original.

Manora in Thailand

In Thailand things are very different, and while Malaysian contempt for the malpractices of Thai officials at the border separating the two countries is strong – a contempt which extends to the supposedly lax Thai theatrical administrative regulations – there is the highest respect for the potency of Thai magic and the effectiveness of Thai *Manora* cures. Such is the reputation of Thai *Manora* that even the infrequent performances of that theatre form in Kedah and in Penang are undertaken chiefly by Thai immigrants. So the *Manora* rehearsal of a troupe under the supervision of their future leader and shamaness, Manee Burinkoat, which I saw at the village of Plaiyuan (see Plate 1) in Nakhon Sri Thammarat, and its subsequent co-performance with another troupe under a male leader at Tung Yai, became the cornerstone of my impressions of this remarkable art form.

Nakhon Sri Thammarat is relatively untouched by tourism, which meant that the *Nora* performances I saw were not diluted but evolved entirely from the needs of the community. Hardly any English is spoken in Nakhon, and the journey by jeep and foot to Manee's hut, where the rehearsal took place, was fraught with difficulties. With the help of torches, we picked our way along overgrown jungle paths through vast plantations of mangosteen, guava, and mango trees, towards the sound of drumbeats reassuringly distinct against a chorus of insects. Market gardening provides *Nora* actors with their main source of income, since their small government subsidies are barely adequate to meet the increasing costs of their elaborately beaded costumes. Even though it was only a rehearsal, I was impressed by the care taken over detail: as in a performance, each young dancer, dressed as a bird-maiden, was required to perform a salutation to her teacher, Manee, as a mark of respect for her unquestioned authority. Acrobatic stunts were rigorously rehearsed, and these provided the element of spectacle in a theatrical form which is mediumistic in nature. In a seance, just before a medium returns to normality, he or she usually takes a high leap into the air to underline his or her magical powers, and all acrobatic stunts within *Manora*, apart from being spectacular and entertaining, betoken its mediumistic character, though achieved through several hours daily of rigorous training under their leader. An exceptionally strong and powerfully built woman, Manee was indisputably in charge. Coming from a strong *Manora* family, she originally felt trapped and tried to evade her vocation, but her husband's severe illness and his miraculous recovery once she vowed to return to the *Nora* fold confirmed her in the inescapability of her current position. The seventy-eight-year-old leader *Nora* Huang Napsipong was there that evening, but only as a shadowy presence, and he reiterated his intention of handing over the leadership to her.

Manora Performance: Ritual in Action

The joint *Manora* performances I saw in the village of Tung Yai in April 1997 as part of the Thai New Year celebration of *Songkran* exemplified the centrality of this art form to the lives of the people of Southern Thailand. A great feast was under way on our arrival, and we were invited to participate in it by a handsome young policeman. Hardly were we seated when a tall and striking figure of indeterminate gender, lavishly dressed in white silk, approached our table and welcomed me. This 'apparition', I assumed, was the male leader of the second troupe performing that evening and, in the capacity of village shaman, had dressed in women's clothes to emphasize the superiority of female magic. In fact, as my guides informed me, the reality was far more bizarre: this figure was the richest and most successful business person in the village, and having married and produced children, had then undergone a sex-change operation, settled his wife and children in another village, and as a 'female' grew in wealth, prosperity, and prestige to become the leading figure in the village. The handsome policeman was her husband.

Watching this phenomenon presiding over that evening's *Nora* performance, like the secular counterpart of an all-powerful shamaness holding an entire village in her sway, I was reminded of the *balian* (priestess-shamaness) and *basir* (asexual priest) among the Ngadju Dyaks of Southern Borneo, who act as intermediaries between humans and the gods. (The term *basir* means impotent, and these asexual priests dress and behave like women.) There was no doubt that the awe in which this person was held by the villagers was linked to her bisexuality: her ambivalence made her the perfect mediator between this world and the supernatural. And so the question of identity became the perfect prelude to an extraordinary evening devoted to renewing the village's unbreakable covenant with the invisible world of spirits – a rare celebration of dual citizenship. By ten o'clock almost the entire village was spread out on the grass in front of the stage, which was built strictly according to religious prescriptions about the departure of spirits at the close of a performance and the direction of the sun's rays by day. This evening's *Manora* would be devoted to the original 'birdwoman' story and as a special attraction Manee's four-year-old son would be playing the 'clown'/'hunter', capturing each birdmaiden in turn, while the daughter of the male leader of the second troupe had been given the role of the star 'birdwoman'. It was only later, after my return to London, that it dawned on me that the use of offspring to play key characters in New Year celebrations was not simply a statement about the regenerative principle in *Manora* but the absolute condition of its continuity: like their parents, these two children would never be able to leave the *Manora* tradition, and would forever be caught in the magic circle of its noose. Like the mythological 'rope' used by the god of force to secure the Japanese sun-goddess Amaterasu, when she emerged from her cave in the famous Japanese restoration myth – which later became the *shimenawa* or 'ritual rope' which demarcated the sacred area for a rite of propitiation – the magical 'noose' in *Manora* is a symbol both of captivity and liberation, the crux of the 'birdwoman' story.

These levels of meaning and participation ran through the whole performance: the young dancers in their bird costumes had been turned into magical beings from another world, in conformity to the law well known to the history of religions, that one becomes what one displays. They wholeheartedly entered the world of make-believe: *Let us be fishes swimming in a lake; let us be crabs and various types of shell creature moving on the beach.* The male leader of the second troupe performing that evening, who also served as the principal drummer, played like one possessed – at the same time flirting with his daughter, who even at a tender age had inherited her father's charisma.

The Lotus as Symbol

Some of the twelve traditional basic steps in the dance she and the other birdmaidens performed, which bear the descriptive name of the lotus in its various stages of flowering – the closed bud, the newly-open bud, the half-open flower, the open flower, and the fully-open flower – have a meaning that transcends description. These movements constitute part of the cycle of twelve basic steps reflecting the twelve months of the year, and so must be regarded as central to the progression of time and life itself.[29] The sexual nuances were at once explicit and implicit, but such was the nature of a public ritual that nothing which transpired on stage was offensive: indeed, the young dancers exchanged repartee which caused ripples of approval to flow through the audience. The 'lotus' in South-East Asia is a well known symbol of the female genitalia, and it was clear to me that the stage representations went beyond the simple reproductive imagery of the lotus. (This is regarded as the 'king of flowers' in the East, and I could remember that as a child I was allowed to stay up all night to watch a certain variant of this species turn from a bud into a flower in our living-room.) The young dancers were divulging, through floral images in the context of a public ritual, intimate details of sexual knowledge which they had imbibed from their elders, and the entire proceedings assumed the character of an initiation rite doubly propitious at New Year. This display of dance, improvisation, song, and badinage represented the transitional milestones in a young girl's journey from pubescence to sexual awakening, from the first sexual encounter to full maturity of experience. In strong contrast to the situation in other parts of Asia, the process of using the 'lotus' image as a way of underlining the central regenerative motif of the 'birdwoman' story was presented with enormous relish. In the famous Chinese play *The Drunken Concubine*, for example, severe political editing has removed the Chinese birdwoman's association with spring flowers[30] and their regenerative symbolism, and so erased the central meaning of the story, which would have connected her with the Thai *Manora*. This, of course, is in line with the current drive of the Chinese Government to excise all traces of sympathetic magic and to place the play firmly in the realm of entertainment.

Much closer to home, such traces do survive: just south of the Thai-Malaysian border, in territory where *Manora* is officially banned, the ritual ceremony known as *cukur rambut* (shaving the hair),[31] is still observed in *kampongs,* those indomitable strongholds of female power. In this rite an infant is passed from the arms of a nubile young girl to those of a blossoming teenager and finally to a betrothed young woman. Barren women, or those who find it difficult to conceive, compete to carry the infant. Three vital accessories to this ceremony, linking it with sympathetic magic, are a basket filled with boiled eggs and decorated with fresh flowers and shoots (symbols of fertility), a young coconut filled with juice to contain the infant's hair, which has been snipped off by young women of varying ages and will be floated down a river (symbols of prosperity and wealth), and a tray full of ten-dollar bills folded significantly into the shape of birds (symbols of female shamanism and magical flight) which will be given to every female participant.

Money, Sex, and Ritual

Money was a powerful symbol too in the *Manora* performance I was watching at Tung Yai. It was New Year, a time of renewal and rejuvenation, and some of the spectators had rushed to the stage to reward with cash the young dancers who had so delightfully re-enacted the power of the regenerative principle – money as celebration of female sexuality in a country where a far darker connection is more common – the *Bangkok Post* on 15 April having carried an article about the Friday busloads of Cambodian and Vietnamese girls 'sold' to Thai soldiers on the Surin border for as little as 100-300 *baht* (£1.50-£4.50) a time. Back in Tung Yai there was no pressure: the dance patterns[32] adopted by the young *Manora* dancers seemed repetitive and interminable, shifting imperceptibly from ritual to entertainment and back until it became impossible to distinguish one from the other. Indeed, this is the hallmark of most South-East Asian shaman-based theatres – a trance-like state being induced in performers by a combination of hypnotic drumming and repetitive rhythmic movement, a state which strongly affected me that night in Tung Yai. I surfaced when the stage seemed to burst alive with acrobatic feats performed by the young dancers whom I had watched rehearsing in Plaiyuan. But although these acrobatic stunts could stand on their own as pure entertainment, and indeed are used as such in performances presented to tourists in the fashionable hotels south of the border, the strongly ritualistic New Year ambience of this particular *Nora* performance presented a different dimension: no mere displacement of normal laws of gravity, but a journey into the super-normal world of the shaman.

What happens when mere acrobatic skill is separated from ritual had been made clear to me during my visit to China in 1994. Here, the actors in Quanzhou, southern China, told me that the ritual sequence called *xi ma*, or 'washing the horse' (an animal associated with sacrifice and exorcism), which in the past preceded an acrobatic display by the groom, prior to the hero mounting a horse, had been banned soon after the Communist takeover in 1949. The sequence required the groom to purify the stage ritually, brushing and saddling an invisible horse, and was thought to be unnecessarily superstitious. I wondered how long it would be before Nakhon succumbed to similar pressures, whether in the interests of tourism or of religious fundamentalism. For the moment I savoured what could be the last vestiges of a hitherto unspoilt theatrical form.

When the young son of Manee appeared on the scene, wearing the sacred *bai noi* (clown/hunter) mask, he received a special ovation since he was making his first stage appearance. His performance of the famous sequence known as *khlong hong*, or 'noosing the birdwoman', was both self-conscious and affectionate: he went from one whirling dancer to another, caressing each in turn and providing the catalyst required to activate the cycle of nature rather than a violent male intrusion into a company of female bathers. In a semi-ritualistic performance such as this, the hunter's role would more usually be taken by an adult actor who would be equipped for the part in a nearby clearing in full view of the audience. He would be given twelve articles necessary for survival on his journey, including a noose, bow and arrow, flint, and salt – twelve also being the stipulated number of basic steps in *Manora* dance.

Hunting and Cleansing

Customarily the sequence following this is known as *thaeng khe*, or 'stabbing the crocodile' – a symbolic way of showing that the capture of the female must be counterpointed by the destruction of her adversary. This motif is taken from a well-known Thai folk-tale known either as *Kraithong* ('The hero who slays the crocodile') or *Chalawan (*the name of the beast itself). A huge papier-mâché crocodile is placed on a slightly raised platform and the troupe leader uses one of his sacred *Nora* sticks[33] to strike and break it up in a ritual destruction of male bestiality. Either because of the extreme youth of Manee's son or the highly celebratory context of New Year *Songkran* festivities, 'the stabbing of the crocodile' was omitted on this occasion. Crocodile or no crocodile, we were back to the initial aquatic scenario of dancers pretending to be fishes in a pool, and the show continued till dawn, ending in the traditional way with the first rays of the rising sun, and so capitalizing through sympathetic magic Nature's promise of a new beginning. This was particularly significant since this performance, staged as part of the Thai Lunar New Year *Songkran* festival (13-15 April), in which the ritual cleansing by water was doubly auspicious: the regenerative core of the play could not have been better served than by the *Songkran* aquatic rituals ushering in the New Year, and nothing is more eloquent than water to express a sense of baptism, renewal, and purification. In this village's syllogism, 'Woman' is associated with water and the intrinsic rhythms of Nature;[34] she is recognized as the regenerative principle, the Great Mother who is the source of the moisture of life, and, according to Eastern belief, she sometimes assumes the form of a Bird, the ideogram of 'god' or divinity. So what I had seen on stage was the dramatic equivalent of the flow of this life force, as indiscernible as the flow of sap in the trees around me. This 'birdwoman' story, celebrating regeneration, was the very element of cohesion, binding together into a community all the villagers gathered in front of the stage, and this bonding was endlessly repeated in all southern Thai villages celebrating *Manora* and *Songkran*. The varying details of the story with regard to its location either in a lake or river, or its inclusion or exclusion of the feather robe motif, were here immaterial: what was important was its strong image of a female regenerative force connected to or identifiable with the elixir of life, a prize beyond the reach of the male. That the female is the legitimate guardian of the immortal fluid is the basic premise built into the unalterable structure of the choreography. One of the twelve basic steps, 'Rahu seizes the moon', is devoted to the fight for the immortal elixir, a reference to the well-known episode in the *Brahmanas* (part of ancient Vedic literature) describing the theft of the elixir which is identified with the moon.[35] The subsequent quest for it was the basis of the age-old conflict between the *Devas* (the gods who are friendly towards mankind) and the *Asuras* (the antagonistic gods). In accordance with the instructions of *Vishnu* (one of the three main gods in Hindu mythology), the ocean had to be churned for the elixir to emerge with all the other healing herbs and jewels, and, while the two antithetical forces were engaged in this task, the Divine Physician, *Dhanvantari*, arose out of the waters bearing the elixir. Though *Vishnu* was determined that only the gods well disposed toward mankind should drink the immortal fluid, *Rahu*, one of the anti-gods, snatched a drop but was beheaded before he could swallow it. What is significant about the inclusion of this attempted theft of the 'moon' or the 'elixir of life' (both terms being used interchangeably, as in the Chinese story about the goddess of the moon and the elixir)[36] is the strong emphasis on female victory and the healing, life-prolonging aspect of the *Manora* art.

The Japanese Connection

In discussing the power of the birdwoman story, which, as we have seen, survives in more than one form in southern Thailand and northern Malaysia, it is illuminating to compare the 'birdwoman' legacy in the current repertory of the classical Noh theatre of Japan, where two plays revolve around her – one directly, through *Hagoromo* ('The Feather Robe'), the other indirectly through *Yôkihi* (*Yang Kuei Fei*), the famous 'birdwoman' concubine of the resplendent eighth-century Tang Emperor, Ming Huang.[37]

The Japanese Noh style of presentation could not be more different from that of the Thai *Manora* with its warmth, sensuality, and reasonable accessibility. The Noh presentation is a model of restraint and economy, and so devoid of any marked dramatic interest that audience involvement is almost imperceptible. Yet *Hagoromo*, in particular, is one of the most frequently performed Noh plays, and the exceptional beauty of its libretto is greatly admired by Noh connoisseurs. The birdwoman story here is far more familiar to the Japanese than the anecdotes from *The Tale of Genji* (one of the two great national epics) on which many Noh plays were based. And, even more than *Manora*, *Hagoromo* might be considered a perfect mediumistic play – an excellent example of a monodrama in which all the various threads of the story are drastically reduced and forced through the single needle eye of the narrator's viewpoint. In this case it is the Angel (a moon goddess) whose feather robe has been stolen by a fisherman, and who is thus prevented from returning to Heaven. This central role is usually taken by the main actor – the *shite* – and his virtually complete dominance of the performance finds a parallel in the solo enactments and dances of shamanistic spirit possession in South-East Asia. As the only 'narrator', the *shite* is the holder of the thread of the narrative, though, in the style peculiar to Noh drama, some of his lines are completed for him by a chorus of six or eight chanters who also comment on the narration, adding a dimension of objectivity. However, there is no question that the *shite is* the sole narrator of, actor in, and commentator on, the narrative, just as a trance medium who is solely in control can speak through several voices.

'Holder of the Strings'

In Sanskrit drama the narrator is called the *sutradhara* (see Chapter Five) – a term derived from puppetry, meaning the 'holder of the strings of the puppets'. Hence, as with several ancient theatres, including the Chinese, the connection between the human and puppet theatres is very close – particularly so with the Noh, whose founder's seminal treatise on acting instructs his actors to perceive themselves as puppeteers, controlling the movements of their bodies through imaginary strings tied to the heart. In large measure this has accounted for the remarkable and concentrated control of the Noh actor, as well as the marked similarity of some of his movements to those of string-controlled puppets. And, above all, this dominating puppet analogy aligns an ancient classical 'human' theatre to the well-attested exorcistic efficacy of puppet performances – while also providing a further parallel with the movements of the *Manora* dancers, whose similarity to puppets is taken for granted in South Thailand by a society which has from time immemorial regarded both these arts as effective means of communicating with the invisible world of spirits. Dancers must thus move like puppets if they wish to be the receptacles of spirits. Similarly, the strong underlying puppet rationale of Noh drama, which defines both its purpose and strategy of stage movement, also attests to its mediumistic character. The single pine tree on the back panel serves as a spirit conductor; and in the two-act structure of a Noh performance, the first features the spirit disguised as an ordinary mortal, the second shows his or her true manifestation, while the dance which the main Noh actor performs to bring the play to a conclusion reminds spectators of the original dance of propitiation by the young goddess Uzume, regarded as the first shaman, actress, and dancer of this theatrical genre. Applying this shamanistic perspective to *Hagoromo*, the 'Angel', played by the *shite*, would be described as the 'middle seat' (the one who goes into trance), and the 'Fisherman' (who steals her robe without which she cannot return to heaven) as the 'front seat' (the questioner). The analogy between trance ritual and theatre continues when the blindfolded 'middle seat' is replaced by the semi-blind *shite*, rendered nearly sightless by his restrictive wooden mask.

At the Hawk's Well

Hagoromo, perhaps because of its muted form, does not feature prominently in the list of birdwoman stories outside Japan. By far the most celebrated play in the West today to have focused on a birdwoman theme is W. B. Yeats's *At the Hawk's Well* (1916), inspired by Noh drama (see Chapter 6). As a coda, it would be illuminating to compare it with *Hagoromo* and *Manora,* both of which preceded it by several centuries.

Yeats's dance-drama features a 'Hawk-Woman' who guards a well containing the elixir of life. It re-tells the classic story from *Hagoromo* about an angel (moon goddess) who is nearly prevented from returning to the moon by a male through his theft of her feather robe. Yeats substitutes water for the feather robe, but in essence deals with the same male quest for immortality involving male-female conflict. The theft of the water is merely an alternative way of dramatizing the classic theft of the feather robe – a dangerous encroachment on female territory.

Although Yeats, in his famous introduction[38] to Ezra Pound and Ernest Fenollosa's *Certain Noble Plays of Japan*, referred to *Hagoromo* in conjunction with *At the Hawk's Well,* this connection has been largely overlooked.[39] *Hagoromo* and *Nishikigi*[40] – focusing on shamanism, courtship, and birds' feathers – were two of several Noh plays included in Pound and Fenollosa's anthology, and it is no accident that Yeats, while discussing the context and inspiration for his *At the Hawk's Well*, should have been drawn to them because of their thematic affinities. It would seem that his 'Hawk-Woman' was conceived in the same mould as that of archetypal female trance mediums like the *Manora* heroine, while Yeats's definition of the essence and beauty of 'Woman' refers directly to her extra-terrestrial dimension, which could only be identified with the resonant image of a bird. Yeats even opens another of his plays – *The Only Jealousy of Emer* – with the line:

> *A woman's beauty is like a white frail bird, like a white sea-bird ...*

There is ample evidence of his involvement with female trance medium activities in the years before the genesis of *At the Hawk's Well*: he attended seances in Dublin with a non-professional medium called Mrs. Mitchell in April 1913, and about the same time was also consulting mediums in London. There is no doubt that his experiences of seances inspired his poetic activities,[41] and it is easy to understand why Yeats, with his strong predilection for the occult and supernatural, should have been drawn to the ancient Japanese drama, not in the spirit of pale imitation,[42] but as a way of interpreting his own occult struggles. However, despite the strong mediumistic overtones of Yeats's play, it would be difficult for a modern western audience, without a common belief, to see the connection between art and everyday life.[43] So while *At the Hawk's Well* is refreshingly accessible through its clarity of structure and text, and the way it focuses on and leads up to the conflict between the 'Hawk-Woman' and her two male assailants, the story is largely irrelevant to its western spectators. In South Thailand, on the other hand, while the 'bird-woman' story, as it occurs in a ritualistic *Manora* performance, is fragmentary and barely discernible, the level of audience participation is huge.

In the ritualistic *Manora* New Year performance which I witnessed in the village of Tung Yai in April 1997, I was seeing something vital to village life: a 'well' from which an entire community had drawn its living water since ancient times. And just as it has always been the function of woman to draw the life-sustaining fluid from the well, so it is the female who still presides over this village – her power being symbolized by the mythical and dramatic image of the birdwoman, endlessly regenerative and eternal. In a region where fact is sometimes indivisible from fiction, and magical reality stronger than everyday logic, the real-life episode of the Tung Yai businessman who 'changed' into a 'woman', married the most eligible local bachelor, and gained control of an entire community, assumed a new meaning for me. As she was driven away from the festivity that evening, the purring sound of her white Cadillac could almost have been that made by fluttering wings. A modern birdwoman still kept us under her spell, and it was the power of her estate, at once real and unreal, which was underwriting the feast and putting in motion once again the story of the birdwoman through the twelve steps of the *Manora* – as relentlessly repetitive and self-validating as the twelve months of the lunar New Year.

The question of her identity no longer vexes me. An answer is not required: as with Parsifal's famous question, 'Where is the Grail?' – which awoke the dying Fisher King and the whole of creation – the art of asking is its own answer, setting in motion the cycle of renewal and regeneration at the outset of the Thai New Year. The Birdwoman remains the most powerful manifestation of an ancient tale which even today takes many forms, and whose image, passing freely between heaven and earth, remains central to notions of female power, the sole guardian of the immortal elixir. In my next chapter I want to relate this notion of power and guardianship to the puppet and human theatres of Southern China. Once again the figure of the Birdwoman is crucial.

Notes and References

1. All performing arts are considered by Islamic purists and the orthodox as *haram* or 'forbidden'. They do not wish to see any kind of human representation, even if it is highly stylized. So the *wayang kulit* or 'shadow puppet theatre' comes under heavy censorship, despite the fact that it was the Muslim philosopher, Ibn Al-Arabi, who saw the *panggung* (puppet stage) as a mini-cosmos, the lamp as the sun, and the puppeteer as God. Many orthodox Malayan Muslims regard this as a heresy, and the shadow puppet theatre as something sinful. Other traditional performing arts are similarly mistrusted. Ironically, even though the *Manora* theatrical art form originated in old Malaya, it has never been totally accepted by the Malays because of its supposedly strong Buddhist base. See Ghulam Sarwar Yousof, *Panggung Semar: Aspects of Traditional Malay Theatre* (Petaling Jaya: Tempo Publishing, 1992), pp. 175, 183.
2. *Manora* was the earliest form of drama known in Siam, and it was believed to have developed in the twelfth century from village performances connected with Buddhist animistic practice in the old Malay kingdom of Patani (just south of Nakhon Sri Thammarat), which is now part of Thailand. In 1909 the British ceded Nakhon and Patani to Thailand under the Treaty of Bangkok. See *The Cambridge Guide to Asian Theatre*, ed. James Brandon (Cambridge: Cambridge University Press, 1993), p. 234.
3. Cf. the role of these two princesses as healers with that of the Japanese legendary Princess Jôruri, who is regarded as the mythical founder of the seventeenth-century *bunraku* puppet theatre initially known as *ningyô* (doll) *jôruri* (narrative recitations). She falls in love with the Genji general and when her lover is taken ill on his way to defeat his enemies, she flies to his side and miraculously restores him to health.
4. See *The Cambridge Guide to Asian Theatre*, op. cit., pp. 23–6.
5. For a fuller account of the *Mesi Mala* myth, see *Panggung Semar*, op. cit., pp. 165–8.
6. It is believed that the drum is made out of the wood of the World Tree which provides communication between earth and sky. Through his drumming, the shaman is able to project himself into the vicinity of the World Tree and can fly to the sky. See Mircea Eliade, *Shamanism* (New York: Arkana Press, 1989), p. 168.
7. The 'clown' figure is frequently associated with divinity and healing, not only in *Manora* but other related Malay dance dramas: for example, in the Malay female court dance, *Mak Yong*, women who have been healed by *bomoh* (witch doctor) clowns in turn become the healers in the community. See *The Cambridge Guide to Asian Theatre*, op. cit., p. 195.
8. Henry Ginsburg, 'The *Manora* Dance Drama: an Introduction', *Journal of the Siam Society*, LX, Part 2 (July 1972), p. 174.
9. The strategic position of Melaka (now spelt 'Malacca'), at the narrowest part of the Straits of Malacca, made it the most prosperous trading port in South-East Asia in the fifteenth century. The port was named after the Melaka tree, under which the first refugee king – Raja Iskandar Shah – rested on arrival. Kingships in Malaya did not begin with the Melaka dynasty, since the Malay states of Kedah

and Patani were known as early as the sixth century. See Wazir Jahan Karim, *Women and Culture: Between Malay Adat and Islam* (San Francisco; Oxford: Westview Press, 1992), pp. 34–8.

10. See Richard Winstedt, 'Indian Influence in the Malay World', *Journal of the Royal Asiatic Society,* Parts 3–4 (1944), p. 188: 'Not many decades ago Perak's Muslim Sultan was still waited upon like a Hindu god, by virgins bare to the waist.'

11. Cf. the legendary history and folklore of China, which abound not only in examples of magical flight but specific instances of linking sovereignty with female divinity. See Mircea Eliade, *Shamanism,* op. cit., pp. 448–9.

12. See the section entitled 'Shamanic Affinities', in A. T. Hatto, 'The Swan Maiden: A Folk-Tale of North Eurasian Origin?', *Bulletin of the School of Oriental and African Studies,* XXIV, London: School of Oriental and African Studies,1961), p. 341.

13. Ibid., p. 334.

14. Ibid., p. 327.

15. Ibid., pp. 333, 343. The 'foreign' wife was frequently associated with sorcery in archaic societies. Medea, the wife of Jason, who was displaced by the daughter of Creon, fits into this category and to be noted was her flight to safety in the golden chariot of Helios (the Sun), pulled by dragons, after killing both the new wife and her own children.

16. Many folk stories were known as *jataka,* and the term exemplified causal connection which, according to Buddhist philosophy, forms the structure of things: every event in the present is to be explained by facts going farther and farther back in the past. See *New Larousse Encyclopaedia of Mythology* (Twickenham: Hamlyn, 1959), p. 355.

17. See Padmanabh S. Jaini, 'The Story of *Sudhana* and *Manohara:* an Analysis of the Texts of the *Borobudur* Reliefs', *Bulletin of the School of Oriental and African Studies,* XXIX, London: School of Oriental and African Studies,1966, p. 535.

18. See Hatto, 'The Swan Maiden', op. cit., p. 327.

19. Mohammad Ghouse Nasruddin, *The Malay Dance,* Kuala Lumpur:Bahasa dan Tustaka, Kementerian Pendidikan, Malaysia,1995, p. 2.

20. For a fuller account of the lives of Tun Kudu and Tun Fatimah, see H. Haindan, *Tun Kudu* (Kuala Lumpur: Pustaka Antara, 1967); *Tun Fatimah: Sri Kandi Melaka* (Kuala Lumpur: Syarikat Buku Uni-Text, 1977).

21. The Valkyries in Teutonic mythology were not only able to transform themselves into swan-maidens but played crucial roles in controlling the destinies of warriors. See *New Larousse Encyclopaedia of Mythology*, op. cit., p. 278.

22. See the article on chastity belts by Kee Hua Chee, *The Star,* 29 March 1997, p. 2. This was written in conjunction with the world's first full-scale exhibition on this subject, entitled 'Infidelity: Violation of Family Values', held at the Muzium Negara, Kuala Lumpur, Malaysia. Cf. the ancient western concept of *mundium,* central to early Germanic marriage, which expressed a man's dominion over his wife to the extent that should she compromise his *mundium,* she could be

smothered in dung (*Lex Burgundronum,* 34.1). See Edwin Hall, *The Arnolfini Betrothal* (California: University of California Press, 1994), pp. 15–16.

23. For a full history of the practice of footbinding, see Howard S. Levy, *The Complete History of the Curious Erotic Custom of Footbinding in China* (New York: Prometheus Books, 1991).

24. The following, from Joseph Campbell, *Primitive Mythology: the Masks of God* (Harmondsworth: Penguin Books, 1976), p. 315, is pertinent: *There can be no doubt that in the very earliest age of human history, the magical force and wonder of the female was no less a marvel than the universe itself; and this gave to woman a prodigious power, which has been one of the chief concerns of the masculine part of the population to break, control, and employ to its own ends. It is, in fact, most remarkable how many primitive hunting races have the legend of a still more primitive age than their own, in which women were the sole possessors of the magical art.*

25. *Women and Culture,* op. cit., pp. 66–7. This translation has been ascribed to Sir Andrew Caldwell, former British Resident of Negri Sembilan in Malaya.

26. Ibid., pp. 141–3.

27. Though, understandably, any form of tampering with the vagina is a delicate subject, several of those I interviewed in North Malaysia and South Thailand maintained that they had a friend or relative who had undergone surgery to tighten her vagina. There is a prevalent belief that the vagina is associated with female sorcery. See R. F. Fortune, *Sorcerers of Dobu (*London, 1932), p. 150 ff., and p. 296, for support of this belief.

28. Wazir Jahan Karim, 1992, p. 68. Verses from the *Qur'an* are often appended to charms and spells in the form of opening or closing statements. The following spell for 'capturing' a person's soul begins: *Bismillahi al-rahmani I-rahimi* ('In the name of God, the Merciful and Compassionate').

29. The twelve basic steps of the *Manora.*dance (with unmistakable sexual nuances) are as follows: 1. Half-open lotus; 2. Lotus in full bloom; 3. Buffalo horn; 4. Closed bud. 5. *Kinnari* (half bird, half woman); 6. Newly-open lotus; 7. Just about to open; 8. 90 degrees opening of the thighs; 9. One leg is stretched out at 90 degrees, the other leg is in a kneeling position; 10. Spider's web (This is meant to enchant the audience. Compare Zeami Motokiyo's aim to 'bewitch an audience' through the principle of *hana* or the 'flower' – 'the element of the unexpected' in the art of Noh drama. See W. Whitehouse and M. Shidehara's translation of *Seami Jûroku Bushû* (Seami's sixteen treatises), *Monumenta Nipponica*, Tokyo, 1942, Vol. V/2, p. 211.) 11. One leg is bent backwards and both arms are wide open; 12. *Melai* (the first step of *manora* dance). *As* in China, where there are twenty-four splendid 'birdwoman' figures in the famous *Kai Yuan* Temple in the Fujian province representing the twenty-four divisions of the solar year in the traditional Chinese calendar, the 'birdwoman' in southern Thailand is seen as the 'presider' over time, but in a lunar year which comprises twelve months. So the number twelve is significantly repeated throughout the *Manora* art: there are twelve steps, twelve stories; twelve songs; twelve parts of the 'birdwoman' costume; and twelve compulsory articles which the hunter takes

with him on his journey. Mircea Eliade writes, in *The Myth of the Eternal Return* (London; New York: Arkana Press, 1989), p. 52, that 'periodic regeneration of time presupposes, in more or less explicit form, a new Creation – that is, a repetition of the Cosmogonic act'. According to Eliade, the Zuni Indians called the months the 'steps' of the year). The number 12, just like the theme of sexuality, features strongly in the performance of *Manora* and in Lady Jôruri's story. See Chapter 4.

30. See an English translation of this unexpurgated scene (with all the spring flowers and their symbolism intact) in Jo Riley, *The Chinese Theatre and the Actor in Performance* (Cambridge: Cambridge University Press, 1997), pp. 239–41.

31. See Karim,1992, p. 211.

32. The dance patterns were either circular or in a figure-of-eight, which is a variation of the circle design: apart from being aesthetically pleasing, the circle symbolizes harmony and continuation while the number eight is associated with shamanism – for example, the eight-legged horse connected with the shamaness/guardian spirit of the Buryat tribe. See Mircea Eliade, *Shamanism*, op. cit., p. 469.

33. The same stick is used as an instrument of healing.

34. See Ian Jeffrey's introduction to *La France: Images of Woman and Ideas of a Nation, 1789–1989* by Ian Jeffrey et al.Uxbridge: Hillingdon Press, 1986, p. 25. Jeffrey refers to the great historian and narrator of France, Jules Michelet, who associated woman with water and nature. So 'the spying on Cézanne's group of female bathers entailed an act of violence, a breaking into the cycle of Nature'.

35. A full account of this episode can be found in *World Mythology,* ed. Roy Willis (London: Simon and Schuster, 1993), p. 71.

36. Chang Ee, the wife of the archer Shen Yi, stole the elixir from her husband, and, while he watched helpless, flew to the moon, which became identified with the immortal fluid. Note the reversal of the theft motif in this Chinese story, where it is the female who steals the elixir from the male. Ibid., p. 95.

37. The traditional Chinese version of the swan-maiden story (dated *circa* eighth century) was translated by Arthur Waley, in *Ballads and Stories from Tun-huang* (London: Allen and Unwin, 1960), pp. 149–55.

38. This introduction can be found in Ezra Pound and Ernest Fenollosa, *The Classic Noh Theatre of Japan* (New York: New Directions, 1959), pp. 151–63. References to *Hagoromo* and *Nishikigi* are on p. 159, p. 161, and pp. 159–60 respectively.

39. The Noh play *Yôrô*, which features a spring of miraculous healing water, has been considered a more likely model than *Hagoromo* for *At the Hawk's Well.* See Richard Taylor, 'Assimilation and Accomplishment: Noh Drama and an Unpublished Source for *At the Hawk's Well*', in *Yeats and the Theatre*, ed. Robert O'Driscoll and Lorna Reynolds (Yeats Study Series, Canada, 1975), pp. 137–8. A close scrutiny of the context of *Yôrô* emphasizes the deep differences between the two plays and, furthermore, Yeats himself made no such connection in his famous essay. It should also be noted that *Hagoromo* is a play strongly associated with the

famous Umewaka family, responsible for the transmission of the great Noh art to Yeats through Fenollosa and Pound. In 1970 the Japanese Ministry of Education made a film of a particularly memorable Umewaka performance of *Hagoromo*.

40. In *Nishikigi* the ghost of a woman who rejected her suitor in life is still carrying a piece of cloth called *hosonuno*, which is woven from birds' feathers.

41. See Roy Foster, *W. B. Yeats: A Life. The Apprentice Mage, 1865–1914* (Oxford; New York: Oxford University Press, 1997), pp. 453–91.

42. In 1949 a Noh play entitled *Takahime* or *The Hawk Princess* was composed by Mario Yokomichi as a complement to Yeats's Noh-inspired *At the Hawk's Well*, and this is regarded proudly by the Japanese as closer to the genuine Noh form than Yeats's 'imitation'.

43. On 17 October 1996, with financial assistance from two Japanese foundations, two productions were organized on the Noh stage at Royal Holloway, with Umewaka Naohiko, the great-grandson of Umewaka Minoru (who introduced the Noh to Yeats), playing the double roles of the Angel in *Hagoromo* and the Hawk-Woman in *At the Hawk's Well*. This was the first time that such a juxtaposition had been made, and it was appreciated as an apt hymn to the Irish-Japanese connection. But, despite the underlining of strong mediumistic resonances in both plays through the distribution of sprigs of rosemary (a sacred herb) to every spectator, the burning of incense, and other devices, audience involvement in the productions was warm but academic.

Chapter Two: The Birdwoman and The Puppet King – a Study of Inversion in Chinese Theatre

Overhanging the Grand Buddha Hall in the Kai Yuan Temple in Quanzhou, Fujian Province, China, are twenty-four magnificently coloured and carved birdwomen. The Hall houses the largest and best preserved altar in China – Ganlujie, first built in 686 during the Tang dynasty. In a country where footbinding was once a widespread custom, confining lotus-footed women to the hearth and the bottom end of the social scale,[1] it is difficult not to feel exhilaration at the sight of these women, their outspread wings elevated to the top of columns and holding up, like caryatids, a most sacred edifice. In the official guidebook one is informed that these figures are representations of the magical singing birds which once flocked to this Great Hall to listen to Buddhist sûtras. Symbolically, they fuse the opposing but complementary forces of the human and natural worlds, whose close alliance is the basis of Chinese life.

Although motifs of birdmen[2] appeared in early Han art (206 BC–AD 220), these seventh-century birdwomen are unique and important. Here is a self-evident glorification of the extraordinary and later forgotten function of women, their bowshaped arms carrying the four treasures of the scholar (writing brush, ink stand, ink slab and paper) as well as musical instruments and fruit, ingeniously interlocked into a complex system of brackets which hold up the columns of the Great Hall. Twenty-four in number, the birdwomen are also meant to symbolize the twenty-four divisions of the solar year in the traditional Chinese calendar, so that besides being immortalized as the attentive listeners to Buddhist scripture and the Guardians of Scholarship (a predominantly male prerogative from time immemorial), they are also seen as presiders over the passage of time. Since the calendar is considered the supreme legislator in Chinese life, 'valid at once for human society and the natural world',[3] these figures assume a position of extraordinary importance. In Quanzhou today, with their image featured on the corners of its town hall (largely devoted to theatrical and musical functions) and on the tee-shirts worn by actors, puppeteers and tourists alike, these birdwomen have become the official emblem of all cultural activities – in particular the theatre – in the province.

There is an underlining irony implicit here since the theatre, for which the birdwoman has become the emblem, has been one of the main instruments for enshrining a conventional image of female confinement: the lotus gait assumed by the *dan* or female role on stage, until fairly recently played only by the male, and considered one of the most striking characteristics of Chinese acting, requires of the actor assigned to mastering such a craft long arduous training, almost comparable in rigour to the tortures once imposed on women by footbinding. But while the training for such roles and the role itself, symbolized by the lotus gait, represent the traditional confinement of women, there has been an extension of female characterization in Chinese theatre, through the liberating role of the *dao ma dan* or woman warrior – which the 20th century's most celebrated actor, Mei Lan Fang, made famous in the play *Fu Mu Lan*. Wearing small wooden shoes, he portrayed a young woman who disguised herself as a man to replace her father and fought a triumphant battle against her country's enemies, far excelling her male compatriots and succeeded in concealing her sex from them. Although there is not such a direct connection between the 'warrior woman' and the 'birdwoman' as there is in western mythology,[4] the affinity is remarkably strong and the superhuman scale of her military exploits equally impressive.

The Image of the Bird and the Theatre

The bird is often associated with creation myths[5] and with shamanism because of the characteristic movements of its flight: rising, activation, change, and vitality. These are characteristics associated with the spirit-possessed shaman and in Siberia, for example, not only is the eagle the prototype of the shaman but the same word is used for both.[6] In early Chinese peasant society it was the reappearance and disappearance of birds which became the pivotal emblem of the system of rotation in Spring and Autumn, of the going out into the fields and the return to the village and of the change from outdoor to indoor activities. This polar opposition of outer and inner reflects the basic elementary classification of all Chinese life into two distinct but complementary orders: female (*yin*) and male (*yang*). Thus, from the beginning, the male worked in the fields[7] while the female laboured at the hearth. This essential division of labour is preserved in the popular stellar myth of the 'Heavenly Cowherd and the Weaving Maiden',[8] who were punished for their love and only met once a year with the assistance of birds whose wings formed a bridge across the Milky Way. From this arose the idea of birds as helpful intermediaries, the envoys of the shaman, and sometimes the shaman herself.[9] The fusion of woman and bird in one image is especially powerful in Chinese thought. What is now forgotten is that initially Chinese society was matrilinear, the surname in ancient times passing down through women.[10] As early as the Shang dynasty (*c.* 1600–1028 BC), the family system had become organized on firm patriarchal lines. But if we go back to the Neolithic era, the situation was reversed. Indeed in some places a matriarchal society survives – for example in certain ethnic minorities in south-west China such as the contemporary *Naxi*, whose women organize production and provide the family surname, with the grandmother as the head of the family.[11] Indeed, in the earliest days of Chinese history it was women who enjoyed supremacy and reverence. The conventional belief in a fiercely male society stems from a powerful Confucian overlay in the sixth century BC.

When we move from society to theatre, we discover a reflection of this overturning of commonly held assumptions in the network of inversions which runs through Chinese theatre, particularly in the string puppet theatre of South Fujian – the *kuei lei hsi* or in Fujian (Min-nan) vernacular *ka le hi*, meaning 'the theatre of auspicious ritual'. The 'Min-nan' vernacular (which I speak, since my grandfather came from the vicinity of Quanzhou) is one of the most archaic dialects in China, traceable to a form of early Chinese carried south seventeen centuries ago. So *ka le hi* in Min-nan demotic not only gives the sound of the local pronunciation but also denotes a puppet form closely connected with Daoist exorcisms.[12] I shall return to this important theatrical form.

Although the power of the 'birdwoman' is distinctly entrenched in Quanzhou, she does not feature directly in a play. But throughout South-East Asia, particularly in North Malaysia and Thailand, there is a prevalent story of a 'birdwoman', captured by a mortal of royal blood, forced into marriage with him, and almost sacrificed by his hostile court – a story endlessly repeated in theatrical performances which are primarily related to shamanistic practices. It is said in these regions that the 'birdwoman' is of Buddhist origin,[13] and so linked to the birdwomen in the Buddhist Kai Yuan Temple of Quanzhou. In the fourteenth-century classical Noh Theatre of Japan, two seminal plays are devoted to 'birdwomen', one directly and the other indirectly. In the former, *Hagoromo,* the birdwoman is an angel, surprised by a fisherman who has stolen her feather robe while she is bathing in a pool; in order to retrieve her robe without which she cannot return to Paradise, she is forced to perform for her thief the 'Dance of the Feather Robe', and the ritual of her robing (see Plate 2) is given nearly as much importance as the dance itself, to emphasize the indivisibility of ritual from performance. In the latter, *Yôkihi* or *Yang Kuei Fei* (in Chinese), the central figure of the 'birdwoman' is the famous concubine of the Tang Emperor Ming Huang (712–756). The action, as in many Noh plays, takes place after her death and is in the form of a seance in which a necromancer contacts her spirit. This indirect portrayal of her as a birdwoman is indistinguishable in essence from direct shamanistic 'birdwoman' performances in South-East Asia.

In the Chinese theatrical tradition, as indeed in Chinese literature, Yang Kuei Fei is only presented indirectly as a birdwoman, but the connection is unmistakable: the Emperor's first glimpse of her is while she is bathing in a pool;[14] she is referred to by the famous Tang poet Li Po as 'the most beautiful flying swallow' trapped in the palace,[15] as well as by many other bird images;[16] while performing for the Emperor the famous 'Dance of the Feather Robe', she is demanded as a sacrifice by his rebellious troops; and in a seventeenth-century play about her tragedy, *The Palace of Eternal Youth,* by Hung Sheng, she is shown as a victim hanging, almost puppet-like, by a silken cord from a pear tree. This is reminiscent of the famous 'Pear Garden' in the capital Changan, which was the first official base of Chinese theatre founded by her royal lover, Emperor Tang Ming Huang. Indeed, in all the stories about the birdwoman, east and west, there is a similar pattern of loss followed by a search for the loved one in another world. In this way there has grown around the myth of the birdwoman the cult and ritual of powerful female trance mediums who specialize in communicating with spirits.

Puppets, Jokes, and Exorcism

There is a connection between female trance mediums, sacrificial victims, and puppets in certain areas of the Fujian province, not found in any other part of the world. Indeed they are all called by the same term, *ang*, which is the local vernacular of the ideograph *wang* and this is also the same character or word used to denote diseased or deformed persons.[17] The fact that puppets, female trance mediums, and diseased persons were all referred to by the same term reinforced their common sacrificial, exorcistic function. Initially, this activity of communicating with spirits was regarded with such male scepticism that the expression *li teh khan bong* in Min-nan vernacular – meaning 'you are raising up the dead' – is still synonymous with 'you're telling a lie'. However, throughout China, in current theatrical convention, puppets are placed first, boy actors second, and adult actors last,[18] and though the literacy of puppeteers is an important factor in raising them to the top of the theatrical scale, what is even more crucial is their special efficacy as agents of exorcism in a society where age-old superstitions die hard. Closely connected with this function of exorcism is the ancient association of the puppet tradition with jesting: as early as the sixth century, puppet shows were known as 'the theatre of Baldy Guo', from the name of a real-life joker who had lost all his hair in an illness.[19] One of the implications behind calling the puppet theatre the joker's theatre is the emphasis on jokes and laughter as part of the infrastructure of exorcism and purification, since the joke, by inverting the accepted order, symbolizes levelling, dissolution, and reunification.[20] As will be seen, the joker in the puppet theatre is a ritual purifier and the patron saint of both puppet and human theatre in Quanzhou, standing for divine jester as well as divine musician.

The two great Tang Emperors who were closely connected with theatre, Ming Huang and Chuang Tsung (923–926), often dressed in the robes of the lowly *chou* or clown to perform with their actors in court. For this and other historical reasons, it is the clown who is chosen to burn incense to the statue of the principal theatre god, believed to be the divine manifestation of either or both emperors. It is held by many scholars that the first actor in Chinese theatre was the jester Meng (610 BC),[21] and in Chinese puppet circles there is a superstition that should *chou* or clown puppets be accidentally placed at the bottom of the box after a performance, they will find their way to the top.[22] The great Tang Emperor Ming Huang not only identified himself with the *chou*'s clown role, but also with the image of a string puppet during the twilight years of loneliness after the loss of his beloved concubine. The following poem was ascribed to him:

They've made an old man,
Wood-carved string-pulled,
Chicken-skinned crane-haired
Like the genuine thing;
The show over in a flash,
Loose-ended,
Once more I am back in this
Dreamlike human life.[23]

This is poignant on more than one level: before Emperor Ming Huang established the famous 'Pear Garden Academy', initially for musicians and dancers, and later for actors, he had set up in 714 a special academy in his inner palace for puppeteers. More than any other royal patron, he provided the impetus for an exchange of stagecraft between his puppeteers and his actors, and under his patronage the movements of puppets and actors merged to such a degree that even today the term *fan hsien*, 'to reverse the string', is used to describe a mistake on the human stage.[24] So it was ironic that the man who had made it possible for the artistry of two different theatrical genres, human and non-human, to overlap saw himself ultimately as indistinguishable from a puppet: highest blurring with lowest, emperor turned puppet in a supreme image of inversion. Arising from this, the ambiguity of puppets being first and last in the Chinese theatrical and social scale is another example of inversion which permeates customs and daily habits. In Shansi Province, for example, on the fifteenth day of the first moon, it has been traditional since the sixth century for a man dressed as the 'Spring Woman' to go from shop to shop stealing lanterns without being stopped by the shopkeepers. It is believed that the thief in this ritual, known as the 'Spring Lantern Theft', would be cursed and the act of cursing would bring good luck.[25] Similarly, role reversal in Chinese theatre, until the rigid Manchu Edicts of the seventeenth century prohibiting the appearance of women on the stage, was an essential part of this general rite of inversion.

Puppet and Human Theatre in Quanzhou

In the summer of 1994 I was awarded a British Academy grant to spend six weeks in Quanzhou in order to compare the stagecraft of its most important string puppet theatre *ka le hi* with that of its principal human theatrical form – *li yuan hsi* or 'Pear Garden Theatre'. Through the Cultural Section of the Chinese Embassy in London, I received an official invitation from the Cultural Bureau in Fujian to document its two chief theatres, which perform predominantly in August, traditionally regarded as the month of *pu du* – a term meaning 'a service for destitute spirits'. Within days of my arrival I realized that *pu du* was a practice frowned upon by the Chinese hierarchy in Beijing, which held ancestral sacrificial offerings, whether in the form of paper wreaths, horses, or of theatrical performances, to be extremely wasteful. None the less a mammoth five-day puppet performance entitled *Mu Lien Saves His Mother* had been scheduled to take place. This was based on a ninth-century text originally taken from the ancient Indian epic *The Mahabharata*, and the scheduled puppet presentation was considered a most powerful form of exorcism. The entire range of dramatic devices deployed in the presentation reinforced the principle of inversion, using jokes, abuse, and constant shifts of tone. These ranged from use of the sacred text pinned on a ledge at the stage front (there were altogether four volumes of text to be recited) to coarse improvisations – which made it sometimes impossible to distinguish between the sacred and the profane. Puppeteer and puppet, human and non-human, blended together, as for instance when a puppeteer unceremoniously offered his own shoe from the side of the stage to represent the boat for a journey required by the puppet he was manipulating. Although the presentation was intended as a hymn to filial piety during a season devoted to honouring ancestors, Mu Lien's mother was subjected to verbal abuse and a range of tortures, conducted with such vigour that it almost seemed necessary for the sanctity of the 'mother' to be inverted for it to be preserved. In a lighter vein (shifts of tone were frequent) a coquettish hag, jocularly called *Ah Chim* in Min-nan vernacular, wearing a red flower in her hair and carrying a parasol to protect her wrinkled skin from the sun, was mocked for the futility of her efforts. On a more serious note, but still in a vein of unmistakable banter, the Confucian subservience of women was expressed in a rhyming couplet:

Cha boh chay ta boh
Ti teng loh kiam ho!

That is: 'If a woman were to sit on a man, Heaven would pour salt rain!' Throughout the performance, in what was said and in the way it was delivered there was a variety of inflections and rhymes which seemed to capture the elemental function and the spirit of banter itself as it might have occurred in early

Chinese peasant societies. When groups of marriageable young men and women from different villages met for the first time in the Spring festival, gender confrontation must have taken place in a spirit of courtship and contest patterned on the calls and answering calls of birds. Banter, in this context, was initially a disguise for shyness; in *Mu Lien* it was a method of inversion and indirect assertion. Then the frequent recurrence of scatological jokes, an essential part of the purification ritual during a month of heavy monsoon rains when pollution was high in an area of poor sanitation, turned *Mu Lien* into a kind of communal laxative, a purging ritual suggesting a turning over in all senses for the purpose of preserving the status quo.

The Puppet King

Before and after the play there was an elaborate ritual of paying homage to the patron deity, in the form of the principal puppet whom the puppeteers addressed as 'Marshal Tian of the Court of Wind and Fire in the Nine Heavens'. In the prelude, sacrificial paper was burnt at the front of the stage and, led by the *'sai hu'* or master puppeteer (aged seventy-four and the last of his kind in Quanzhou), the troupe chanted magical incantations while the 'Puppet King' or Marshal Tian was hoisted up at the back of the stage. From here he presided throughout the performance, both as the most important puppet and as 'puppeteer'. In the postlude, he was lowered from his elevated position and made to perform a dance at the front of the stage by the puppet master (see Plate 5), concluding with a deep bow to the audience in a self-evident posture of inversion.

The choice of Marshal Tian as the 'Puppet King' as well as the 'Leader of the Actors' in Emperor Ming Huang's Pear Garden Academy is in itself a significant example of inversion: a royal patron fostering a close interdependence between the two theatrical forms in a two-way dialogue. Through this, the puppet theatre provided the human theatre with many of its steps and gestures, and some of the movements of the stage actors were found by puppeteers to be useful when they were manipulating puppets.[26] In this context, the traditional story of the origin of the 'Puppet King', so far ignored by western scholars, offers fascinating evidence of his importance:

> In the company of his high priest, Emperor Ming Huang went to the moon where he heard many pieces of heavenly music. When he returned to his own palace he was nostalgic for the melodies he had heard. Not long after, Heaven sent him a jade flute but no one could play it. In Quanzhou there was an exceptionally gifted musician. He was the grandson of the Su family but born without a father. As this was considered inauspicious, the baby was abandoned in a field. A tenant of Su's, called Lei, picked up the foundling and looked after him. Four years passed, and one day when Su came to collect rent, he recognized his grandson through an identification mark and took him home. As it was a difficult decision whether the boy should be called Su or Lei, he was named Tian meaning 'field', after the place where he had been abandoned. He was so musical that he could play any musical instrument given to him, but unfortunately he could not speak. One day, while the villagers were sinking a well, they found some ancient musical scores which no one except Tian could decipher. Ming Huang heard about him and summoned him to his capital. He was endowed with the gift of speech by the Emperor and was the only person who could play the jade flute. For this he was promoted to the status of 'Imperial Scholar'. He was only eighteen years old. After his death he became known as 'The Leader of the Pear Garden'. The actors of 'The Pear Garden' or 'Li Yuan' theatre addressed him as 'Hsiang Kung Yeh' (honourable young lord) as well as 'Tian tu yuan shuai' (Marshal Tian). In front of his shrine (Han Lin Yuan) they added two words: 'Jade Sound' and, on either side, they wrote this verse:
>
> > At eighteen he started to laugh,
> > Was very drunk and fell down on the golden step;
> > A jade girl descended to support him in her arms.[27]

This account may read like a fairy story, but the precision of the details of parentage and geography suggest that the cult of the 'Puppet King' is based on fact and that Marshal Tian was a real person, born some time in the eighth century in Quanzhou Province.

The Continuity of Tradition

Both the string puppet theatre and the Pear Garden Theatre of which he is the patron deity are flourishing and seminal theatrical forms. The pattern of inversion is unmistakable: a small village foundling is elevated by the Emperor to the distinguished position of 'Imperial Scholar' and the 'Leader of Actors' in the first official theatrical Academy. Actors (excluding puppeteers) had been forbidden to take the imperial exams because they were classified with criminals, prostitutes, and riff-raff as belonging to the lowest strata of society.[28] Not only is this story important in justifying the continuity of the current *Li Yuan Hsi* or Pear Garden Theatre in Quanzhou from the original eighth-century Pear Garden Theatre established by Emperor Ming Huang, but it emphasizes the function of laughter particularly in the puppet theatre. The image of Tian as the 'laughing drunk youth', comforted by a 'jade girl', is highly significant: this account of his deification is analogous to a Daoist initiation rite which enables a disciple to pass from the world of humans to that of the gods through the mediation of the 'jade girl', one of the servants of the mightier gods and goddesses, sent to be his mate.[29] It symbolizes a very special kind of union, better described as 'ritual intercourse', which has a uniquely Daoist meaning. Tian is clearly perceived as, or associated with, the *he he shen* or 'god of union'. Indeed, marionettes (of which Tian is the patron deity) are shown at weddings for the purpose of obtaining from Heaven the happy union of the couple.[30] Tian's extraordinary musical gift reinforces his role as 'unifier': as the only one who could play the heaven-sent 'jade flute', he was capable of placing the world in harmony with the order of the universe through his music. But equally important is his capacity for foolery: the laughing drunken aspect of his image. Tian is also the 'divine jester': his roles as unifier and jester are inseparable, as is supported by the fact that the ideograph *he*, which means 'union', is also the Chinese onomatopoeia for laughter. Puns and onomatopoeia abounded in the puppet *Mu Lien* performance I attended, affording endless laughter.

Here it is crucial to emphasize the unique role of the laughter which is associated with Tian and the puppet theatre of which he is the patron. It has an exorcistic resonance which makes it radically different from the purely entertaining and therapeutic function of laughter in western theatre. Apart from being the divine unifier, musician, and jester, Tian is also an exorcist closely associated with the supreme exorcist god, Chao Kung Ming. According to Chinese ritual, the open laughing mouth of the Exorcist is capable of swallowing the demons of disease and acting in a comic way, exercising the power of gathering and expelling evil spirits.[31] Laughing and jesting were part of a pattern of 'spiritual acrobatics' or inversion which is sometimes directly reinforced: at the exorcistic ceremony preceding the sending off of spirit boats carrying the demons of pestilence in South China, jesting priests often somersault and turn cartwheels, literally turning themselves upside down.[32]

If the story of Marshal Tian, at once Head of the Pear Garden Actors and Puppet King, is one of inversion, so is the most famous play in the Pear Garden repertory, *Ch'en San Wu Niang,* which is sometimes referred to as *The Story of the Lychee and the Mirror.* Written in 1566, this is the oldest and only surviving text of the Pear Garden repertory (there is a copy of it in the Bodleian Library). Since this theatre is meant to be a continuation of the first Pear Garden Theatre in Emperor Ming Huang's reign, it is religious in character, incorporating many hand patterns of Buddhist figures in the Dun Huang caves in north-west China,[33] and free from the acrobatics which characterize the relatively new nineteenth-century Beijing Opera. Outwardly, the story of this play is typical of the Pear Garden repertory, which specializes in impoverished scholars who sit for the imperial exams in order to gain advancement. Ch'en San is a poor scholar who falls in love with Wu Niang at a lantern festival. Her father betrothes her to a rich man, but she has fallen secretly in love with the poor scholar and agrees to elope with him to the Fujian province – in defiance of the strict Confucian code enjoining women's absolute obedience to father, husband, and son. Yet this flagrant act of disobedience is celebrated in Quanzhou not only through performance of this play, but by honouring the couple's unswerving love, which is associated with a tree known locally as the 'One Tree Forest' – a combination of the *banyan* and *chongyang* tree. It is indisputable that paternal authority constitutes the framework of this classical play, but equally undeniable that romantic love is celebrated. There is deliberate ambiguity as to whether the play is a reinforcement or subversion of Confucian ideals, but if anything it comes down in favour of inverting the established order.

Enter Bertolt Brecht: A Western Misunderstanding

That great lover of subversion, the German playwright Bertolt Brecht, first came into contact with Chinese theatre in Moscow in 1935, an event which was to bring that theatre to the attention of the West and to lead the playwright to formulate his most influential dramatic theory. When he saw the great Chinese actor Mei Lan Fang perform in Moscow in that year, he perceived Chinese theatre, out of context, as a detached unemotional form which exactly corresponded to his ideal 'epic' theatre. He was reacting strongly against the theatre of close emotional identification between actor and role, and audience and actor. He felt that if the actor could distance himself from his role, the spectator would do the same, allowing the latter to take a critical stance towards the stage action. So, of course, arose Brecht's famous *Verfremdungseffekte* or 'alienation effect', intended to counter the magical associations of stage illusion and the tendency for spellbound audiences to identify emotionally with characters on stage, both of which Brecht found abhorrent. What Brecht missed in the 'neutral' setting of a Moscow theatre, however, was the intensely religious and sacrificial nature of the theatrical form he was watching. I have already argued that in both puppet and human forms the idea of sacrifice and of ancestor-worship is minutely bound up with the text and style of performance; but the setting in which that performance takes place offers even more striking evidence of the close connection between theatre and religious ritual – a connection which survives to this day, in spite of objections from Beijing.

Traditionally, most Chinese theatre stages have been built directly opposite temple altars, and although many were destroyed during the Japanese occupation of China from 1937 to 1945 and in the Cultural Revolution of 1966, a large number survive. The Tien Hui Keong, in which I watched performances during my stay in Quanzhou, is typical: the stage is set in the temple courtyard facing the altar of the chief deity, with the audience sitting in the intervening space. Most performances are intended primarily as acts of homage to gods, their highly entertaining aspects regarded as secondary. So it is hardly surprising that the extract from the Chinese classic *The Fisherman's Revenge*, which Brecht saw Mei Lan Fang perform in Moscow as part of the celebration of the Fifth International Decade of Revolutionary Art, should have seemed a world away from its cultural background. Brecht was present at the invitation of the German director and theorist Erwin Piscator; he was hungry for a revolutionary theory that would exorcise the ghost of the nineteenth and early twentieth-century European 'romantic' theatre; and he was watching what amounted to an acrobatic turn entirely removed from its traditional context and setting. Brecht thought he had finally found a weapon to fight the old theatre of magic, emotion, and trance – but had he watched the kind of performance that I witnessed in Quanzhou, he might well have come to an opposite conclusion. For here was a theatre intended as a sacrificial offering, made by actors and their deeply involved audiences, in a vernacular dialect that implies the closest intimacy in a multi-dialect nation, in order to appease the wandering ghosts of ancestors. (These ancestors, of course, *only* spoke in the vernacular, literacy being a relatively modern phenomenon.) The spectators, usually consisting of small family groups and close friends, have gathered to affirm Confucian platitudes which they know by heart. Brecht's *Verfremdungseffekte* is hardly applicable here. Indeed, the close link between the actor and his role in traditional Chinese theatre is supported by the history of the female role in the Pear Garden Theatre of Fujian: there is a record of an edict of 1811 or 1815 by a sub-prefect of Amoy (now called Hsiamen) forbidding performances by boy-actor troupes in which the boys playing the roles of young women had pierced their ears and in some cases even bound their feet, and were using the theatrical performances as a means of attracting lovers.[34] And Chinese theatrical history is full of stories of actors who lived in the houses of prostitutes in order to study every detail of their behaviour so that they could render a more lifelike portrayal of this class of women.[35] The highest approbation from the Chinese spectator is 'true to life'.

The Paradoxes of Chinese Theatre

The outward detachment in Chinese acting which impressed Brecht in Moscow was a cover for the most inward identification with the role. Brecht was correct in his comment about the detached stylization of the movement; what he did not realize was that Chinese actors patterned their movements on puppets – but that this would not have alienated a Chinese audience so deeply entrenched in the puppet tradition that they see *themselves* as puppets in the control of spirits and demons.[36] When Brecht saw Mei Lan Fang act in Moscow, the actor's movements appeared self-consciously puppet-like because Mei was extremely aware of the inextricable connection between actors and puppets.[37] But we also know from his biographies how strongly he resembled a woman in real life: 'he is of a willowy build and his voice is high, gentle, and soft; in fact it sounds very much like that of one of his heroines on stage'.[38] In conformity with the traditional Chinese theatrical practice, he had been cast as the *dan* or female role type because of his natural affinities with it – ironically the very actor-role identification which Brecht wanted his *Verfremdungseffekte* to eliminate.

Inversion is the principle which underlies the fundamental strategy of Chinese theatrical movements on stage: for example, if an actor intends to turn towards the right, he will initially point his feet to the left; a momentary feeling may be extended into a long aria, while conversely a distance of several thousand miles is compressed into a few steps. And, in one of the most celebrated sequences in Chinese Opera, popularly known in the West as *The Fight in the Dark*, two actors fight on a brightly lit stage, miming the darkness and only missing each other by a hair's breadth, in full view of the audience.[39]

It may come as a surprise that the criteria for assessing the value of a Chinese theatrical performance, so outwardly visible and spectacular, are as follows: three marks for appearance; six for strength; eight for feeling; and ten for the unseen.[40] This is prompted by the strong Chinese aesthetic of minimalism which insists that the eye see what it knows to be there rather than what *is* there. Strictest economy is therefore the salient characteristic in the deployment of props: if a horse is required, for example, the actor carries a symbolic horse whip – and Brecht eulogized Mei Lan Fang's use of a paddle to depict a boat.[41] But as an extension of this argument, which places the unseen at the top of the scale in a theatre of inversion, it is not difficult to understand that beneath its matter-of-factness and so-called detachment there is an undertow of strong emotion that binds actors and audience together in offering the presentation in homage to *unseen* spirits.

Back to the Birdwoman

What is crucial in Chinese theatre is that the entire stage paraphernalia of ritual, superstition, and magic, before, during, and after a performance should be perceived as a sacrificial offering to ancestral spirits and deities. The true theatrical scenario consists of a multitude of small and local performances taking place in the vernacular (there are just as many vernacular theatres as there are different dialects in China) such as those I saw in Quanzhou. These resemble ancestral seances and are accompanied by the relentless din of orchestras – all part of the exorcism.

Although there are large scale performances of Beijing Opera in *pu tung hua* (the national language) which appear wholly entertaining and secular, local vernacular theatres are still the touchstone of real communication with ancestral spirits. And as I sat with the local audience in Quanzhou in the summer of 1994, watching theatrical performances, sharing a common vernacular dialect and ancestry, I felt an intense emotional involvement which I imagine would have much disquieted Brecht. Indeed, the Chinese regard their theatre as 'Stanislavskian', and in 1954, just two years before Brecht's death, the same Mei Lan Fang who had inspired his *Verfremdungseffekte* was proclaimed the Master Stanislavskian actor of the year in Beijing.[42]

So through the twenty-four magnificent birdwomen overhanging the largest Buddhist altar in China; through Yang Kuei Fei, 'the most beautiful flying swallow' trapped in Emperor Ming Huang's palace; through this same Emperor who regarded himself as a puppet; through the musical foundling he turned into the 'Puppet King'; through the use of puppets as objects of both reverence and scorn; through a theatre in which actors and spectators are emotionally linked in an act of sacrificial homage to ancestral spirits; and even through its detached, ironic, and fundamentally caricatured representation in the theatrical theory of Bertolt Brecht, there runs a pattern of inversion which is indivisible from the basis of Chinese theatre.

On my last day in Quanzhou, after bidding farewell to the birdwomen in the Kai Yuan temple, I purchased a wooden carving of Marshal Tian, the 'Puppet King', as a souvenir. Just as I was about to leave the store, the manager pressed into my hand a small carving of the 'Laughing Buddha' in white jade. Its smile resembles that of the 'Puppet King', and this gift of an amulet juxtaposing the sacred and the profane is still in my possession, providing me with a powerful symbol of the principle of inversion – a principle which I am still trying to fathom.

Notes and References

1. Women's bound feet were called *jin lian* or 'golden lotus'. By the end of the nineteenth century, there were around 100 million women in China whose feet had been bound. See Christina Madden, 'The Art of Confinement', *The Independent*, 24 April 1996, p. 44.
2. Anil de Silva, C*hinese Landscape Painting in the Caves of Dun Huang* (London: Methuen, 1964), p. 86.
3. Marcel Granet, *The Religion of the Chinese People,* trans. Maurice Freedman (Oxford: Oxford University Press, 1975), p. 47.
4. See the section on 'Valkyries', the supernatural warrior women/swan maidens who lived with Odin (the principal god of the Teutonic peoples) in Valhalla, in *New Larousse Encyclopedia of Mythology* (Twickenham: Hamlyn Publishing, 1959), pp. 255–79.
5. In Egypt it is believed that the first deity took the form of a bird which arose from the dark, watery abyss called the 'Nun'. See Roy Willis, ed., 'The First Gods', *World Mythology* (London: Simon and Schuster, 1993), p. 38.
6. Joan Halifax, *Shaman* (London: Thames and Hudson), p. 23.
7. The ideograph for 'male' includes the radical for 'field'.
8. Granet, op. cit., pp. 54–5.
9. Although there are male and female shamans, the latter are regarded with special reverence. This is because the eagle, believed to have been the first shaman, transmitted its essence to a woman sleeping beneath a tree. She became pregnant and gave birth to a baby son, the first shaman. See Halifax, op. cit., p. 23.
10. The ideograph for 'surname' contains the radical for ' woman'.
11. Cecilia Lindqvist, *China: Empire of the Written Symbol* (London: Harvill, 1991), pp. 43–4.
12. See K. M. Schipper, 'The Divine Jester: Some Remarks on the Gods of the Chinese Marionette Theatre', *Journal Bulletin of Ethnology,* 1966, p. 1.
13. The 'birdwoman' story in South-East Asia is taken from the 'Jataka' which is the technical name in Buddhist literature for a story about one of the previous lives of Buddha. See Ghulam Sarwar Yousof, *Dictionary of Traditional South-East Asian Theatre (*Oxford; Singapore: Oxford University Press, 1994) pp. 99–100.
14. In all 'birdwoman' stories, east and west, it is while the birdwoman is bathing in a pool that her 'plumage' is stolen by a male. See *New Larousse Encyclopedia of Mythology,* op. cit., p. 278. With regard to Yang Kuei Fei, in the poem of the great Tang poet Po Chui I – 'The Song of Endless Sorrow' – (see *A Further Collection of Chinese Lyrics and Other Poems*, trs. Alan Ayling and Duncan Mackintosh in collaboration with Ch'eng Hsi and T'ung Ping-Cheng, London: Routledge and Kegan Paul, 1969, p. 221.), *she was invited to bathe in the cool of spring in the Hua-ching pool* and the Emperor spied on her from a secret vantage point. The Hua-ching pool, fed by warm springs, was on Li-shan, the hill about twenty miles east of the capital, Ch'ang-an, now called Xian.
15. Anil de Silva, 1964, p. 132.

16. In Hung Sheng, *The Palace of Eternal Youth,* trs. Yang Hsien-yi and Gladys Yang (Peking: Foreign Language Press, 1955), p. 13, Yang Kuei Fei and Emperor Ming Huang were referred to as the 'phoenix couple'. On the seventh day of the seventh month, on which is celebrated the yearly meeting between the 'Weaving Maiden' and the 'Cowherd' through the mediation of birds, the royal pair vowed that in Heaven they would be 'as birds embraced that fly on one another's wings'. See Po Chui I, 'The Song of Everlasting Sorrow', in Alan Ayling and Duncan Mackintosh, *A Further Collection of Chinese Lyrics,* op. cit., p. 233.
17. See J. J. M. de Groot, *The Religious System of China,* Vol. VI, Leyden: E.J. Brill, 1910, p. 1194. From 409 to 377 BC, the ruler Muh wanted to expose such diseased persons to the sun in order to persuade Heaven to send rain in time of drought.
18. See Piet van der Loon, *The Classical Theatre and Art Song of South Fukien* (Taipei: SMC Publishing, 1992), p. 35.
19. William Dolby, *A History of Chinese Drama* (London: Paul Elek, 1976), p. 10.
20. See Mary Douglas, 'The Social Control of Cognition: Some Factors in Joke Perception', *Man,* Journal of the Royal Anthropological Institute, III, No. 3 (1968), p. 374.
21. See Josephine Huang Hung, 'Introduction', *Classical Chinese Plays* (Taiwan: Vision Press, 1972), p. 3.
22. Roberta Helmer Stalberg, *China's Puppets* (San Francisco: China Books, 1984), p. 69–70.
23. This is translated in Dolby, 1976, p. 10.
24. Hsu Tao Ching, *The Chinese Conception of Theatre* (Seattle: University of Washington Press, 1985) p. 152.
25. Piet van der Loon, 'Les Origines rituelles du théâtre chinois', *Journal Asiatic,* CCLXV (Paris: Asiatique Societé, 1997), p. 147.
26. Hsieh Yong Chien, one of the teachers in the Pear Garden Theatre in Quanzhou, teaches stage movements to both actors and puppeteers. In the Lingao county theatrical performers play the same roles on stage as the puppets they manipulate. See 'Chinese Puppetry', *China Today,* XV, No. 6 (Beijing: China Welfare Institute, June 1996), p. 69.
27. This is a close translation from Wu Jie Chiu, *Li-yuan yu li-yuan hsi hsi-lun* [*The Origin of the Pear Garden: an Examination of the Pear Garden Theatre*] (Fuzhou: Fujian Theatrical Research Institute, 1985), p. 63.
28. The Imperial exams began in the Han dynasty (206 BC–AD 220) and were only abolished in 1905. See H. G. Creel, *Chinese Thought* (New York: New American Library of World Literature, 1953), p. 168.
29. See K.M. Schipper, op. cit., p. 92.
30. Ibid., p. 81.
31. Ibid., pp. 85–6.
32. Ibid. See Plate 2, entitled 'The Sending Off of the Spirit Boat: the Jesting Priest' (Tainan, 12 October 1964, at night).

33. For example, hand patterns known as 'Kuan Yin' ('Goddess of Mercy') hand, 'Buddha' hand, 'Mother Chiang' or 'root ginger' hand were based on those of religious figures painted on the walls of the Dun Huang Caves founded in AD 433 by the monk Lo Tsun.
34. See Piet van der Loon,1992, p. 24.
35. This is taken from *Ch'in yun hsieh ying hsiao-pu,* p. 56. See Colin Mackerras's translation in his *The Rise of the Peking Opera* (Oxford: Clarendon Press, 1972), p. 83.
36. Dolby, 1976, p. 82.
37. Roger Howard, *Contemporary Chinese Theatre (*London 1978), p. 29.
38. A. E. Zucker, *The Chinese Theatre* (Boston: Little, Brown, 1925), p. 187.
39. Kenneth Tynan, *Curtains* (London, 1961), p. 389.
40. This teaching was ascribed to the distinguished nineteenth-century actor Chi Yu Liang. See *Chinese Literature*, No. 9 (Peking: Foreign Language Press, 1969), p. 82.
41. Bertolt Brecht, 'Alienation Effects in Chinese Acting', in *Brecht on Theatre,* ed. and trans. John Willett (London: Methuen, 1964), p. 92.
42. See Uchiyama Jun, 'Doctrine: China, Theatre after 1949', *The Drama Review,* XV, No. 3 (Spring 1971), p. 253.

Chapter Three: Puppet Dominance in Chinese Thought and the Art of *T'ai Chi Ch'uan*

Emperor Qin Shi Huangdi and his Puppet Obsession

As the first Chinese Emperor of a short-lived dynasty who unified China under a centralized political system in 221 BC (which lasted till 1911), Shi Huangdi is remembered for his ruthless control of China and by the remaining evidence of his endeavours to maintain security and power: the Great Wall and his terracotta soldiers, skilfully crafted to protect him in death and still to be seen in his tomb at Mount Li in Xian, Shensi Province. He is at once famous for his achievements and notorious for his burning of books in 213 BC[1] The purpose of this was not so much to destroy learning as to guarantee his monopoly of it, so that copies of precious books – collections of poetry, historical documents, books of philosophy and literature covered by the 'hundred schools' – were only available to academicians working in his Imperial Library.[2] The *I-Ching* ('Book of Changes') which is said to contain all the possible social situations in which the superior man might find himself, stemming from the time of King Wen and his son, the Duke of Chou (c.1000 BC), was however spared. Unlike the later Tang Emperor Xuan Zhong or Ming Huang, who is associated with the string puppet, Emperor Shi Huangdi has no strong claim on Chinese affection despite the size and scale of his remaining monuments. A man so obsessed with control was unlikely to inspire it and the nature of that obsession in terms of his empire, subjects, and every aspect of government, as carefully documented by the great historian Sima Qian (145–86BC), expressed itself best in the manipulation of his collection of robots or animated dolls. The greatest law-maker in Chinese history, the first to standardize the system of laws and examine and codify duties and responsibilities so as to establish unchanging practices,[3] found that the absolute power that he yearned to exercise over his human subjects was unobtainable and so retreated into the world of mechanical toys.

'The Thread from Heaven': Control and the Transmission of Power

Just as Lord Brahma in Hindu mythology is acknowledged as the Ultimate 'Holder of Strings', so in the Chinese world picture, 'Heaven' or 'The Heavenly Emperor' *Huang[hao] T'ien Shang Ti* ('Sovereign-on-High-August-Heaven') is perceived as the guardian of the 'thread'[4] or controlling device which is handed down to the reigning Emperor known as the 'Son of Heaven'. The Emperor became the supreme religious head and all the administrative cults which were established had value only in so far as they were reflections of the imperial cult.[5] As the sole spiritual authority, he was the basis of the official religion and nothing could be instituted unless it was carried out by him or by those to whom he had delegated his spiritual powers. So the network of control stemming from Heaven to Emperor to People is envisaged through the image of a string puppet in which the Emperor/Controller assumes the role, sometimes of puppeteer and sometimes of puppet in a system which is transposed from heaven to state, and from state to paternal or family control. If we look, for example, at the traditional ceremony for honouring family ancestors in which their spirit was invited to possess the living grandson[6] and often spoke through him, there is little doubt that the grandson behaved like a manipulated puppet in the control of an ancestral spirit, the image of puppet manipulation therefore becoming a metaphor for the transmission of power. Emperor Shi Huangdi played the role that was expected of him in this transmission to such an extent that he ended, as we know from the *Hsi Ching Tsa Chi* ('Various Notes on the Capital of the West') attributed to Ke Hsuan (3rd century AD) in a world of make-believe, preferring the metaphor to the problems of government. According to Ke Hsuan, Liu Pang (founder of the Han dynasty, 206BC–220AD) discovered many robots and a magic mirror in Qin Shi Huangdi's palaces.[7]

It was, of course, a much later Emperor (see Chapter 2) who best expressed the wider definition of the 'Thread from Heaven' but when Emperor Tang Ming Huang compared himself to a string puppet in the poem I have quoted, he was only reflecting a national sentiment. This is reflected in the following lines from the well known play – *The Lute* – by Gao Ming (c.1301–1370),[8] which recounts the story of a successful Imperial Examination candidate who was forced to reject his faithful wife and parents and marry the Prime Minister's daughter. One of the neighbours in the humble village of his origin comments:

> *Zhang Guancai: Ah, so that's how it was. In that case,*
> *(Sings) After all he had no choice,*
> *It looks as if the gods and demons*
> *Pulled all the strings.*
> [Act 37, 'Sweeping the Pines']

The string-puppet image had become a common metaphor in China by this time, expressing an unresisting acceptance of the human predicament which could only increase the Chinese fear of the supernatural world. This fear had been part of Chinese thought and religious practice for a long time and is seen particularly clearly in Emperor Shi Huangdi's increasingly frantic search for the elixir of life and ever deeper involvement with the world of robots and mechanical toys.

Jean Lévi's *The Chinese Emperor*

The French novelist Jean Lévi has created a compelling narrative on this subject – *The Chinese Emperor* – derived from, and closely depending on, Sima Qian's *Annals of Qin* in his *Historical Records*.[9] In the afterword to his novel Jean Lévi states that the idea of robots or puppets was suggested to the Emperor by one of the anecdotes in *Lie Zi*, a Daoist work. This is the story of the famous puppeteer Yang Shih in the reign of Emperor Chu Mu Wang (ruled 947–928BC) in the Zhou dynasty. There is no historically documented account of this connection but it is very plausible that the great Emperor would have known of this story and Jean Lévi convincingly builds a portrait of an Emperor obsessed with objects which can be mechanically controlled at his will and pleasure. There is a vivid account of how one of his craftsmen was ordered to cast a bronze orchestra comprising twelve marionettes.[10] Two tubes ran beneath the dais on which the twelve bronze musician puppets sat cross-legged on a mat playing various instruments. Two men hidden behind a screen that concealed the ends of the tubes manipulated the strings through one while blowing into the other, thereby causing the figures to come to life. The Emperor was completely enchanted and in time grew dissatisfied with his real concubines and dancing girls, preferring marionettes, though when his concubines, either in flattery or mockery, dared to simulate their puppet-like movements, they were summarily executed. He then had servants made of lacquer and wood and manipulated to offer him food and wine, his obsession with puppets growing to such an extent that he ended up wanting to populate his entire empire with them.[11] Even in death, as we have seen, he was surrounded by a version of them, his vast tomb, constructed by over 700,000 convicts,[12] being filled with an army of mortuary figures, as well as human slaves, buried to serve him in death. In later centuries moveable figures of clay or wood were substituted for human sacrifices in the tombs of the rich and powerful, further underlining the puppet connection, but already in Emperor Shi Huangdi's tomb we have a picture of the 'Son of Heaven', Heaven's 'puppet' as it were, having received the sacred 'thread' which turns him into the Controller/ Puppeteer of his subjects, ending his days not only with accompanying sacrifices of slaves and concubines,[13] but with a resplendent army of terracotta warriors as well as a horde of 'robots', hydraulically powered to dance and sing for him[14] in the next world.[15] There is almost a sense of puppet mania running through the Imperial Court at this period, driven by an increasingly obsessed Emperor, which was bound to foster the later dominance of the puppet in Chinese theatre, religious beliefs, and even in healing practices.

Puppets and Healing: The Merging of the Medium/Healer, Puppet and Scapegoat

It is understandable that from the point of view of 21st century scholars, stories of spirits entrapped in puppets and used for healing, seem to belong to folklore if not of dangerous magic. This was certainly the view taken by the authorities in Beijing in 1994, when I spent six weeks in the Fujian Province. It was thus almost impossible to see any of the old religious practices and the sale of extravagant paper wreaths and ornately decorated vehicles customarily used as burnt offerings during traditional ancestral worship was somewhat restricted. So the following references, for example, to the practice of *ang i* ('puppet aunts') in Amoy (modern Hsia-men), in the early 20th century, have to depend on the detailed descriptions of De Groot[16] and on accounts given by relatives who emigrated from that part of the world to Malaysia at about the same time. In my opinion such descriptions and accounts accurately reflect the high premium placed on puppets as agents of healing. Deep superstitious beliefs die hard and whatever the official line promulgated by Beijing, I am convinced that the use of puppets by, and as, mediums still takes place.

In certain parts of the Fujian province, certainly in the Amoy or Hsia-men vicinity mentioned above, the same word *ang* (in Min-nan dialect) or *wang* (in Mandarin) is used for a 'puppet' as well as for a female medium (called *ang i* or 'puppet aunt'). In ancient documents the term *wang* can also refer to a female sacrificial victim, literally meaning a 'queer hag' or someone deformed, of a nervous temperament and given to possession, who in the reign of the ruler Mu (BC 409–377), was exposed to the sun in the hope that Heaven would take pity and send rain to the earth.[17] In this area at least, the female medium was closely identified with the puppet and spirit possession. In fact she was regarded as the surrogate mother of the puppet spirit in the same way as Indian puppeteers regard their puppets as *puttalika* 'little sons' and the 10th century BC puppeteer Yang Shih referred to the puppet that offended the Emperor as 'his son' (see Chapter 5) – an indication of high esteem and affection.

The *ang i* or 'puppet aunts' in Amoy are known to employ 'spirits' which they carry with them in the body of a puppet hidden in their bosom or a sleeve of their garment in the course of ministering to clients. This would be a familiar story in Kelantan where I researched the art of *Manora* (see Chapter 1) because it is a common practice in the villages I visited for 'witch doctors' (*bomoh*) to keep spirits in huts. The puppet used by the female Amoy medium is usually made out of peach or willow wood because there is a strong belief in its extra spiritual and magical properties[18] and the way such a puppet is made helps us to see the process through which it is believed life or vitality can be siphoned into it. The 'puppet aunt' sneaks into the home of a pregnant woman and stealthily conceals a piece of peach or willow wood by her windowsill, carefully choosing a place which the woman is likely to pass over or be in contact with. This is primarily to enable the vitality of the foetus to be transferred into the wood. As soon as the baby is born, the puppet aunt removes the piece of wood and with appropriate magical spells, carves it in the likeness of the baby with particular attention to its correct sexual organ. This little figure is carefully preserved until the baby begins to utter sounds resembling speech. At this point the 'puppet aunt' takes it into a temple and hides it somewhere on, or behind, the altar so that a priest, while performing sacrificial rites or uttering magical conjurations to induce spirits to the sacred table, will inadvertently summon the soul or spirit of the real baby into the puppet. If by this means the entire soul of the baby is siphoned into the puppet, the baby will die; if only part of its vitality has been transferred, it will develop a fairly serious illness. Meanwhile, the 'animated' puppet, thus brought to life, is then taken away by its surrogate mother who, by exposing it nightly to dew, ensures that its vitality does not totally evaporate and that she now possesses a puppet inhabited by a live spirit which, hidden in her sleeve or close to her stomach, is used for healing, sorcery, divination and other contacts with the spirit world. The puppet has thus become a spiritual power-centre essential to, and indivisible from, the power of the medium herself and it is not therefore surprising that the same character *wang or ang* came to stand not just for 'puppet', 'female medium' and 'sacrifice' but also for 'scapegoat'.[19]

So strong is the Chinese belief in the ability of puppets to provide a habitation for spirits, that there have been cases where it is claimed that the transfer of tormenting evil spirits from humans into wooden likenesses of their

Puppet Dominance in Chinese Thought

victim which are immediately destroyed, can free the possessed.[20] Closely related to this practice is that of using a puppet to absorb an evil spirit from a physically sick person, there being a strong Chinese belief in the correlation between illness and spirit possession. A puppet is sent for and passed all over the sick person, while an appropriate spell is uttered to induce the spirit into it. Once it has absorbed the evil spirit, the puppet is burnt, the spirit dispelled and the patient cured. It is therefore no surprise that in this part of China, the idea and reputation of the puppet as an effective agent of exorcism, is firmly entrenched. String-puppet performances, called *ka-le-hi* ('the theatre of auspicious ritual'), are used to propitiate or expel evil spirits, particularly on occasions like weddings, birthdays, or the completion of buildings, when an absolutely clean start is required. The consequent respect accorded to puppets because of their special powers, was traditionally extended to their operators – puppeteers of the *jia-li* (auspicious ritual) theatre – who, unlike actors, – relegated to the bottom of the social scale on a par with criminals and prostitutes, were permitted to sit for the civil service examinations.[21] If actor troupes were to pass a *jia-li* troupe on the street, they were required by etiquette, to send a representative to pay respects to the patron deity of puppets, Marshal Tian – also referred to as *Xianggong yeh* ('Reverend Lord Minister').

The Exorcistic Power of the Dancing Puppet and *T'ai Chi Ch'uan*

There is a close link between the puppet figure of Marshal Tian and the ancient callisthenic art of *T'ai Chi Chuan*, represented by the well-known circular symbol surrounded by eight 'trigrams' or three-lined figures consisting of broken or unbroken lines or a combination of both. (See diagram below). In an important rite of exorcism, the puppet figure is made to dance on the *T'ai Chi Ch'uan* symbol as an act of exorcism, change and propitiation, a rite involving the harnessing of the fundamental strategy of *T'ai Chi Ch'uan* (see Plate 4). If we examine the three Chinese characters denoting this art, the first two translated as *T'ai Chi* mean 'Supreme Principle' referring to the fundamental concept that all of life has been set in motion by the interaction of two vital forces – *yin,* the passive and *yang,* the active – the opposing and yet complementary male and female energies which have given rise to everything under the sun. The third character *Ch'uan,* represents 'fist' but without any of the pugilistic connotations associated with this word in the West, since in ancient Chinese thought *ch'uan* implies concentration, containment and control over one's actions suggesting that mobility is governed by immobility, the outer by the inner and the body by the mind.[22] In other words *Ch'uan* connotes power and control over one's actions and suggests a technique of organized harmonious forms designed to protect the practitioner from destructive forces. So though the result is mental and physical co-ordination, the mind is the chief controller, and aptly *T'ai Chi Ch'uan* has been called the exercise 'controlled by the mind' *(ting tou yuan).*[23]

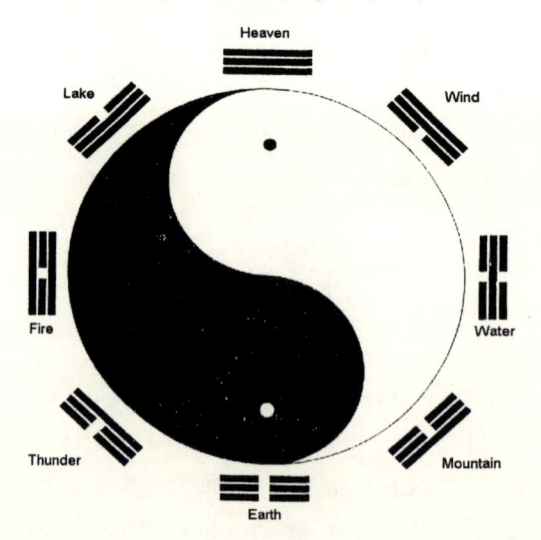

Diagram showing the circular *T'ai Chi* symbol containing the two contrasting but interlocking pear-shaped bodies – *yin* and *yang* — which have given rise to everything in the universe. [Note that the white and black dots reinforce the principle of opposites by representing elements of *yin* in *yang* and vice-versa.] This symbol is surrounded by eight trigrams supposed to have been

originally seen as markings on the back of a 'Divine Tortoise' by the legendary Emperor Fu Hsi about 3,000 BC.

The Chinese regard the famous *T'ai Chi* symbol as an ancient mathematical model of the universe. The eight trigrams symbolise the primal forces of creation and destruction and suggest the possibility of change. Most significantly, the entire design is governed by the principle of opposites represented by the interlocking, but opposing, pear-shaped bodies held in harmony within a circle as well as in the opposing sets of eight trigrams contained within the harmony of the universe. (For example, the 'heaven' trigram consisting of three unbroken lines is placed directly opposite the 'earth' trigram made up of three broken lines). Nowhere is the primal power of opposites as the key to functioning and indeed to life itself, so clearly articulated: it is the interaction of the opposing breaths of 'heaven' and 'earth' which has given rise to the 'ten thousand things in the universe'; and it is the application of this strategical principle of opposites which has found its way into the conduct of daily affairs including warfare[24] and into the charting of effective theatrical movements observable in Chinese and Japanese theatres (see Chapter 5).

With increasing political restrictions from Beijing, it is rare to find such exorcistic rituals taking place in modern China, though they can still be found in Singapore which has a large Fukienese community.[25] Where it does still take place, in a ritual considered so potent that it does not even require spectators for the rite to work, it is clear that the figure of the moving puppet on the eight trigrams is itself an archetypal model for exorcism. The art of *T'ai Chi Ch'uan* is a set of movements based on the sixty-four permutations of the 8 trigrams. These movements consist of 108 forms, as many forms as there are believed to be malignant influences in the world. In other words there is a correlation between the performance of the movements and a confrontation with evil, a confrontation that assumes the nature of a metaphysical battle, a war-like concept which is underlined by the martial title and nature of Xianggong or Marshal Tian who, as we have seen, is closely connected with the exorcism of evil spirits in a kind of spiritual war. This interpretation is further supported by the presence of five triangular flags, each mounted on thin poles inserted at the back of the litter (*lien*), an indispensable piece of furniture for the altar of every deity dealing in oracles and representing the Divine Emperors who rule over the five divisions of the Universe, each the commander-in-chief of a celestial army who suppresses the work of evil spirits.[26] There are, of course, no historical documents spelling out the connection between the Xianggong puppet figure dancing on the eight trigrams and the art of *T'ai Chi Chuan* and the modern Western practitioner of *T'ai Chi* may find it difficult to accept that the 108 forms she or he goes through are any more than physical exercises. It remains true, however, that according to Amoy Chinese religious beliefs, the movements serve to counteract the seventy-two *te soah* ('earthly evil influences') and thirty-six *t'ien kang* ('celestial evil influences').[27] What is unarguable is the therapeutic effect of practising them and as long as the words 'evil vibrations' are substituted for 'evil spirits', and the concepts of 'purification of space' and 'physical well-being' replace those of 'spiritual exorcism' and 'purging of evil influences' there is no fundamental disagreement. After all, the result is very much the same and in both cases the power of the dancing puppet (i.e. puppet movements) – the practitioner of *T'ai Chi* being told to see herself or himself as a string puppet attached to the ceiling by an invisible string fixed to the top of the head – is identified with primal energy generated by the two creative forces of *Yin* and *Yang*.

The Dancing Puppet and Primal Energy

These two creative forces are also called the 'Dual Powers' or the 'Two Breaths' (*Erh Ji*) and it is said that all life is the result of the conjunction between the 'male' breath of heaven (yang) and the 'female' breath of earth (yin). The vital energy which the exercise of *T'ai Chi Ch'uan* is meant to generate is termed *ch'i* ('breath') and it is this distinctive quality which has been transferred to theatre and distinguishes the gifted or charismatic performer (see Chapter 5). The interaction of, or tension between, these two opposing forces is life enhancing when used in the practice of *T'ai Chi Ch'uan* which deliberately makes use of a series of opposites: inhalation-exhalation, solid-empty, right-left, forward-backward, rise-sink, etc. The puppet dancing on the *T'ai Chi* symbol links two seminal forces: puppet power and the 'Supreme Principle' of life. In other words, to move like a puppet is to return to the primal source of energy produced by the interaction of the same *Yin* and *Yang*.

Without being a religion, the concept of *yin/yang* has given a dualist orientation to Chinese thought and established itself as fact. Together with the theory of *Wu Hsing* ('Five Elements'), the categorization of things into the familiar five elements of wood, fire, earth, metal and water (all products of various combinations of *yin* and *yang*) it has been particularly important to the Chinese from Han times (206BC–220AD), a period of great material prosperity, as the Chinese empire gradually spread to Central Asia and Korea. Indeed the concepts of *yin/yang* and the 'Five Elements', from earliest times constituting the bedrock of Chinese consciousness, grew in these more prosperous times, to permeate the art as well as the thought of the Han people so that an artist considered that only the correct balance of the two forces and five elements could bring happiness and prosperity. The achievement of such a balance would be duly rewarded by being 'allowed to visit the land of the immortals and to enter Heaven riding a flying dragon or a floating cloud.'[28]

Wu-Hsing: **The 'Five Elements' Theory**

If we enumerate the elements in the order of the sequence of the seasons they symbolize, Wood represents Spring (beginning of the year), Fire stands for Summer, Earth is the central pivot of the changing year, Metal equals Autumn and Water represents Winter. There is no clear explanation as to why the division of the world into five elements was identified with the yearly sequence of the seasons but it became accepted as the decree of heaven in the same way that in the sphere of human government, the tendency towards dualism was marked by the opposition of the 'golden mean' and 'excess' – action requiring a middle course in opposition to extravagance and excess. The number 5 was clearly perceived as a magical number, being the same as the central number of the 'magic square' which is itself the same as the 'River Chart' brought out of the River Luo in Honan, according to legend, by the Divine Tortoise. (See note under *T'ai Chi* diagram). These legends are sometimes confused because the 8 trigrams of the *I-Ching*, arrived at by arranging two of the *T'ai Chi* symbols in every possible grouping of three and supposed to have been seen on the back of a 'Divine Tortoise', seem to be part of the same divine revelations as those associated with the sacred Luo diagram or the magic square of nine, arising from the same river.[29] Importantly, and I will be returning to this point below, the ancient way of writing the character *tian*, meaning 'field' – the same character that is used for Marshal *Tian* – resembles this same magic square, but what I'm concerned with here is to emphasise the special importance given to the number 5 in both legends and to see how it runs through both the theory of the elements and the practice of *T'ai Chi Ch'uan*. For example, in the magic square of nine in which the horizontal, vertical and diagonal line of three figures add up to 15 it is 5 which is clearly positioned in the middle. Each cell is accorded a number as follows:

4 9 2

3 [5] 7

8 1 6

The magical importance of the number 5, seen in the centre of the square, links with the number of elements (5) which are themselves the ramification of the *yin/yang* concept since each element is made up of one of the trigrams. For instance, water is composed of two broken lines encasing an unbroken line:

– –

—

– –

and not only is every person identified with one of these five elements for divination purposes but the five basic attitudes in the practice of *T'ai Chi Ch'uan*:

'Advance', 'Retreat', 'Look to the Left', 'Look to the Right', and 'Central Equilibrium', are directly derived from the five elements, demonstrating that every move in this art has been carefully and strategically worked out . The strategy is expressed thus in a 14th century treatise:

When four ounces move a thousand pounds it is obviously
Not a matter of strength.
Looking up, the other feels my height; looking down, the other
Feels my depth; advancing he feels the distance lengthening;
Retreating he is more crowded.
A small bird cannot take off; a single fly cannot land.
Others do not know me, but I alone know others.[30]

So the incorporation of the magical 5 into the basic attitudes of *T'ai Chi Ch'uan* invests it with something of the oracular power of the legendary river chart.

The Synchronisation of Marshal Tian with Two Key Symbols in Chinese Thought

It is nowhere documented, as we have seen, that the practitioners or founders of the art of *T'ai Chi Chuan* consciously connected the recommended string-puppet-like stance of the performer of these ancient movements with that of the dancing marionette figure of Xianggong (Marshal Tian). The connection is however very plausible, since the dancing puppet figure on the *T'ai Chi* symbol expresses, as I have shown, a potent rite for exorcising evil spirits and clearing the ground for a new venture – no new temple can be opened unless this rite is performed – and the dancing puppet has itself become the God of puppets for the people of Southern China, whose traditional string-puppet theatre has become, as a genre, the most sacred form of Chinese drama. Marshal Tian as the figure deliberately positioned at the centre of the *T'ai Chi* symbol (see Plate 4) brings together two key symbols of Chinese thinking: the interlocking of *yin* and *yang* and the motif of the 'magic nine squares' with which, as I've indicated, Tian, is associated. The old way of rendering the character for 'field' (*tian*) is that of a square with nine divisions. So the puppet Tian, seen as both puppet and God, and standing at the centre of opposites, becomes both life-giving healer (as field nourisher) and exorcist (resolver of tensions).

Trigrams and String Images

The creation of trigrams is attributed to Fu Hsi who after seeing the patterns on the back of the 'Divine Tortoise', devised eight sets of broken and unbroken lines in various combinations as symbols of the fundamental nature of the universe. Each of the eight trigrams stands for an aspect of nature, society, and the individual. These predate the sixty four hexagrams which are described and tabulated in the *I-Ching* and were preserved on wooden tablets long before King Wen (the author of the *I-Ching*) recorded them in 1150 BC in the form of predictions. His son, the Duke of Chou, added a commentary to the text of the *I-Ching* and Confucius contributed to it by writing a detailed treatise on the philosophy of the book which he called the *Ten Wings*. Eventually the 'Book of Changes' or *I-Ching* became the most important of the five Confucian classics.[31] It was also, as we have seen, the only book to be spared by the great lover of puppets Emperor Qin Shi Huangdi in 213 BC when he ordered the burning of books. Apart from divination, this book also offers information on government, numerology, astrology, cosmology, meditation and military strategy, and although it originated in China, it became an integral part of the cultural heritage of Japan, Korea, Vietnam and other Far Eastern countries.[32] All *T'ai Chi Ch'uan* movements are based on the 64 hexagrams of the *I-Ching*, and they, like their model, carry strategic as well as exorcistic value. The strategic element of *T'ai Chi Ch'uan* implies a sense of control which the treatises that shape its movements often relate to string puppet imagery and it is interesting in this context that Zeami, one of the founders of Noh drama, while using the string

Puppet Dominance in Chinese Thought   77

puppet/puppeteer imagery located in the heart, as a means of teaching his actors how to move, also saw acting in terms of military tactics.[33]

Lessons in strategy are in fact encoded in *T'ai Chi Ch'uan* movements. It was watching the fight between a snake and a crane and observing the way the snake fended off the crane's attack that inspired the 10th century Daoist priest Chang San Feng[34] to codify the movements in *T'ai Chi Ch'uan*. What fascinated him was that although the crane flew down and tried to stab the snake with its sharp beak, the latter, by twisting and bending, was always out of reach, and furthermore, was able to use its tail to attack the crane's neck. It represented an unforgettable lesson in strategy and he felt that he had been given the golden opportunity of observing the principle of the *I-Ching* in living form. Another good example of strategy is the 21st form in the *Yang* style of *T'ai Chi Ch'uan* known as 'Carry Tiger in your arms and return to Mountain' and is related to the *I-Ching* Hexagram 52, *Ken* which signifies Stillness and Mountain. The hexagram gives the image of an embraced 'tiger' which is in some way related to the 'mountain'. In performing this movement the practitioner releases the 'tiger' and allows it to return to the 'mountain'. This is for his own protection. The Commentary on the Decision says:

When it is time to stop, then stop.
When it is time to advance, then advance.
Thus movement and rest do not miss the right time.[35]

This sense of strategic movement is often shaped in the treatises by special reference to the body as string-puppet:

Remember that the entire body is strung together, let there
not be the slightest break.

In each movement the entire body must be light and it is especially important
that all parts of the body string together.[36]

Use force as if drawing on silk.[37] *A feather cannot be added, nor a fly land without effecting a change in balance.*[38]

If the ch'i is correctly cultivated, your spirit of vitality will rise and you will feel as if your head were suspended by a string from above, thus eschewing bodily slowness or clumsiness.[39]

Holding the head as if suspended by a string from above, the entire body feel slight and nimble.

In any action all parts of the body must be connected like pearls on a string.[40]

If the puppet string image is strong in the art of performing *T'ai Chi Ch'uan* movements, it is fundamental to the execution of Chinese theatrical movements which are of course themselves underpinned by the principles of *T'ai Chi* (Supreme Principle). So not only did the great 20th century Chinese actor, Mei Lan Fang, comment on the actors' movements as puppet-like[41] but there are accounts of Chinese acting which report that, for example, when a certain Kao Ming-kuan was performing in a play, there was a sequence which was as if puppets had come on stage.[42] The teachers of the Pear Garden Theatre in Quanzhou told me that as a standard rule, the body is divided into five sections – head, eyes, hands, trunk, and feet – but these must move as though strung together by an invisible string. This seemed very similar to the vertical alignment of head, neck and torso needed in *T'ai Chi* where the practitioner, as I have said, is usually instructed by the teacher to imagine she or he were suspended from a control-string attached to the top centre of her/his head. In other words the pupil has to become a marionette and with the subsequent concentrated balance of weight, she/he will move with the lightness of one.

Marionette Movement and Embryonic Behaviour

In the early 20th century, an American scientist, George E. Coghill,[43] beginning the first systematic observation of embryonic behaviour, chose as his subject of study a kind of salamander. After watching its early stages of development very carefully, he noticed that all the activity of this creature seems to originate in the musculature of its head before travelling to its tail and, more significantly, remained controlled by the head and trunk even after the development of its limbs. He was then able to extend his research to cover human embryonic behaviour which led him to the very significant conclusion that humans have inside them the 'marionette' principle, a principle which becomes vitiated by civilized habits like sitting on a chair. It has been noticed that little children, in so far as they are marionette-like in their natural state of relaxation and total lack of anxiety, quite often escape unscathed from accidents. 'To become little children' is another model which *T'ai Chi* instructors use, and as I will show in my discussion of Heinrich von Kleist and his advocacy of the marionette art (See Chapter 6), the equation of the marionette condition with the primal state of innocence, the pre-conscious state which is the true springboard of creativity, should be taken very seriously, as it has been in the theatres of the East.

The Power of *T'ai Chi Ch'uan*

Since 1970 when western theatre directors like Peter Brook,[44] Robert Wilson,[45] and Bill Gaskill[46] incorporated *T'ai Chi* movements into their productions, this ancient Chinese form of movements has passed in and out of fashion. It is now well-entrenched in the field of healing therapies which have turned eastwards for inspiration and many practitioners go through the movements as a form of relaxation, a strengthener of the back for those with back problems and an effective antidote against hypertension and insomnia. When I was in Quanzhou in 1994 groups of about thirty or so regularly gathered outside temples in the early morning to perform these movements and it is the alignment of these movements with Nature which takes us to the heart of their meaning. For if we survey its ancient history as I've tried to do in the preceding pages, it would seem that locked into the River Chart of Nine Magic Squares – etymologically linked to Marshal Tian – and the Dual Concept of the Two Breaths of *Yin* and *Yang*, is our very first embryonic blueprint of life. The moment we realize this, it is as though we return to the primal marionette principle which is in us and which we have not completely forgotten. If an embryo moves like a puppet, it follows that the movement of a puppet is synonymous with the primal movements of life, in which we return once again to the Hindu concept of fusing two seminal activities in one god – the Lord Shiva – god of puppets and of all movements. Lastly, if we consider the '*Ch'uan*' component of the term – *T'ai Chi Ch'uan* – it is evident from all the resonances which this art form has triggered, that it does not only refer to the literal 'fist', suggesting a physical confrontation. Its carefully structured 108 forms which are meant to counteract 108 evil influences in the heavenly and terrestrial spheres, demonstrate in no uncertain terms that the objective of *T'ai Chi Ch'uan* is indeed the waging of a spiritual battle, mirrored in a physical way by the use of the art as a means of self-defence. So from both a spiritual and physical perspective, it is efficacious for the practitioner in terms of protection from evil spirits and of physical healing, perhaps different ways of describing the same phenomenon, since illness is sometimes perceived as a form of demon possession and the exorcism of evil spirits as a form of healing. Behind this ancient art, whether considered as a metaphysical battle or as a series of health-giving exercises, stands the figure of the string-puppet, both as a model for movement and a symbol of renewal. In the words of Heinrich von Kleist in his remarkable essay on the marionette theatre (see Chapter 6) 'we must eat again of the tree of knowledge in order to return to the state of innocence.'

The following lines from a *T'ai Chi* treatise by a distinguished pupil of Chang San-feng aptly summarise the power of this art form:

T'ai Chi as the ultimate form arises out of Wu Chi, the formless,
It is the origin of movement and quietude, and the mother of

Yin and Yang.
In movement it opens, in quietude it closes. ...The quietness is like that of a mountain range.[47]

This sharp image of life and death, emptiness and form, opening and closing, is encapsulated in an often repeated form in a *T'ai Chi Ch'uan* movement known as the 'Bird's Beak'. It is an eloquent marking, if not celebration of inaction, the return to stillness or nothingness which is the starting point of all creation. The following poem which catches the almost inexpressible sentiment behind this form has been ascribed to the 4th century BC Daoist philosopher Zhuang Zi:

The bird opens its beak and sings its song
And then its beak comes together in stillness,
So living and Nature must meet in stillness
Like the closing of the beak after its song.[48]

The circular nature of existence, expressed so perfectly in this poem, as it is by the interlocking *yin* and *yang* symbol, and in the circular journey of the 108 movements of *T'ai Chi Ch'uan*, brings me back, in my quest for the meaning of this ancient form of callisthenics, to the 3rd century BC puppet-loving First Emperor of a unified Chinese Empire, Qin Shi Huangdi and his miraculous exemption of the oracular *I-Ching* from the flames. The puppet-like movements of *T'ai Chi Ch'uan* have, like the book on which it is patterned, been saved from the fire, and, more enduring than the Great Wall and terracotta warriors made to guard a human Emperor in life and death, continue to rise up, phoenix-like, to renew us.

Notes and References

1. Sima Qian, *Historical Records*, tr. Raymond Dawson, Oxford, New York: Oxford University Press, 1994, p. vii.
2. This was burnt down at the end of the Qin dynasty resulting in a great loss of learning.
3. Dawson, 1994, p. 82.
4. Ibid., p. xix.
5. Granet, 1975, p. 104.
6. C. H. Wang, *From Ritual to Allegory: Seven Essays in Early Chinese Poetry,* Hong Kong: Chinese University Press, 1988, Essays, pp. 42–43.
7. See Jean Lévi, *The Chinese Emperor,* translated from the French by Barbara Bray, London: Viking Press 1988, pp. 337–38.
8. William Dolby, 1976, p. 82.
9. See Jean Lévi, 1988.
10. Ibid., p. 301.
11. Ibid., 302.
12. Dawson, 1994, p. 85.
13. Ibid., p. 86.
14. Jean Lévi, 1988, p. 305.
15. Dawson, 1994, p. 85.
16. J.J.M. De Groot, 1910, pp. 1338–9.
17. Ibid., pp. 1193–4.
18. See Donald Mackenzie, ed., *China and Japan: Myths and Legends,* New York: Avenal Books, 1985, pp. 137 & 330. The peach tree is supposed to grow in Paradise among the Kun-lun mountains in Tibet, and it is believed that under the care of Si Wang Mu (Royal Mother of the West) it supports the universe. The willow is venerated in Siberia and is supposed to be capable of renewing youth, prolonging life and curing diseases.
19. J.J.M. De Groot, 1910, p. 110.
20. Ibid.
21. Stalberg, 1984, p. 49.
22. Compare Zeami's golden rule in Noh drama: 'Move the mind ten; move the body seven.' Without doubt this proclaims the sovereignty of mind over body.
23. For a fuller definition of *ch'uan* see Delza, 1973, p. 7. See Note 34.
24. See Da Liu, *T'ai Chi Ch'uan and I Ching, A Choreography of Body and Mind,* London: Routledge and Kegan Paul, 1974, p. 7.
25. Singapore enjoys freedom of worship and ancient ritualistic practices such as for example, *tang-ki* (divining youths) medium rites, banned in China, are permitted to take place on the island.
26. J.J.M. De Groot, 1910, p. 1316.
27. See K.M. Schipper, 1966, p. 81, who emphasises the significance of the number 108 by quoting Warner's *Dictionary of Chinese Mythology,* pp. 946 and 506. Every complete group of marionettes consists in principle of 72 puppet heads

and 36 bodies implying that the troupe as a whole represents the total of spirits in the universe.
28. Anil de Silva, *Chinese Landscape Painting in the Caves of Tun Huang,* London 1964, p. 54.
29. Arthur Waley (tr.) *Analects of Confucius,* London: George Allen and Unwin, 1938, pp. 48–9.
30. Edward Maisel, *Tai Chi for Health,* New York, Chicago, San Francisco: Holt, Rinehart and Winston, 1972, p. 207.
31. The four others were the Book of History, Odes, Ritual, and Spring and Autumn.
32. Da Liu, 1974, p. 7.
33. See *Kadensho: A secret book of Noh art* by Zeami, translated by Nobori Asaji, Osaka:Union Services Co., 1975, p. 18. 'For instance, concerning military tactics, it sometimes happens that a small army defeats a powerful force through the resourceful mind of an able commander, and also by dint of his surprisingly clever stratagem. If we view it from the defeated army, what does that mean but that they were deceived by the unexpected strategy of the enemy? And that is the very secret to get victory in all arts.
34. Though the Daoist Chang San-Feng, c.960 AD, of Mt. Wutang in Hupeh Province has been credited with devising the exercises known as *T'ai Chi Ch'uan,* their origin could have begun with Emperor Yu in 2300 BC as a way of promoting health. According to this story, the Emperor noticed that stagnant waters from a devastating flood were causing epidemics across the land and ordered that a series of exercises called the 'Great Dances' be performed regularly by all the people. He was putting into practice theories of blood circulation inherited from his ancestors who believed that 'the blood flows continuously in a circle...and that unceasing circle movement is life-giving'. (See Sophie Delza, *Body and Mind in Harmony. T'ai Chi Ch'uan: An Ancient Chinese Way of Exercise to Achieve Mental Health and Tranquility* , New York: Cornerstone Library, 1973, pp.179–180). There are however no records to substantiate this claim. The Daoist idea that water (and nothing could be more yielding than water), is able to erode the hardest stone made a forceful impression on Chang San-Feng. For a while he was a prominent magistrate in the Chung-san district in China though he gave it up to become a hermit. He took to travelling from place to place, studied under various Daoist masters, and learned techniques of meditation as well as martial arts. The origin of martial arts probably began with Shao-lin exercises (18 movements for relaxation and self-defence) devised by the Zen monk Bodhidharma for the physically degenerate monks in Shao-lin monastery in Hunan province in 535 AD. There is no doubt that some of these seem similar to *T'ai Chi Ch'uan* exercises. It is generally held that Chang San-Feng incorporated some of Bodhidharma's Shao-lin exercises and also those of a woodcutter, Hsu Hsuan-ping, who lived around 750 AD into a system of exercises now known as *T'ai Chi Ch'uan.* See Da Liu ,!974, pp. 3–4.
35. Ibid., p. 59.

36. Maisel, 1963, p. 204.
37. Ibid., 211.
38. Sophie Delza, 1973, p. 183
39. Cheng Man-ch'ing & Robert Smith, *T'ai Chi: The "Supreme Ultimate" Exercise for Health, Sport, and Self-defence*, Rutland, Vermont: Charles Tuttle Co., 1967, p. 110.
40. Ibid., p. 106.
41. See Roger Howard, *Contemporary Chinese Theatre*, London: Heinemann Ltd., 1978, p. 29.
42. See Colin Mackerras, *The Rise of the Peking Opera 1770–1870*, Oxford: Clarendon Press,1972, p. 107.
43. See Maisel, 1963, p. 61.
44. As early as 1968 the actor Colin Blakely in an interview with *The Drama Review*, Vol. 13, No.3, Spring, 1969, p. 122, spoke enthusiastically about the relevance of *T'ai Chi Ch'uan* exercises to the group's work in preparation for Brook's production of *Oedipus* in 1968.
45. Robert Wilson used *T'ai Chi Ch'uan* exercises for his production of *Journey to Ka Mountain* at the Shiraz-Persepolis Festival in 1972.
46. When Bill Gaskill directed David Hare's *Fan Shen (*based on the book by William Hinton), which was first shown at the I.C.A. on 22.4.75, it was publicised that he used *T'ai Chi Ch'uan* exercises as part of the training of his actors in rehearsal.
47. Maisel, 1963, p. 206.
48. Although this poem has been ascribed to Zhuang Zi by many *T'ai Chi Ch'uan* teachers, and there is no doubt that its sentiment echoes the philosophy of the great 4th century BC Daoist philosopher, I have not yet been able to locate it in his oeuvre.

Chapter Four: In Search of Lady Jôruri

The small stage revolves and two men are revealed to the audience; one is the storyteller, one is the shamisen player: narrator and accompanist. Both are dressed in clothes which have been ritually blessed and put on, and both are kneeling, heads bowed. From the back of the main stage the oldest puppeteer appears, black-hooded, to make the opening announcement – *Tozai* or 'East-West' – which refers both to the breadth of the auditorium and to the locations of the two paradises of the Buddha. A performance of the greatest puppet-theatre tradition in the world, the Japanese Bunraku, is about to begin. But *bunraku* derived from the name of a puppeteer called Uemura Bunraku-ken,[1] is not the original name of this powerful art form. Until 1871 it was known as *ningyô jôruri* (*ningyô* meaning 'dolls') and it is the figure of Lady Jôruri, whose name lies behind this older title, a figure ambiguously poised between prostitution and Buddhist sainthood and conveniently forgotten by scholars and practitioners alike, that I want to concentrate on in this chapter.

Just as Otozuru,[2] a relatively unknown female dancer/courtesan, inspired the evolution of aristocratic Noh drama and Okuni,[3] of similar reputation, brought about the genesis of the sensational Kabuki with its wider appeal, so Lady Jôruri spearheaded Japan's third great dramatic form, the Bunraku. The connection between this woman and puppetry is literal and metaphorical: not only did she originally give her name to the puppet theatre but her brief life of love, devotion, healing and sacrifice for the sake of her famous lover and his military cause, encapsulates the tyrannical role of loyalty and duty (*giri*). Indeed the fierce system of control and manipulation exercised by the military powers from the 12th to the 19th centuries reduced those in its grip to little more than puppets and Lady Jôruri's life exemplifies in a human story the mechanics of puppet control. When she finally drowns herself after being abandoned by her lover, she surrenders to the momentum of events like driftwood flowing down a torrential river, resembling one of those *ningyô* dolls at a 'Purification Doll Festival'[4] – a sacrificial offering carrying the sins of the community. Though struck off official records, like the other outcasts who initiated and sustained the classical theatrical genres, Lady Jôruri represents the host of unsung heroines whose invisible support was crucial to the military struggle and the political and cultural life of the nation.[5]

As with most Eastern names, *'Jôruri'* has a meaning: the word taken as a whole, literally means 'pure crystal' and is also a reference to the Eastern Paradise of the 'Healing Buddha' who offers relief in this present world as opposed to the 'Amida Buddha' of the Western Paradise who promises salvation in the next. *Jô* on its own means 'pure' and *ruri* refers both to lapis lazuli, a type of 'rock crystal', and to *Rurikô*, one of the titles of the 'Healing Buddha'. *Ruri* in this instance means 'light' and is a reminder of one of the twelve vows the Buddha made on attaining Budhahood: that he would have a spotlessly pure body, within and without, transmitting a light brighter than the sun and moon.[6] The other name of the 'Healing Buddha' is *Baisajya-guru* the 'Medicine Master', known in Japanese as *Yakushi-rurikô-nyorai*, and he is characteristically portrayed with a medicine jar in his right hand. In the *Yakushiji* (Yakushi Temple) in Nara, the Healing Buddha is seated on a medicine chest flanked by the standing figures of *Nikkô* (the bodhisattva of the sun) on the right, and *Gakkô* (the bodhisattva of the moon) on the left. At the very top of the Eastern Pagoda of this temple, seeming almost to fly free in the sky, are 24 angels engaged in music-making and praising the Buddha by sprinkling flowers[7] (see Plate 6). They serve as guardians against fire and are, in effect, the Japanese counterparts of the 24 birdwomen who hold up the pillars of the Kai Yuan Temple in Quanzhou (see Chapter 2). In this Buddhist setting, by virtue of her name and by what I hope to show as her function, Lady Jôruri is invested with an aura of purity, light, healing and relief in this world.

Who was this extraordinary woman? How do we know about her? Did she even exist? My research in Japan in the spring of 2000 revealed a complicated but fascinating story that has connections with the Birdwoman myth in other parts of Asia, with the puppet theatre of Southern China and the shamanistic purpose of the Thai Manora. As so often, we have to begin with a piece of fiction, a story that has taken on the power of myth.

Lady Jôruri – A Japanese Heroine?

The original title was *Jôruri Monogatari* ('The Story of Jôruri') though it later became known as *Jûnidan zôshi* ('storybook in twelve sections'). This was because the early reciters of *Jôruri Monogatari* were the same *biwa hôshi* (blind monks playing on a two-string lute) who sang the famous Japanese epic *Heike Monogatari*[8] ('The Tale of the Heike') which was divided into twelve parts – the number twelve assumes considerable importance in 'The Story of Jôruri' as it is also associated with the twelve vows and twelve generals of the Medicine Master. On the surface these two tales could not be more different: the Heike Story is a national epic recounting the military conflict between two major rival families – the Minamotos and the Tairas – which plunged the entire country into civil war; the Jôruri Story is ostensibly a slight romance between a relatively unknown woman and a famous Minamoto general. The Heike Story is regarded as a glorious narrative celebrating the military exploits of brave male warriors whereas the Jôruri story brings out in relief the sad tale of an individual woman who loved a handsome Minamoto warrior without counting the cost, was abandoned and subsequently took her own life. The general populace had grown tired of grim war tales and found this romantic story a relief. And yet these two outwardly different tales have a great deal in common and represent, as it were, the twin faces of war. The Heike tale can be seen not just as the story of heroic male struggle, brutality and bloodshed but also as the story of a supportive network of female suffering and sacrifice, often discounted or completely taken for granted; the Jôruri tale, on the other hand, while serving as a memorial for the thousands of slain warriors, acknowledged and lauded for their great deeds, also stands as a liturgy for the forgotten multitudes of nameless women trapped in wars not of their making. Spanning seven centuries of warfare (12th to the 19th) from the Kamakura to the Edo period, the story of Lady Jôruri is stitched into a gigantic tapestry of invisible female support without which the entire male effort to gain supremacy through bloodshed would have been fruitless. So like her sisters in suffering in the Heike epic – Giô[9], for example, who ironically permits someone she has helped to replace her in the great Kiyomori's affection,[10] or Kenreimon-in,[11] who lives perpetually in the memory of her young son's suicide – Lady Jôruri, by demonstrating an endless capacity for love, stands for the kind of Japanese heroine who in the end liberates and heals the whole of her sex. Although there are some variations in the existing versions of the Lady Jôruri story,[12] the following[13] is a synopsis of a widely accepted one.

The Tale

The setting is Yahagi, a small town in the old province of Mikawa (present day Aichi). As the town is specified by name, this brings it into the category of legend rather than that of folk tale.[14] It is springtime (a period of regeneration), the year is 1175, and the story takes place during the Minamoto/Taira clan conflict. The hero is Minamoto Yoshitsune, famous for his beauty, musical talents and military skills, variously known as Ushiwaka-maru, Hôgan-dono and On-zôshi. Accompanied by his servant, he is fleeing from the Tairas and while pressing northwards, arrives in Yahagi. Through an opening in a fence he sees a group of women admiring flowers, playing musical instruments and composing songs in the garden of a beautiful house. He is told that the house belongs to a rich man who has died leaving a wife and a daughter. For many years after their marriage the couple was childless and sought the intervention of the Healing Buddha at the temple (*Hôraiji*) on Mount Hôraiji.[15] Their wish was granted and they named their daughter *Jôruri*, the emphasis being on her semi-divine nature as she was born of immaculate conception.[16] Lady Jôruri is among the group of women being observed by Yoshitsune and our first glimpse of her is through his eyes. His Peeping Tom view[17] of her, engaged in composing music and poetry and admiring flowers, surrounded by two hundred and forty female attendants (a deliberate playing on the mystical multiplicity of the number twelve), provides a clue to the role or function of genteel women in a rule-ridden society. One is reminded of Prince Genji's meeting with Lady Yûgao in the 'Tale of Genji'.[18] The scene is of women amusing themselves in a way that accords with male perception: living out a male fantasy, their movements highly contrived and controlled. The emphasis is on seclusion, oppressive vigilance and control. Lady Jôruri is a paragon of beauty and our hero immediately falls head over heels in love with her.

The focus is now a close-up of Lady Jôruri making music with twelve of her attendants and Yoshitsune notices the absence of flute accompaniment to complete the harmony. He is an accomplished flautist and he takes out his flute, a present from his mother, to supply the missing element and so complete the orchestration. The wish for sexual fulfilment is expressed in a musical trope and because Yoshitsune's musical rendering is so exquisite a great yearning is created in Lady Jôruri's heart so that she sends one of her maids to find out the identity of the musician. The maid mistakes Yoshitsune for a retainer since master and servant have changed dress to fool their enemies but Lady Jôruri is not deceived and sends another maid, Jûgoya (meaning 'Fifteenth Night') to identify the remarkable flautist. She detects an aura of nobility about his person and is convinced that he must be a member of the celebrated Minamoto family. The open doors in Lady Jôruri's sleeping quarters proclaim how eagerly the 'Visitor' is awaited. Yoshitsune is conducted to her bed where she lies protected by four screens representing the changing seasons of the year. It is now the season of spring, a time of fecundity and renewal, and he is escorted with due ceremony as though a key player in a fertility ritual.[19] Each of the four seasons is described in detail, as are the furnishings and books. It is evident that the lady in question is one of exquisite taste and high accomplishment. Yoshitsune extinguishes twelve of the thirty lights in her bed chamber and like Prince Charming in the Western story of the Sleeping Beauty, wakes her up and declares his love. Lady Jôruri, who has done everything to promote the affair, now, as perhaps is expected of her, displays resistance to his proposals, for fear of being discovered by her mother. She puts him off by telling him that she is saying sûtras (sermons originally given by the Buddha) for the recent death of her father. Yoshitsune retorts by saying that since the age of three, he has had ten thousand sûtras recited for the loss of his father so that the loss of a beloved parent should serve as a bond between them and then resorts to using the example of great lovers in Chinese, Indian and Japanese poetry to break down her resistance. For a while she does not respond for fear of being punished by various buddhas, but finally succumbs to his persuasiveness and their love is consummated.

At dawn Lady Jôruri's mother rushes to her daughter's bed chamber because she entertains great suspicions of Yoshitsune's real identity. But before her arrival, Yoshitsune leaps over a ditch and continues his journey northwards, accompanied by his servant. Reaching a beach, he suddenly becomes very ill and is left in the care of some beach dwellers while his attendant continues with the journey. The local inhabitants try to steal Yoshitsune's sword but it turns into a snake, twelve fathoms long. Meanwhile Lady Jôruri has been banished from her home and is living in a brushwood hut. In the guise of an old man, the god Hachiman, the protector of the Minamotos, appears to her in a dream and tells her of Yoshitsune's illness. Immediately she flies to her lover's side and prays to the Healing Buddha who restores him to life and a band of wandering priests help them to a nearby hut belonging to a nun. The nun turns out to be the Healing Buddha in disguise and after twelve days of care and healing, Yoshitsune recovers, for the first time revealing his true identity to Lady Jôruri. He tells her that he has no choice but to continue his journey alone in order to escape capture by his enemies. They exchange vows of eternal love and he promises to join her as soon as he defeats the Tairas. She gives him a hair ornament as a parting gift and Yoshitsune summons goblins (*tengu*) to transport her home before he goes on his way.

There are supposed to be at least forty different versions[20] of the Jôruri story but it has never been performed in its entirety, the long version being kept for private reading and not for recitation. The original version was probably written in the last quarter of the seventeenth century but a later shorter version[21] alluded to by the scholar Charles J. Dunn, is determined to give the story a happy ending so that all references to the Healing Buddha and Yoshitsune's illness are excised. The focus in this version is on the courtship, using the two maids as messengers and a detailed description of the four screens, to suggest the inevitability of their love and its consummation, ending with the words: 'the joy in their hearts is beyond the power of words to express'. This brings the Jôruri story, historically set in the twelfth century, nearer the ideal of a seventeenth century love story where lovers are prepared to make many sacrifices for love. In other versions, particularly those circulating in Yahagi, the tale ends on a tragic note.

The Yahagi Connection

Yahagi is a small town within the larger city of Okazaki in the Aichi prefecture of Central Japan. Outside this town, Lady Jôruri is usually considered a fictional character but within it she is regarded as a real person whose tragic love affair with a famous Minamoto general ended in her suicide. In order to support the claim that she really lived and died in Yahagi in the 12th century, the inhabitants of this town have, since the sixteenth century, constructed memorial sites to mark the places where it is claimed she lived and died, and where she is still lovingly remembered. Some of these sites were recorded in a 1522 document called *Munenaga Shuki*,[22] the diary or handbook of Munenaga who lived from 1488–1533 and a map exists[23] which shows seventeen sites connected with Lady Jôruri or Yoshitsune. In April 2000, accompanied by Norikazu Shingyo, a medieval historian who is a specialist in the Lady Jôruri 'legend', I was able to see for myself the fresh floral offerings which the locals still place on her grave and closely related memorial sites. There is no doubt that in this town a sanctity has grown around every detail connected with Lady Jôruri and for its inhabitants the 'truth' of her story has always been vital for the psychic life of the community. Her brief and eventful life has become symbolic of the community's perception of the role of women during the brutal military conflict which for so long destroyed fine emotional feelings and individual lives. For the people of Yahagi, myth and truth have become one and the story of a 12th century heroine has become both a source of spiritual strength and the focus of historical events. Because it will lead us into the social and dramatic life of the time and in particular the Bunraku puppet theatre, I want to look at this map rather more closely.

A 'Map of Life'

The first memorial site (see map in illustration section), the *Jôjuin* temple, contains a portrait of Yoshitsune and Lady Jôruri, as well as a nineteen volume work, the 'Tales of Lady Jôruri', written by Kyôchôshi Fumimaro and 'The History of Lady Jôruri' which states clearly that she died on 12th March 1177. This temple used to be called Reisei-ji, the Buddhist name of Lady Jôruri's maid, Jûgoya, after she became a nun. It was Jûgoya who had conducted Yoshitsune to her mistress's bed. The second memorial, *Jôruri ga Fuchi*, is meant to mark the spot on the bank where Lady Jôruri stood before she drowned herself in the river Otogawa. As the prevalent belief in this community is that she came to a sad end, every attempt is made to particularise this event in terms of date and location. The third site, *Hime Kuyôtô*, is the tower erected for the repose of Lady Jôruri's spirit. *Hime no Ashiatoiwa* or 'Lady Joruri's footprint rock', the fourth memorial, represents an effort to canonise her and imitates the legend that three or four hundred years after Buddha's death he was only represented by his footprints carved on stone because his believers felt that it was impious to make statues of his likeness.[24]

The fifth memorial, *Jakô Ike* meaning 'musk pond' is supposed to exude the fragrance of Lady Joruri's favourite perfume, an intimate detail calculated to indicate how real and close she is to the consciousness of the community. The sixth memorial site, *Jakô Dsuka*, represents the spot where it is believed that Yoshitsune buried Lady Jôruri's perfumed pouch after her death, an action curiously reminiscent of a detail in perhaps the greatest love story in China (see Chapter 2) which recounts the deep but brief love affair between Emperor Tang Ming Huang or Tang Xuan Zhong (*Gen-sô* in Japanese) and Lady Yang Kuei Fei

(*Yôhiki* in Japanese). When her royal lover returned to the site of her grave – she had been forced to commit suicide by his rebellious troops and had been hurriedly buried – to give her a proper reburial, it was reported that all that remained in her grave was the perfumed pouch he had once given her. This emphasis on a similar detail in the course of the sad love affair between Lady Jôruri and Yoshitsune underlines the importance given to the Jôruri story by the community of Yahagi.

Senbon Toba, the seventh memorial erected in Lady Jôruri's memory, marks the place where Yoshitsune read a thousand *Hokekyô* or 'Lotus sûtra' for the repose of Lady Jôruri's spirit while the eighth memorial has been raised in honour of Lady Jôruri's maid, Jûgoya,[25] and takes the form of her tomb, known as *Jûgoya no haka*. The ninth site is Kômyôin Temple, formerly called *Myôgen-ji*, which houses portraits of Yoshitsune and Lady Jôruri and also one of the latter's guardian, Yakushi-Rurikô-Nyorai or the Healing Buddha. The 10th memorial is another dedicated to the maid Jûgoya, using her Buddhist name 'Reizei',[26] and the 11th memorial is labelled *Jôruri Kûruwa*. *Kûruwa* is another word for the prostitute quarter, a connection which I will explore below, and this place is supposed to be the second residence of Lady Jôruri's father', Kanetaka Chôja, the second word meaning the 'manager' of a prostitute establishment. The 12th memorial is referred to as *Murasaki Iwa Ishi* meaning 'Purple rock stone.' This purple stone, it is said, used to be in Kanetaka Chôja's garden and is now buried deep in the ground. The thirteenth memorial is the Seiganji Temple which possesses Yoshitsune's famous flute, known as *Usuzume*, a gift from his mother, later given to Lady Jôruri. Among other things, this temple possesses one of Lady Jôruri's mirrors, and two portraits, one of Yoshitsune and the other of her. It also has the history of the temple and a chronological history of Lady Jôruri, again recording that she died on 12th March 1177. The 14th memorial is marked as the formal tomb of Lady Jôruri – an old Japanese practice sometimes accords a person two tombs, one where the corpse is buried and the other where memorial services are offered for the departed, a system that originated from the sense of abomination felt towards the unclean corpse.[27] The 15th memorial site, *Daimon* or

'Big Gate', is supposed to be the entrance gate to Kanetaka's residence and *Misokasu Iwa*, 'the dregs of miso rock', the 16th memorial site, is named after the story that Kanetaka Chôja had such a huge household that they had to dispose of the dregs of their *miso* (soya bean) consumption daily. These dregs turned into rocks and memorial sixteen displays some of them. This is to reinforce the solidity of Lady Jôruri's father as a man of great wealth. The seventeenth memorial on the map is the Takisanji temple which houses Lady Jôruri's *kôtô* (musical instrument). The powerful brother of her lover, Shogun Yoritomo, who is supposed to have hounded Yoshitsune to suicide, has a memorial statue here. It is outwardly a statue of *Sho Kannon*, the 'Goddess of Mercy' commissioned by his nephew and built according to Yoritomo's height, with relics of his finger nails and a lock of hair locked inside it. Clearly it is important for the people of Yahagi that the first Shogun should be associated, however indirectly, with their heroine.

An analysis of the seventeen memorial sites, more than half of which had appeared by the seventeenth century, shows that the way Lady Jôruri was forced by circumstances to take her life, is strongly emphasized in Yahagi, though perhaps not taken quite so seriously outside this town. Three memorial sites, Jôjuin, Jôruri ga Fuchi and Seiganji, refer to her sad death on a specific date. Jôruri ga Fuchi in fact marks the spot where she stood on the bank of the river Otogawa before plunging to her death. But the local inhabitants were very concerned that when the body was recovered she should be buried within the precincts of Okazaki castle on the bank of Yahagi river (see Plate 8) and, as will be shown, although her story was set in the 12th century, every attempt has been made to link her with the powerful 17th century Shogun, Ieyasu Tokugawa, who was closely associated with Okazaki castle. This emphasis on the suicide of a woman disappointed in love in the 12th century, seems to predate the fashion for suicide and strong governmental disapproval of it in the 17th century. This disapproval sometimes took the form of dishonouring the bodies of those who took their lives.[28] However, because there was a ban on any form of criticism of the Tokugawa authorities, the continued exaltation of a suicide like Lady Jôruri, could well be taken as an oblique attack on existing laws. The decreed desecration of the bodies of those who had killed themselves as a result of thwarted love in the 17th century was certainly in contrast to the great honour paid to Lady Jôruri in Yahagi precisely because she had ended her life so tragically after being abandoned by her famous military lover.

The frequency with which Yoshitsune is mentioned in the memorial sites indicates his importance to the Lady Jôruri tale as far as the Yahagi community is concerned. For them it is vital that Lady Jôruri interact with a famous historical general and the backdrop of that terrible military conflict between two great family clans. Hence the studious marking of the sites of contrition on the part of the man who abandoned her. The plight of Lady Jôruri is in a sense so real to this town that she can only be conceived of as an actual local girl whose courtship, love, abandonment and suicide together with the contrite hero's eventual return to Yahagi, seem to bind this society together. In fact there is a strong view offered by Takeda Isamu that a statue of Buddha, originally called *Krôsonbutsu*, but now referred to as *Kurohonzon*, still in existence and kept as hidden treasure in the Zôjôji temple of the Tokugawa line in Tokyo, can be used as proof that Lady Jôruri was a real person.[29] According to this argument, Yoshitsune returned to Yahagi sometime during 1178–1182 and learned that his former love had taken her own life after the birth of their child.[30] She had been living in a hermitage after being evicted from her parental home, and it was in this refuge that Yoshitsune placed the statue of Buddha, specially commissioned by him, in the hope that it would console Lady Jôruri's spirit. Eventually a temple called Rurikô-san Ansei-ji was built on the site of the hermitage and the statue was moved into it.[31] When that temple became desolate, the Myôgenji temple, now called Kômyôin, was chosen to house this precious memento. Enter Ieyasu Tokugawa who apparently decided to take the statue into his possession and moved it into his castle. It is today supposed to be jealously guarded in the precincts of the Zôjôji temple[32] in Tokyo and according to Isamu Takeda, this furnishes evidence of Lady Jôruri's reality. Whatever the truth, the fact remains that an entire community is determined that such a statue should be an inerasable part of their memory and perception of the Jôruri story and this is written into the records of the Komyôin temple.

As to the emphasis on the role of Lady Jôruri's father in her tragedy, it is worth commenting that he represents patriarchal authority. Not only does he emerge blameless but there is an assumption that despite his harsh treatment of his daughter, he has every right to take possession of the *Kurohonzon* which her lover had commissioned as an act of contrition. Ultimately the statue is in the hands of the most important patriarchal figure in the land, Shogun Ieyasu Tokugawa himself, who had it placed in the same *bodaiji* (family temple) in Edo where his own funeral service was to be conducted. The meaning is clear: patriarchal authority in the home is reinforced and justified by Shogunal patriarchal power over the nation and in the name of national order and stability, such authority is sacrosanct. So from this perspective, Lady Jôruri's sacrifice was determined by a trinity of male authorities, state, lover, and father, and her death was far more than a desperate reaction to a lover's desertion. It touched a deep vein in Japanese culture concerning the necessity of individual or collective sacrifice to the stability of military government.[33] From this point of view, no sacrifice, however small, was irrelevant because it acted as a way of servicing the system and was part of the culture of total self-surrender and loyalty which defined the warrior ethos.[34] Within such a system, no affair of the heart, which might distract the warrior from his mission, was ever tolerated by the State and the sacrifice of Lady Jôruri's life almost predetermined. Her lover's desertion and her disinheritance merely sealed her fate.

It is not surprising then that the historical records of the Kômyôin should have linked Ieyasu Tokugawa with the Jôruri legend. This was clearly an attempt to mitigate the harsh exclusion laws imposed on women who were deemed unfit to gain Buddhahood or even to go near any of the big centres of Buddhist learning like Mt. Hiei or Mt. Koya.[35] The fact that it was her lover, Yoshitsune, who attempted to reverse this regulation by commissioning the instrument of her salvation (i.e. the Buddha statue), shows how strongly the Yahagi community perceived the great wrong that Lady Jôruri had suffered and the need for some form of reparation to be made by him. In a sense the way that the memorial sites have been arranged represents the community's rewriting of the story and the manner they would like it to end. What was supposed to have happened was too painful and so the memorial sites with regard to Yoshitsune's contrition, the dominance of her father and the fact that his tyranny merged with Shogunate authority and reparation, were a way of reconciling the far too painful truth with fantasised reality. There is no doubt that Kanetaka Chôja stood for Confucian male authority which formed the bedrock of Edo governmental regulations within an indisputable framework and it is interesting that in this version, the role of Lady Jôruri's mother is greatly reduced: while there are two memorials in the Seigan-ji temple, one dedicated to Lady Jôruri and the other to her father, there is not a single memorial site devoted to her mother. In the fifteenth century chronicle of Yoshitsune, there is a reference to the mother as the most famous courtesan on the Tôkaido road between Edo and Kyoto.[36] On the map of the memorial sites there is a marking described as Jôruri Kûruwa which is also referred to as the second residence of Kanetaka Chôja. Since the term *kûruwa* is suggestive of the prostitution quarter it is apposite that we should consider to what extent the label of prostitute applies to Lady Jôruri.

There is a strong argument put forward by Norikazu Shingyo[37] that the tale of Lady Jôruri was based on the true life story of an actual prostitute whose sad love affair with a prince was woven into a miracle story concerning the Healing Buddha. He links the popularity of the tale with the fame of Yahagi as a great centre of business and trade in the 15th century which certainly facilitated the wide acceptance of the story by people outside the area who wanted to share its prosperity. As Yahagi prospered, so did the number of temples multiply, in particular those dedicated to the Healing Buddha. One of them was reputed to have been built by Odai no Kata, the mother of the Shogun Ieyasu Tokugawa who lavishly endowed it.[38] There is in fact a version of the Jôruri story which perceives her as an earthly manifestation of Yakushi-Rurikô-Nyorai (the Healing Buddha) himself. Set all this against the widespread famine and disease sweeping over Japan in the 15th and 16th centuries[39] and it is not surprising that a story about love and healing, strongly connected with the Medicine Master or Healing Buddha, should gain so much popularity both inside and outside Yahagi. Certainly at the time of Yahagi's prosperity, a figure such as Kanetaka Chôja, the father of Lady Jôruri, would have commanded sufficient respect and business credibility as the rich manager of a brothel in Yahagi and this served to increase the popularity of the tale. It would seem that the great prosperity of Yahagi, combined with the power of its temples, helped the tale to gain such wide acceptance that fact and fiction became indivisible as far as local people were concerned. Pragmatism and expediency may have had a part in turning Lady Jôruri into an honoured local figure, who had loved unreservedly and was punished for that.

The Prostitute Element

As noted above, Lady Jôruri's father, Kanetaka Chôja, was reputed to have been the manager of a brothel (*Chôja* meaning 'brothel manager') but there is a division of opinion between two leading specialists over the identity of Lady Jôruri and her impact on Yahagi, particularly on the issue of her connection with prostitution. Takeda Isamu in his article 'A Study of Lady Jôruri' (referred to above) is sure that there is no such connection and uses the Buddha statue left by Yoshitsune to put her forward as a candidate for Buddhist sainthood. On the other hand, Shingyo Norikazu, who escorted me to the site marked Jôruri Kûruwa or the Jôruri prostitute quarter, in April 2000, and who has used the same sources of information about the origin of this story as Takeda Isamu, concludes that Lady Jôruri was based on a real life prostitute. It so happens that a third theory, put forward in 1954 by another scholar, Tanabe Hisao, sheds further light on this question as well as making a link with the early Japanese puppet theatre.

In the 15th century, when the Lady Jôruri story begins, the province of Mikawa in which Yahagi lies had become a centre of prostitution, entertainers and wandering puppeteers known as *kairaishi* or *kugutsu-mawashi*.[40] Tanabe Hisao[41] strongly suggests that the villages of Mikawa province provided the appropriate context for the origin and propagation of the story and it is not difficult to imagine the women of these villages offering their services in a world where entertainers and prostitutes were often indistinguishable. There is very little documentation of the activities of nomadic puppeteers but they were definitely recognized as belonging to the official list of entertainers in the 11th century and the *Shin-sarugaku-ki* ('New Account of Sarugaku'),[42] written around 1055, lists *kairaishi* among the various kinds of *sarugaku* performers (practitioners of popular entertainments imported from China). The arrival of such groups among the outcast community of entertainers and prostitutes in Mikawa, provides the perfect setting for an appealing story about a rather special kind of prostitute and a very different type of customer. Indeed Tanabe Hisao feels that the Jôruri tale was probably concocted by the prostitutes themselves as publicity to attract a better class of customer and wrote about the origin of this story in conjunction with his observations on the growing importance of two musical instruments, the *biwa* and the *shamisen* in this area. Until the arrival of the *biwa*, reciters of the Jôruri tale used a fan to provide the rhythmic accompaniment to the recitation, but the later introduction of the *shamisen* with its more erotic tones from the Ryûkyû islands into Japan in 1580, certainly increased the growing eroticism and popularity of this tale.[43] The fact that Yoshitsune, a popular figure from the *Heike Monogatari*, was the hero of the new tale helped the reciters to feel that they had not completely broken away from its model which was just beginning to be wearisome to audiences. And the addition of a beautiful heroine, who was no common prostitute and had not been previously included in the *Heike Monogatari*, provided the excitement of new material.

Whichever version of Lady Jôruri's story is true, she is, despite a highly Buddhist name, often referred to as *chôja no musume*, meaning daughter of a 'chôja' and is presented as a Circe-like figure whose alluring charm draws Yoshitsune to spend the night with her. As for the connection between prostitution and puppetry, an entry in a tenth century dictionary says that the word with the

Sino-Japanese pronunciation *kairaishi* is pronounced *kugutsu* in Japanese and that *kugutsu*, which is the first name given to puppets in Japan, is also the word used for a female prostitute.[44] While it would be an oversimplification to maintain categorically that it was the double meaning of *kugutsu* which prompted the naming of a genre of ballad recitation and puppet accompaniment after Lady Jôruri – in any case, she gave her name to the recitation first, and the puppet accompaniment came later – there is a highly suggestive possibility here which is reinforced by a significant document, the only one about these wandering puppeteers to survive from the 12th century.

A Contemporary Account of the Puppeteer's Life

This document, written in Chinese, is an account of the activities of these wandering puppeteers and the fact that both its content and style seem somewhat exaggerated and fantastic, has been of concern to scholars, particularly since there are no corroborating reports elsewhere. But I would like to argue that because this is the only document on the activities of *kairaishi* entertainers, one should try to ascertain if the thrust of what it is trying to get across contradicts the scanty information we have about puppet entertainment from the 12th to the 16th century.[45] There are only four other references to puppet entertainment over four centuries: in a 13th century dictionary *Chiribukuro* ('Bag of Dust'), there is mention of *kugutsu* entertainers to the effect that they were formerly very popular, but the situation has changed though the women continue to serve as prostitutes; the second in the 15th century is a passing reference to puppet entertainers in the diary of Sadafusa, the father of the emperor Go-Hanazono, who wrote of *tekugutsu* (puppet manipulators) coming and performing *sarugaku* on the 25th day, 3rd month, 1416; the third is recorded in the diary of a court lady, Oyudono no ue, who writes that from 1561 to the end of the century, *ebisu-kaki* (puppet manipulators attached to the shrine of the deity Ebisu) perform in the palace; and the diarist, Matsudaira Iketada refers to visits by a *hotoke-mawashi* ('one who causes a buddha to dance') over the period from 4th day, 3rd month 1585, to 2nd day, 6th month, 1588.[46] These are clear but pithy entries over four centuries, and it is fascinating to put the relevant points of this 12th century document by the court scholar Ôe Masafusa (1041–1111), entitled *Kairaishi-ki* ('Account of *kairaishi*') alongside them. In this context, I want particularly to focus on the activities of *kugutsu* women, who were traditionally attached to migrant puppet troupes, so as to provide a wider context for Lady Jôruri's one night sexual encounter with a guest/traveller:

The women are wont to heave sighs, roll their hips, and smile alluring smiles. They use rouge and white powder, perform songs and lewd music, and thus they seek to fascinate men. In this they are not restrained by their parents, husbands or sons-in-law. They do not hesitate to spend a night of pleasure with travellers and wayfarers, even though they have only a brief acquaintance with them.... On account of their attractions, they are given large sums of money. They possess embroidered garments, brocaded clothes, and golden hair ornaments and caskets. This is true of all of them, without exception.[47]

What comes across clearly is an exotic picture of the behaviour of the wives of nomadic puppeteers, much taken up with amorous one-night affairs with wayfarers and travellers. Presumably they also assisted their husbands with their jobs as puppeteers but they seemed mainly preoccupied with prostitution and this is supported in the 13th century dictionary entry, *Chiribukuro* (quoted above), which went so far as to say that when puppetry declined, all that was left was prostitution. The intertwining of these two activities among the *kugutsu mawashi* ('wandering puppeteers') must have given support for the term *kugutsu* being used to refer interchangeably either to prostitutes or puppets.

The derivation of *kugutsu* from *kugu* is also illuminating in shedding light on the 'prostitute' aspect of the term and therefore relevant in a discussion of the sexuality of *kugutsu* entertainers. According to Origu Shinobu, the word *kugu* means a 'basket' or 'box' which is used for collecting seaweed or shellfish.[48] In addition, this basket or box *(kugu)* also served the puppet entertainers as a stage for their puppet shows. But *kugu* goes beyond this practical definition. In ancient China, 'basket' imagery contains sexual nuances. For example, the basket used to trap fish becomes a metaphor for the female while the fish which swim into the basket represent the male. The word in Chinese for a square basket is *k'uang* and it is used principally for gathering and offering food. But metaphorically, it serves as a natural feminine receptacle for magical treasures.[49] Such a 'basket' or *k'uang* was used for example, as a sexual image in the poem entitled *Lu Ming* ('Deer Cry') in the *Shih Ching* ('Book of Odes'), in which the real and metaphorical image of a canister suggests a scene of feminine enticement. In the first stanza which is reminiscent of the welcome Yoshitsune received from Lady Jôruri and her maids, a fortunate guest is entertained with music and then propositioned:

> *I have a lucky guest*
> *Sound the zither, blow the mouth organ.*
> *Blow the mouth organ, sound the reeds.*
> *The receiving canister, take hold of this.*[50]

There is clearly the suggestion that it is the music and the receiving canister, overflowing with offerings, which attract the 'guest' and he is enticed and drawn into the feminine presence. So the 'basket' metaphor is a veiled reference to an amorous or lascivious woman in Chinese myth and poetry and seems congruent with the suggestion that *kugutsu*, which incorporates *kugu* or 'basket' also means 'prostitute'.

If we look at most versions of the Jôruri story, a great deal of care is taken to emphasize the enchantments of the heroine and her surroundings in such a way as to romanticise the consummation of their love after so brief a meeting. So although there is no proof that Lady Jôruri, who gave her name to the 17th century puppet theatre, was a direct descendant of the 12th century female *kugutsu* entertainers, there is ample evidence in the way her story unfolds to suggest that metaphorically, if not historically, she belongs to the same tribe of female entertainers who 'do not hesitate to spend a night of pleasure with travellers and wayfarers'. Though she displays some modesty when Yoshitsune is stealthily guided to her bed by her maid Jûgoya, she is certainly not the pure blushing maiden implied by her name. In the early part of their courtship it is she who takes the initiative by sending several messengers to ascertain the identity of her tantalising guest and clearly indicates more than willingness for their relationship to become intimate. The details which the Yahagi community have decided to highlight, as shown in the memorial markings, offer an insight as to how they really feel about the true intentions of mistress and maid.

Considerable attention is given to the roles of the maids: the first one, having fallen in love with Yoshitsune herself, mis-identifies him in the hope of securing him later as a lover for herself. Questions have been raised as to the importance of the second maid, Jûgoya, but if we consider the meaning of her name, 'Fifteenth Night',[51] and the fact that it was a popular name adopted by female Kabuki performers who were by day theatrical artistes but prostitutes in the evening,[52] we will be able to understand how seriously the 'prostitute' element in the Jôruri story was taken by the locals in the town in which the tale arose. The fact that the name *Jôruri* is a Buddhist synonym for purity and also stands for the Eastern Paradise of the Healing Buddha, in no way disqualifies her from being equally highly regarded as adept in the art of love. Interestingly, the prostitute quarter is sometimes referred to as the 'Western Paradise of Amida'[53] and if we examine the configuration of buildings which make up the Jôruri-ji Temple in Kamo-cho, Kyoto prefecture, there is clearly an attempt to unify both the Eastern and Western Paradise of Buddha: the main building which houses the nine wooden statues of *Amida Nyorai* ('Lords of the Western Paradise') is suitably located on the West bank of a small lake, while the three-storied pagoda, which houses the wooden statue of *Yakushi Rurikô Nyorai*, the 'Healing Buddha' or the 'Medicine master', is located on its eastern bank. And paradoxical as it may seem, though this temple which shares the same name as Lady Jôruri,[54] dissociates itself from her story, its layout so exquisitely balances the Western and Eastern paradise in shape and meaning, one with its width and the other with its height, that it captures the nature of the heroine's divided self.

There are of course celebrated examples of prostitutes with Buddhist names: the clearest case is that of Hotoke Gozen – celebrated in the Noh play *Hotoke no Hara* by Zeami. She wins the favour of the great Taira chieftain Kiyomori principally because Giô, who was his current favourite, intercedes for her so that she is permitted to dance for him. Ironically the fresh new dancer so captivates Kiyomori that he sends Giô away so that Hotoke can replace her in his honour and affection. The newly-installed favourite is so stricken with remorse by her unwitting part in displacing someone who has been kind to her that she soon leaves Kiyomori's court to become a nun like Giô. This story is so replete with the Buddhist sense of the transitoriness of power and glory and the compassionate nature of prostitutes that Hotoke's Buddhist sounding name is not the least incongruous. And what is most striking is the Zen Buddhist circular conclusion of the tale: the replacer and the replaced are one just like the beginning and the end – a cryptic truth pointedly expressed in the perfect circle on the certificate awarded a Zen aspirant or a sword master.[55] Perhaps the most beautiful and celebrated Japanese courtesan of all ages is the poetess Ono no Komachi: in the Noh play of the same name by Kan-ami she displays her deep knowledge of Buddhism by defeating two priests in an argument about Buddhism. The piece opens with Ono no Komachi appearing as an unsightly beggar woman who sits down on a Buddhist stupa for a rest. For this she is reproved for her disrespect by two passing priests. There is no doubt as to who comes off better in an argument which clearly demonstrates the courtesan's instinctive closeness to Buddhist teaching.[56]

There seems to me then to be a strong case for saying, on the basis of what documentary evidence we have, that Lady Jôruri, so precisely called into life by the people of Yahagi, and whose name was given to a great puppet theatre tradition, came from the world of prostitution and, by no means for the first or last time, united both the 'floating world' of pleasure and the longed-for state of

Buddhahood. The meeting of Buddhist teaching with Confucian principles in medieval Japan underlines this unity.

The Impact of Buddhism

There is no doubt that Buddhism with its teaching that women were sinful souls and should therefore be barred from attaining Buddhahood, and its upholding of the suppression of desire and deferment of rewards combined with Confucianism and its emphasis on family obligations, loyalty and harmony above everything else, provided the impetus for many warriors and merchants to seek relief in the prostitute quarter from the overpowering responsibilities and ethical constraints of their daily life. It is not difficult to understand why the prostitute quarter was also called 'Amida's Western Paradise' and though there seems to be some disagreement as to whether or not there were licensed prostitute quarters in the 12th century[57] when Yoshitsune and Lady Jôruri met, the point is that absolute historical accuracy in the presentation of the plot is irrelevant to the meaning of this story. As there were strict laws forbidding the criticism of any aspect of Edo governmental regulations with regard to the ordering of society, any allusion to a brothel whether high class or otherwise, had to be veiled: in other words transposing the context of Edo licensed quarters to an earlier age (i.e. the 12th century) is a way of bypassing rules forbidding discussion of sensitive contemporary subjects and using them to illuminate the heroine's situation.

The year 552 (as given in the *Nihonshoki* or *Nihongi*, 'Chronicles of Japan'), has been given as the date when Buddhism was officially introduced to Japan. This was accomplished through the agency of the chief of the Soga clan who built the first Buddhist temple on its estate. And just like the young maidens who were chosen to attend to spirits or *kami* in Shinto shrines, three ordained nuns who were really young maidens ranging in age from eleven to seventeen, were selected by the priest of this newly established Buddhist temple to wait on the spirit of Buddha.[58] As it was this same Soga chief who had, by skilful intrigue subordinated the other clans, he was able to arrange the nomination of Empress

Suiko (592–628) as the first female to receive the charisma of the Imperial office. The scene was also set for Buddhism to be established not only as a religion of a certain class but the new religion of the throne and the empire.[59] The responsibility for this transformation fell on the shoulders of the young nephew of the Empress, Prince Shôtoku. It would seem that he was attracted to Buddhism not because of a personal faith in this new religion but because he recognized it as the frame for a great civilization which could help uphold the throne as the central authority. The second of his seventeen articles promulgated in 604 and regarded as the first constitution of Japan, enjoined the nation to 'sincerely revere the Three Treasures. *Buddha, Dharma, and Samgha*, are the supreme refuge of all beings, and are objects of veneration in all nations.' Prince Shôtoku recognized the potentiality of Buddhism for uniting the diverse clans which had been politically and religiously divided. He saw the State functioning, not just as the patron of a new religion but as the controller of a 'religious' police force and using it as a means of enforcing order. Using the metaphor of a tree, he conceived of Buddhism as the fruit, while equating the trunk with Confucian ideology and the root with indigenous Shintoism.[60]

In 685 every province in Japan received an order from the throne that 'in every house a Buddhist altar should be established, and an image of Buddha with Buddhist scriptures placed there. Worship was to be paid and offerings of food made at these altars.'[61] The reciting and copying of various sûtras particularly the *Kônkômyôkyô* ('The Sûtra of the Golden Light') which justified exalted kingship from a Buddhist view point, was encouraged so that together with the *Hokekyô* ('Lotus Sûtra') and the *Ninnôkyô* ('Benevolent King's Sûtra'), they were regarded in a political light as the 'Three Scriptures Protecting the State'. By 741 there was a State-sponsored Buddhist official temple in every province and in 751 *Tôdaiji* ('The Eastern Great Temple') in Nara was made the national Buddhist *Sô-kokubunji* ('the chief temple') among all the state-supported official temples.[62] It was clear that the State was sponsoring Buddhism not so much for the people's salvation as for its own protection to achieve a social and political end. When deemed necessary, Shintoism and Buddhism were bracketed together to provide succour to the ruling regime. In the event of outbreaks of drought and disease, for example, both Shinto and Buddhist functionaries were summoned to supplicate the Heavens for rain. The Shinto god Hachiman (protector of the Minamoto clan) was sometimes portrayed in the robes of a Buddhist priest.[63] Large estates were donated to Shinto shrines and Buddhist temples for their services to the State. But in the Nara period, government support of Buddhist temples far exceeded its donations to Shinto shrines and it became clear that Buddhism was considered the chief civilizing agent for solidifying the nation.

These fine distinctions between the various different philosophical schools of Buddhism based on different interpretations of scripture went over the heads of the majority of the Japanese people.[64] What really appealed was the portrayal of Buddha as a great healer and this sprang from the *Mahayana* – the 'Buddhism of the Greater Vehicle' – which arose five centuries after the death of Gautama, the historic Buddha (ca. 563–483 BC). The *Mahayanas* flourished in East Asia and regarded Buddha as a transcendent being. One of his transcendent forms was as the 'Healing Buddha' or *Yakushi-rurikô-nyorai* in Japanese. And so in the famous 'Songs on the Buddha's Footprints' of the eighth century, Buddha was portrayed as a great healer and a *marabito* which is a traditional Shinto term for a *kami* or spirit who visits villages from a far-off place at the time of harvest and other important seasons.[65] So the notion of the Healing Buddha as one of the Manifestations of the Cosmic Buddha aroused the primitive faith and healing instincts of the Japanese. At the apogée of the Nara civilization in the reign of Emperor Shomu (724–49), who is remembered as one of the most devoutly Buddhist Emperors, there was a great rage in Nara for the copying of sûtras to obtain health and prosperity. The notion that it was possible to persuade the Healing Buddha to counteract disease by granting health appealed as a form of potent magic. The *Yakushiji* Temple, Head Temple of the Hosso Sect in Nara began in the reign of Emperor Temmu in 680 for expressly this purpose. His beloved consort was gravely ill and he instituted the building of this temple as a means of concretizing his supplication to the Healing Buddha for her recovery. Seven years after the project began, Emperor Temmu died. His wife, fully restored to health, succeeded him as Empress Jito and completed the complex of temple buildings in 698.[66] To be noted is the double framework of healing: the healing power of the 'Medicine Master' is manifested in the recovery of the Consort who in fact completed the building and such is the profundity of faith in the power of the 'Healing Buddha' over the years that even today a Yakushi Festival is held on the 8th of every month to offer a 'Mass' to him. On this day, the door of the three-storied pagoda, which houses the statue of the Healing Buddha in the *Jôruriji* Temple in Kyoto is opened.[67] The fact that a thousand steps lead the pilgrim to the "Healing Buddha" in *Hôraiji* temple in the Aichi province does not deter those who are riddled with disease or the childless who, as Lady Jôruri's mother is said to have done, make the steep climb to seek assistance.

The Origins of the Story

The theme of healing in the Jôruri story is multi-layered: thanks to the Healing Buddha, the childless wife of Kanetaka Chôja conceives and Lady Jôruri is born; the latter with his help miraculously heals her ailing lover who is then able to proceed with his journey leaving behind his mistress/healer/shamaness. There was no doubt in the minds of the original tellers of this story that it must be narrated as a tale within a context of healing. The originator of this tale was one called Ono no O-Tsû who has proved to be as mystifying as her heroine. Whether or not she was a real person is perhaps less important than the fact that a cult has grown up around her 'creation'. However every effort has been made to render her real by connecting her to historical personages: as evident in the passage below she is firmly linked to the great Oda Nobunaga. It is alleged that when his army besieged Kyoto in 1568, among his soldiers were men from Mikawa who recited the tale about Lady Jôruri as invented by Ono no O-Tsû:

"The origin of the story of Jôruri was as follows: on one occasion Lord Nobunaga was ill; he was very depressed and unable to sleep. Three lady attendants never left him – Seigen Koto, Kakuto and Ono no O-Tsû; they never quitted his side by day or night. Apart from these a great number of other attendants waited upon him. Night and day they read to him stories of all kinds, but his depression was not lifted. Thereupon Seigen and Kakuto spoke together to their master: 'Ono no O-Tsû is skilled in writing, and so, if she composed some interesting story and read it to you, it might relieve you.' Thereat Nobunaga asked O-Tsû to do as they had suggested. She made all kinds of excuses, but as he repeated his request time and time again, there was nothing she could do but take up her writing-brush. She cast about in her mind what she should write about. In the end she composed a story about a lady called Jôruri, the daughter of a rich man at the posting station at Yahagi in Mikawa province. She read it to her master and he found it particularly entertaining. All the servants, male and female, from Seigen and Kakuto down, listened with all their attention, and all were struck with admiration for it."[68]

During the flourishing of the puppet theatre in Japan in the 17th century, this version, ascribed to Ono no O-Tsû, was widely accepted. But the credibility of the story teller was questioned in the 19th century when Ryutei Tanehiko, a novelist and antiquarian pointed out that Oda Nobunaga, the lord on whom Ono no O-Tsû was attending, was born in 1532, a year after the reference to Lady Jôruri in the diary entry of the poet Sôchô.[69] (He seemed to be unaware of earlier dates when the story had begun circulating.) What rattled him was that there was a considerable time-lapse between the 1531 documentation of the story and the time (presumably in the 1560s) when Ono no O-Tsû was compelled to compose the Jôruri story as a healing balm for the battle-beseiged general. Ryutei Tanehiko further emphasized that the attribution of the Jôruri story to Ono no O-Tsû only occurred sometime between 1648 and 1678. The former is a reference to a work called *Yodarekake* ('Collection of Drivellings')[70] in which the origin of the story is given but no author is mentioned and so it does not have to be taken into consideration for the purposes of this discourse. The latter date is however pertinent as it refers to *Shikidô Ôkagami* ('Great Mirror of the Art of Love')[71] and in this work Ono no O-Tsû is clearly given credit for being the author of the tale. What is interesting is that these revelations of date discrepancies have not significantly affected the nostalgia with which writers hold on to Ono no O-Tsû's tale either in conjunction with Oda Nobunaga or Toyotomi Hideyoshi.[72] Many different theories have arisen to account for the varied views on the subject of origin and authorship of the tale with relation to male or female groups of reciters,[73] but this is largely irrelevant to my subject and I would like now to focus on the *Shikidô Ôkagami* of 1678 which is both a substantial and relevant source. What should be borne in mind with reference to the discussion above is that discrepancy of dates does not necessarily invalidate data as transmitted through stories. There are far too many references to the Ono no O-Tsû anecdote in conjunction with the Jôruri story for it not to be taken seriously.

Sex and Healing

Fujimoto Kizan's *Shikidô Ôkagami*[74] is the most thorough treatise on prostitution of his time (see below). It maintains that Lady Jôruri's story was the original material of the recitation which has been given her name. Furthermore it attests that Ono no O-Tsû, who told the story as a healing balm for the sick Oda Nobunaga, devised it from her inventive mind. The story of Lady Jôruri is one of love, sex and healing and the fact that it was included in a treatise on the art of sex suggests an underlying connection between sex and healing. This connection features clearly in the story itself: Lady Jôruri and Yoshitsune's one night of love is tenderly portrayed and in addition to the gift of her body by one so adept at lovemaking, she extends the therapeutic benefits of sex to healing him when he is later stricken with illness. It is interesting in this connection to bear in mind that in ancient China (and even today), the Chinese regarded sexual relations not only for the sake of procreation and in satisfying mutual desire between male and female, but as a vital part of the therapeutic arts. Along with breath cultivation, sexual intercourse was one of the methods of *yang sheng* or 'nurturing life'[75] and there is a belief that young virgins emanate a vitality which is rejuvenating for the male. Unfortunately none of the books on this subject in the royal Han Library in the first century BC are extant but only portions of Chinese sex manuals which date perhaps from the Later Han and Six Dynasties have been preserved. The main source for the fragments of the sex manuals is chapter 28 of the 10th century Japanese medical compendium *Ishimpô*.[76] What is indicated is that if intercourse is carried out properly, the act can nurture the body and promote health.

From the way Lady Jôruri and Yoshitsune were presented it is clear that they were both considered great adepts in the art of love. In particular, Lady Jôruri, being enclosed in her father's household, very young and fecund, is a powerful source of regenerative energy. The art of sexual play she engaged in with Yoshitsune was not unlike the 'play' or *asobi* engaged in by shrine maidens in their courtship of spirits.[77] These were spirits who could be persuaded to avert disease or bring rain in times of drought. One has only to remember how Lady Shizuka, regarded as Yoshitsune's favourite and most beautiful mistress, danced in the presence of the Retired Emperor and miraculously ended the drought that had afflicted the country for one hundred days.[78] Such was her shamanic power as an extraordinarily gifted dancer that she was able to influence the spirits which brought disaster. But precisely where her role as a shamaness ended and where that of a dancer and a prostitute began, is difficult to establish. It would seem that though the essence of shrine maiden activities, which included wooing and dancing to entertain spirits, was religious, very often the sacred shaded into the secular, and many female shamans drifted into the world of female entertainers and prostitutes.[79] And for this reason, looking at the role of Lady Jôruri as an accomplished entertainer, and then as a highly desirable partner in bed which shifted into that of a healer, it is impossible not to regard her in the same light as many female entertainers, from the 12th to the 17th century, who combined dramatic performance with shamanism and prostitution.

Pleasure Houses and their Power

Generally referred to as *chôja no musume* meaning 'daughter of a manager of prostitutes', and clearly included as the heroine of a story invented by Ono no O-Tsû in Fujimoto Kizan's famous book on the art of love, *Shikidô Ôkagami*, it would be difficult for Lady Jôruri, despite her highly sounding Buddhist name, to escape the label of 'prostitute'. There were at least five hundred terms describing the different kinds of prostitutes reflecting the subtle divisions of meaning between each type.[80] The designations of rank differed from locality to locality and from generation to generation. For example, when I compared the love play between Lady Jôruri and Yoshitsune to the erotic, sacred wooing of spirits by shrine maidens which is referred to as *asobi*, I found that there was in fact a type of prostitute called *asobime*.[81] From the highest rank of prostitutes, the *tayû* to perhaps the lowest *yujô* ('bath girl'), they constituted an extremely powerful and influential group without which the entire social, political and cultural fabric of the Edo era would have crumbled. Indeed the highest ranking courtesans (*tayû*) were regarded as models of womanhood excelling in the arts of conversation, traditional dancing, singing, and the composition of poetry. They were also leaders in fashion and their imitators came from the highest ranking women in the country. Their coiffure and dress sense far exceeded those of the townsman's wife and even the ladies in the Shogun's court were anxious to learn from them. And at the height of their popularity in the 17th century, it was impossible to find a play either in the puppet or Kabuki theatre which did not make a reference to them.[82]

Furthermore no stigma was attached to a customer for visiting a pleasure house. The rigours of the Confucian code which underpinned Edo society were so oppressive that as long as the stability of the family was not threatened, the male head-of-the-house was permitted to take his pleasure in the brothel quarter. But what was not sanctioned was for the samurai or *chônin*[83] to fall in love with the prostitute. This would have disrupted the State's rigid control of prostitution and endangered the stability of family life which functioned as a cog in the political wheel and led to stability in the nation. Families seemed to have been bonded not so much by love as by duty and the function of every member of the family was to serve the State. Consequently very little emotion was displayed in the home and certainly romance played no part in its constitution. In other words the nation and the family were regarded as sacred political institutions: the former demanded total loyalty, while the latter demanded absolute filial piety. But should the father oppose the Shogun (whose person embodied the Nation), the children were meant to take the side of the Shogun and ostracize the father:[84] loyalty to the State took precedence over filial piety. Not only were marriages arranged by the family but warriors and men of higher rank could not marry without official sanction. Such rules proved so restrictive that the prostitute quarter offered release, and because her profession was legally sanctioned, the high-class prostitute became an important part of the social structure, able to refuse a customer who was not to her liking.

The licensing of prostitutes meant confining them to certain districts, leaving those who were unlicensed to ply their trade wherever there was demand, though even these were under constant police surveillance. Licensing prostitutes as a means of controlling them more effectively meant confining them within thick walls. It was under Toyotomi Hideyoshi in the 1500s that brothels were brought under control for the first time principally for the sake of military security. While building Osaka castle in 1585 Hideyoshi established a licensed quarter in Osaka believed to be the first example of an enclosed segregated district and in 1589 he gathered the brothels of Kyoto into a single area called Yanagimachi. It was said that the Shogun himself, usually disguised by a large wicker hat, patronised this quarter which had been organised by one of his retainers.[85] When Nijo castle was built in Kyoto by Ieyasu Tokugawa in 1602, the brothels were moved to a quarter known as Misuji-machi which in 1640 was transferred to the south-west corner of the city wall beyond the compounds of Buddhist temples. This area came to be known as Shimbara, measuring 200 metres by 240 metres and was surrounded by an earthern wall and a moat three metres wide, with a single entrance on the east side. A similar policy prevailed in

Edo where the brothels were gathered to form the Yoshiwara quarter outside the city. The fact that there was need to confine and segregate the brothels was a tacit acknowledgement of their power. As early as the 1650s there were specialized manuals published as guides to these districts: for example, Kyoto guide books gave brothel and theatre quarters as much attention as they did the Imperial Palace and the Kiyomizu temple.[86] The Edo *bakufu*,[87] while deploring the brothels and theatres as necessary evils, admitted and recognized their importance in rendering the cities under their control attractive and seductive enough to attract commerce. It was felt that because the brothel and theatre were kept separate, each group could be better controlled and keener supervision could be maintained between these 'outcasts' and the rest of society. These two enclaves were referred to as the two *akusho* meaning 'bad places', and there was so much interaction between these two 'bad places' that both assumed an even more potent position in society. But before looking at the impact of the brothels on the theatres, I want to consider an important book on the Art of Love and consider its bearing on the story of Lady Jôruri.

The Art of Love and the Context of Sacrifice

Fujimoto Kizan (1626–1704) spent twenty years writing his treatise on the art of love, *Shikidô Ôkagami*, and started to visit prostitutes at the age of twelve. At that time brothels and theatres were the twin inspirations of Japanese popular culture. Since prostitutes were often the leaders in literary taste and fashion, to visit a prostitute was like participating in the most refined artistic activities of the time.[88] On the one hand they were considered the daimyo's plaything; on the other, they seemed deserving of the luxuries lavished on them. The story is told of a rich merchant who was so enamoured of a prostitute that he bought up all the eels available in the district on one particular day so that she would be the only one who could feast on this delicacy for dinner.[89] Kizan was completely mesmerized by the strange power of the brothel quarter which stood in a kind of no-man's land between the rigid control of Confucianism in this world and the promises of

Buddhism in the next. Indeed the brothel for him represented salvation in this world and led him, probably slightly tongue-in-cheek, to portray the art of lovemaking with the seriousness with which Confucianists pursued the *Dao* ('Way'), or Buddhists sought enlightenment. Ironically, this portrayal was not far from the truth since the growth and prosperity of the brothel districts seemed to go hand-in-hand with the enforcement of Confucian and Buddhist beliefs. The Confucian relegation of women to the lowest rung of society and their domestic enslavement in order to serve their husbands unconditionally, meant the creation of dutiful, emotionally restricted households alongside pleasure-filled brothel quarters. Such quarters offered men at least a temporary paradise. Kizan devoted his energies to constructing a new religion or a new 'Way', comparable to that of the Confucianists and Buddhists and in 1657 wrote in his treatise which was a series of evaluations of prostitutes in Osaka:

> *I have been a devotee of this Way ever since that long-ago autumn*
> *of my thirteenth year when I first squeezed a hand under a trailing sleeve.*
> *I claim moreover that it was I who first established it as a*
> *true Way, and gave it the Name of the Art of Love.*[90]

There was every attempt to make *Shikidô Ôkagami* a book of learning: it was interspersed with quotations from Chinese and Japanese classics and its tone was dignified and erudite just as many high class prostitutes were women of great refinement and learning. In one section of his book he splits it into 28 subsections based on the way the Lotus Sûtra is divided.[91] There is of course a conscious or unconscious echo of Chapter 28 of the *Ishimpô*, the Medical Compendium on the sexual practice of the ancient Chinese. Of great interest is the way Kizan decorates his own rake's progress with many appropriate classical quotations and the rake, just like a Zen aspirant or a sword master, is rewarded with a certificate of the highest achievement in the form of a drawing of a perfect cicle on attaining his ultimate goal.[92] In Kizan's configuration, the strict ritual which constitutes the sex ceremony seems part and parcel of the strict ritual inherent in Buddhism and Confucianism.

All this is important in putting Lady Jôruri's sacrifice in perspective, since, in the ritualistic context of society, courtesans were in the practice of making such sacrifices in order to prove their serious attachment to the customer. After discussing tatoos devised by the male customer, which could be applied to any part of the prostitute's body, Kizan brings up the courtesan's custom of sending a severed finger to a former patron as the supreme proof of her devotion even though he had deserted her.[93] We are told that the recipient of such a pledge would normally return and resume his relationship with the woman, but almost in the same breath, we are informed that in the nature of things, such a return could only be temporary. The Patron could of course redeem a prostitute's contract and set her up as his mistress or even his wife in society outside the quarter, but that was very rare. A grimmer possibility for prostitute and customer was double suicide but customers generally seemed satisfied with the relaxed atmosphere of the brothel where companionship and sex were much better than what was available in the home, and it was also rare for the male customer to make any such outrageous sacrifice in the pursuit, or as a consequence, of pleasure. In the case of Lady Jôruri and Yoshitsune there was no question as to who was meant to pay the price and though the people of Yahagi were insistent that Yoshitsune returned to make atonement, we know that he later formed a deeper attachment to Lady Shizuka, his most beautiful and famous mistress.

This ultimate depreciation of the woman's sacrifice in order to maintain the status quo and return everything to Confucian order and control goes back to the ancient value system which led Chinese emperors to send prostitutes to the front line with the men who were meant to protect the nation.[94] The role of the prostitute in this case was purely to function as a political tool to keep the war machinery in motion, comforting and relieving the war-worn soldiers and then expecting to be discarded. If we consider Lady Jôruri's role in the Minamoto/Heike conflict, she was similarly used and abandoned. While high class prostitutes set the fashion for aesthetic refinement and turned the purchase of their favours into a ceremony of sex, the position of the prostitute lower down the scale was intolerable. Essentially a slave to the whims of her customers, she was condemned at an early age to prostitution because her parents were unable to pay the land tax or other debts. The Tokugawa feudal regime looked to Confucian China for its rules and traditions and it was the Chinese attitude towards prostitutes which once again provided the model.

There were prostitutes in China as early as the Spring and Autumn Period (770–476BC). As it was the custom of feudal lords to entertain their guests with music, dance, and prostitutes, prostitution started as a way of establishing good relations with influential neighbours for trading purposes which could lead to economic advantages for both parties. But legal prostitution only began in earnest with the Han dynasty (206–220AD) when Emperor Wu forced prostitutes into war camps specifically to comfort his soldiers.[95] That those who provided the solace could themselves become casualties of war was hardly ever considered just as no account seems to have been taken of their personal privations and sufferings so long as they fulfilled this necessary state service and eased the pressure on males in a fiercely controlled Confucian society. Toyotomi Hideyoshi, who was responsible for instituting the first prostitute quarter in Kyoto and for freezing the social divisions in society which he saw so necessary for stability, is a good example of this point of view. There is a record of a letter he wrote to his wife in 1590, while he was away besieging a castle, which exemplifies his approach:

I wish to send for Yodo [his concubine]. I wish you to tell her and make arrangements for her journey, and tell her that next to you she is the one who pleases me best ...[96]

Putting his wife at the top of his list of bed partners was merely a gesture since there was never any doubt in the documentary records that Yodo was the one he adored most. Controlling his concubine through his wife was just one of the ramifications of the control system which prevailed during the Edo era. The aim was the security and stability of the nation but at the expense of common human feelings.

The Impact of Confucianism and the Chinese Concept of Sacrifice

Since the turn of the 5th century when Emperor Ojin was supposed to have appointed Confucian scholars from Korea to tutor his children, Confucian ideology had been infiltrating Japan. On his death he was succeeded by his son Emperor Nintoku, who instituted a Confucian-inspired reign and came to be regarded in Japan as one of the ancient sage-kings of China. Confucian China was such a crucial template for the Japanese attitude towards sacrifice that it deserves consideration as it introduces the concept of *li* (propriety), a word which was used to cover the whole range of conventions determining the correct code of ceremony and conduct relevant to a person's obligations according to his status, a concept which cemented Chinese society together and was even endowed by Confucius with a moral connotation.[97] The character for *li* incorporates the character for 'sacrifice', an example, as Arthur Waley has shown, of the way the importance of a term is often reflected in written Chinese.[98] An act of sacrifice was also considered the most efficacious means of moving the gods to compassion: in the *Ancient Book of History,* for example, it is the Duke of Chou's offer to sacrifice his life to save his sick brother that persuades the gods to spare the latter's life.[99] According to the 3rd century Confucian writer Hsun Tzu (quoting from an earlier document) sacrifice is seen as 'the supreme expression of loyalty, love and respect...and the climax of all those ritual prescriptions which we embody in patterned (*wen*) behaviour.' It is also, as I have shown, central to Japanese warrior culture, most succinctly expressed in the *Hagakure (*'Hidden under the Leaves') a work which emphasises that the samurai must be ready to give his life away at any moment. That Chinese inspiration is acknowledged is indicated by the fact that this book which was started in the 17th century by Nabeshima Naoshige was also known as *Nabeshima Rongo* in imitation of the Confucian Analects (*Rongo*).[100]

So since the fabric of society must be preserved at all costs, it follows that individual or group sacrifices such as that of the forty-seven *ronin*,[101] will be necessary. The related concept of *kenshenteki* or 'self-sacrifice' which underpinned Edo society will be discussed later. In a fiercely regimented framework where the government assumed complete power over the people, human sacrifice was taken for granted, while a fierce system of policing enforced public obedience across society. It was therefore not surprising that the popularity and prosperity of the brothel quarters grew while the division between prostitution and Buddhism crumbled and the pleasure quarter became known as *Gokuraku* (Amida's Western Paradise).

The Kabuki and the Puppet World

Whatever the reasons for, and the extent of, Confucian control over every aspect of Japanese life, the connection between the brothel and the stage was never in doubt. There was in fact no sharp division between Lady Jôruri as *chôja no musume* or 'daughter of a house of prostitution' and Lady Jôruri as the founder of the puppet theatre, because no such distinction existed between the pleasure quarter and the theatre during the Tokugawa era. As is well known, Okuni, attendant at the Izumo shrine, and undoubtedly a prostitute as well, began the Kabuki theatre in 1603 with a dance on the bank of the River Kamo in Kyoto. This was the famous area called the *Shijô Gawara* ('Fourth Street River-bed') which later became the location for the first formal puppet theatre, established by a puppeteer from Nishinomiya. Okuni's first theatrical performance told the story of a dandy visiting a brothel and was so successful that it prompted the establishment of a series of female troupes in imitation.[102]

Other imitators like the brothel owners at Misujimachi and Fushimi, also set up what seemed like theatrical stages on the east bank of the Kamo river near Shijô as showcases for their prostitutes. It became almost impossible to distinguish between women's kabuki (*onna kabuki*) and prostitutes' kabuki (*yûjo kabuki*). The word *tayû* describing a 'top grade prostitute' was in fact taken from the theatre where it referred to the most talented performer. Ambiguity and mutual borrowing seemed to be the order of the day, as expressed by the many deliberate blurrings between the theatre and the brothel, between what was play acting and what was real,[103] and in the dizzy reversal of gender roles. The random assignation of male roles to women performers and female roles to males so that a rake was often played by a woman and a prostitute by a male turned the scenario into one of indecency and confusion and gave rise to many indecent skits which were a thinly disguised means of soliciting clients for the brothel owners. This prompted the Shogun's Confucian-inspired scholar, Hayashi Razan, to write:

The men wear women's clothing; the women wear men's clothing...they sing base songs and dance vulgar dances, their voices are clamorous, like the buzzing of flies and the crying of cicadas.[104]

To be noted is the Confucian comparison of 'prostitutes and females who make mischief on the streets at night' to 'the insects that infest any country...a necessary evil'[105] that cannot be entirely stamped out but must therefore be tolerated. The merging of the prostitute and theatre world meant that in the first decade of the seventeenth century, many star performers were *tayû* prostitutes. And certainly when the first Kabuki theatres sprang up in the Shijô entertaining district, just outside the formal wall prescribed by Hideyoshi to demarcate the 'riverfolk marginal people' from the rest of society, many prostitutes from the unlicensed brothels in the Gion district and the southern riverbank plied their trade among the foodstalls and the complex of sideshows with their storytelling, acts of magic and recitations from military epics, as well as taking part in the performances. As a result many brawls occurred among, and about, the licentious activities of these women, so that in 1629 all women were officially banned from the stage and in 1640 prostitutes were moved to Shimbara on the opposite side of the river from the theatre. There was a general policy in other cities to separate prostitutes from actors: in Osaka, for example, a separate theatre district was set up in Dotombori and 'prostitute-plays' were banned from Shimbara.

But no amount of reform could divorce the theatre from the vigour of brothel and prostitute life, the Kabuki actors even modelling their stage roles on well-known prostitutes as well as on the puppet plays that had become such an important part of the floating world. This could lead to exciting results: for example when young Kabuki actors were faced with the challenge of finding a subtle way of playing women, they focused on the essential elements of a woman's gesture and hit on certain exaggerated characteristics which derived from the amplified movements of the puppet theatre. In turn, the puppet theatre began to replicate the movements of particular Kabuki actors so that the audience were able to recognise the characteristics of their favourite performers, while across the road at the Kabuki, the puppet-like grace of the 'onnagata'(male specialists in playing female roles) was imitated by the women in the audience who then began to import puppet-based characteristics into their daily human movements.[106] This remarkable interconnection between theatre, puppet and brothel should help us recognize the same link in the Lady Jôruri story.

Forgotten Women

Though it is interesting to examine Lady Jôruri's story in terms of the diverging detail in different versions, it is more challenging to consider why she and her lover, Minamoto Yoshitsune, have been identified either directly or indirectly, singly or taken together, with so many powerful rulers ranging from Kiyomori[107] to Yoritomo, and from Oda Nobunaga to Toyotomi Hideyoshi and Ieyasu Tokugawa. Looking at the message of the Jôruri story against the wider context of links with powerful figures over nearly five centuries, it becomes clear that she is representative of a huge kaleidoscope of women whose stories of unacknowledged support and sacrifice cry out to be articulated. They range from the wives, concubines and sisters of three powerful Edo Shoguns to the humblest serving maids, illustrating how women, irrespective of rank, were shamelessly exploited, like Lady Jôruri, in order to ensure the stability of the military government.

One of the most high-born of these women had one of the most miserable lives and is a strong example of how human emotions were totally discounted in the pursuit of political power: Oichi no Kata, the sister of the Shogun Oda Nobunaga.[108] One of sixteen children, she sensed from an early age the rivalry and hatred between her brothers over the leadership. When Nobuyuki, the younger brother of Oda Nobunaga died it was clear to all that the latter had engineered it. As far as he was concerned, his sisters were pawns to be disposed of in marriages of convenience in order to help him obtain the Shogunate. Oichi allowed herself to be given in a political marriage to Nagasamu Asai and, following his death, to Nobunaga's retainer and disciple, Katsuie Shibata. By now the poor woman was inevitably involved in her brother's political intrigues and had no choice but to follow her new husband to his death when he was defeated by her brother's great rival Toyotomi Hideyoshi. Before committing suicide, Oichi sent her three daughters out of his castle and committed them to the mercy of Hideyoshi. One of them, Yodo, was taken as concubine by the victorious Hideyoshi, bore him two sons and after his death and a great deal of political in-fighting also committed suicide in Osaka Castle along with her surviving son Hideyori, power passing to the equally unscrupulous Ieyasu Tokugawa. This was the man who had virtually ordered her death and whose granddaughter, Senhime, again for political expediency, had been married, aged seven, to the eleven year old Hideyori.

It was no better for lower-class women like Okiku,[109] Lady Yodo's maid, who continued to serve her mistress when she and her ill-fated son Hideyori had gone into hiding in Osaka castle. Even in her old age Okiku recalled vividly in her stories the hair-cutting ceremony specially arranged for the child bride, Senhime, granddaughter of the tyrant Ieyasu. The little girl had to stand on a checker board while her bridegroom, Hideyori, cut off a few strands of her hair with a knife. Okiku's description of the event is one of the few eyewitness accounts of this kind of heartless marriage of expediency and the little details of life under siege in Osaka castle while the rice-cakes pile up uneaten outside the apartments of the court ladies and the courtyard is full of the screams of the dying are extraordinarily powerful. Okiku's father was one of the soldiers given 300 kokus of rice as part of his wages for defending Osaka castle against Ieyasu's powerful army and she made him a flag of white and red cloth which he took to his death. Miraculously his daughter escaped while her mistress and her son committed suicide and were engulfed in the flames of the burning castle.

It is difficult not to regard the feelings of women like Lady Yodo and Okiku who were involved in the brutal civil wars of the Edo era, as just as authentic as war statistics and numbers of dead. They certainly bring home the fate of women within the broader historical framework and help to provide a background for the Lady Jôruri story, of which there are divergent versions and frequent gaps. She is not, for example, mentioned in the *Heike Monogatari* or in the Noh plays[110] devoted to her famous lover, Yoshitsune and yet her name has been given to a type of recitation (*jôruri*) and to a type of puppet performance (*ningyô jôruri*); the town of Yahagi has made huge efforts to treat her as a real person and yet she has nothing like the stature, outside Yahagi, of Lady Shizuka, Yoshitsune's famous and beautiful mistress, who was similarly abandoned and suffered dreadful tribulations at the hands of her lover's powerful brother, Yoritomo. So if we place her in the category of 'failed' heroines in the sense that her famous lover was also considered a 'failed' hero, earning himself the sobriquet *hôgan biiki* (meaning 'underdog'),[111] it can be argued that her claim to fame and honour lies precisely in the fact that she was a low-key figure, in many ways resembling a wayside flower, plucked, sacrificed and discarded by a historical general who won fame in the civil war which tore the country apart. She thus becomes a symbol of the many abandoned women whose plight as casualties of war, history does not deign to catalogue and to Yahagi's credit, Lady Jôruri's story has been carefully preserved in temples and memorial sites, in contrast to the indifference shown to her story in the world of the puppet theatres of Osaka and

Awaji island, to which she originally gave her name. Her very marginalisation links her to the many female shamans, entertainers, prostitutes and healers whose relevance to the established, mainstream, theatrical arts of Japan is indisputable though never clearly acknowledged.

Lady Jôruri and the Diaries

The word *Jôruri* can refer both to a type of recitation and to the subject of her story, Lady Jôruri herself. This can lead to confusion over what is meant but the earliest known reference to Lady Jôruri's story was in 1485 in a travel-diary written by Banri Shûku. This is in the form of a poem near the beginning of Book Two of *Baika Mujinzô* ('Inexhaustible store of plum-blossom') written in Chinese. The poem described how the author travelled from the castle of Kariya to Yahagi on the 15th day of the 9th month, 1485, and there he was told that the son-in-law of a rich man in the town belonged to the Minamoto family.[112] Though this date has often been referred to as the first known reference to Lady Jôruri's story, no one has commented on the inaccuracy of a major point: the distinguished member of the Minamoto clan did not marry Lady Jôruri but merely spent the night with her, continuing his journey the next morning. The seriousness of his mission made marriage at that time out of the question and it is clearly documented that he married twice later: his first wife was the daughter of an Eastern warrior, Kawagoe Shigeyori, and his second wife, the daughter of Taira Tokitada, was forced to commit suicide with him when his omnipotent brother, Yoritomo, decided that he had to be dispensed with.

The second reference, also a diary entry, is equally problematic because although it refers to a relic of Lady Jôruri, most likely a tomb, in a temple in Yahagi where the author, Sôchô, a famous teacher and composer of linked verse, spent a night in the fourth month of 1527, there is no mention of the story itself. But one can infer, as Dunn did, that it was the reputation of Lady Jôruri which led to a tomb being built in her memory and that her story was probably fairly well known in the town of Yahagi.[113] In other words this diary entry contains inductive evidence. Four years later in 1531 Sôchô described in another diary entry how much he delighted his guests on the 15th day of the eighth month, and the 13th of the ninth, when he summoned a *ko-zatô* (a little blind performer) to sing *jôruri*. However the subject of the recitation was not mentioned though Dunn suggests that "it would not be unreasonable" to assume that it was about Lady Jôruri. In 1540 there were references to a *zatô* (one of several grades of blind performers who earned their living by reciting passages from the *Heike Monogatari*), a recitation of *jôruri*, and *Ushiwaka* the childhood name of Yoshitsune in a group of three verses written by the poet Arakida Moritake. As Yoshitsune was only fifteen when he met Lady Jôruri, it is most likely that he would have been referred to by his childhood name of 'Ushiwaka'. The consensus of opinion is that it seems certain that the *zatô* must have been reciting Lady Jôruri's story.[114]

Two more diary entries, one by the court noble Yamashina Tokitsugu on the 25th day, 7th month, 1571, and the other by his son, Tokitsune, on the 15th day, 8th month, 1592, refer to a performance of *jôruri*, without specifying whether it was just the type of recitation to which Lady Jôruri had given her name or the story of Lady Jôruri herself.[115] It is mentioned in *Jôrurishi* ('History of Jôruri')[116] that the first puppet theatre performance took place in Kyoto in the Keichô period [1596–1614]. Menukiya Chôzaburô, the reciter and musician, collaborated with Hitta, the puppeteer from Nishinomiya, to perform the story of Lady Jôruri, and one of Menukiya's own compositions, *Miyako Meguri* ('Round the Capital'). Again diary entries give more specific dates and titles. The grandson of Tokitsugu refers in his diary of 1614 to a 'jôruri' piece called *Amida no munewari* ('Amida's Riven Breast') and Tokiyoshi, in his diary referring to the same performance, called it Amida no munekiri. In fact, according to Sanko *kikagi*, a local history of the Kanazawa area, there was a puppet performance set up in a theatre there in which three pieces, given the general name of jôruri, *Amida no munewari*, Goô no hime, and Ushiwaka-maru jûnidan, the last being the most popular, were presented.[117] These three pieces also have in common the theme of female self sacrifice and the fact that they were presented at the same time had the effect of reinforcing its similar motif. Theatre reflected real life and the year 1614 was one of brutalities as Ieyasu Tokugawa asserted his hegemony. Female sacrifice was the least of his concerns when Osaka castle was beseiged in May 1615 and Yodo was forced to commit suicide with her son.

Female Sacrifice, Puppets and Society
Lady Jôruri's suicide after her abandonment was not as spectacular as that of Yodo's or as sensational or melodramatic as Lady Tenju's in *Amida no munewari*.[118] In this play, Matsuwaka, the gravely-ill, twelve year old son of an extremely rich man, required the liver of a girl born on the same day and hour as himself in order to be healed. A sacrificial victim presented herself in the shape of Lady Tenju who only asked that after her death, her younger brother,Teirei, should be taken into the household of the rich man. Her intended sacrifice was indeed for her brother's sake, their dead parents, and of course for the dangerously sick patient. The rich man promised that a temple would be erected for the repose of her parents' souls, and that not only would her younger brother be brought up together with his son but would also share his inheritance. The story is clearly an allegory for the sick state of Japan which can only be healed through female sacrifice and it has, at least, a happy end: Lady Tenju's liver was duly extracted and administered, after many purifications, to the sick son who immediately recovered; the rich man entered the sanctuary (where the sacrifice had taken place) and saw a stream of blood pouring out of the split chest of the statue of Buddha (hence the title of the play: *Amida no munewari* or 'Amida's Riven Breast') where the siblings lay enfolded in each other's arms seemingly oblivious to everything. The rich man in awe and gratitude took Lady Tenju as his daughter-in-law while her brother became the priest of this temple. The moral of the story is the redemptive healing power of female sacrifice but delivered so heavy-handedly and allegorically that Lady Tenju did not capture the national imagination nor win sufficient sympathy to be turned into a national heroine.

Closer to the Jôruri story is that of *Goô no hime*: Yoshitsune is in hiding from the Tairas in Kuruma and being caught in a thunderstorm, takes shelter in the gateway of the house of Lady Goô, who is just fifteen. She lives with her aunt who is a Buddhist nun, and Yoshitsune is entertained royally. Stereotypically, she falls in love with the handsome hero who brings out his famous flute on which he plays several airs to return their magnificent hospitality just as in the Jôruri story. He is suddenly taken very ill just before he intends to depart and the two women, as in the Jôruri story, though with certain crucial differences, devotedly nurse him back to health. Far from being a conscientious, good-hearted healer, the aunt is avarice personified and after discovering that their guest is a Minamoto general she decides that she will betray him to Kiyomori for a reward. In order to ensure the safety of the guest with whom she had fallen in love, Lady Goô allows herself to be subjected to a range of appalling tortures including fire, snake-bites, arrows, cold and boiling water, ending with her own death, since she refuses to betray the whereabouts of her beloved Yoshitsune.[119] Her sacrifice makes it possible for him to return to temporary safety in the temple at Kuruma in the north of Kyoto. That the female was expected to sacrifice herself, for the sake of the male, particularly in the interest of national stability during the Edo period was taken for granted by the audience. In any case, by 1614, puppet *jôruri* had been well established according to the *Sanko kikigaki*, a reliable local history, and in the plays the dominant theme of female self-sacrifice (*kenshenteki*)[120] reflected both a feminine aesthetic in theatre and, more importantly, real life. The theme of female self-sacrifice in the first three *joruri* puppet plays ever presented in the Kanazawa theatre was so taken for granted that no comment on it was either expected or forthcoming.

The lonely voice of protest came in a strange tale about karmic retribution concerning a *sekkyôbushi*[121] puppeteer and his female puppet circulating around 1770.[122] This story invested the female puppet with such animation, vigour and initiative in order to reverse the status quo that it can perhaps be read as wishful thinking on the part of women – an attempt to take on an independent existence which can only be achieved by killing the male manipulator. The tale runs thus: a very popular chanter of *sekkyôbushi* from Kyoto called Higurashi Kodayu began in the 1680s to lose his grip on his audiences who were hankering after more elaborate costumes and more sophisticated puppets. So in despair he was forced to abandon his occupation and become a vagabond. Having destroyed all the puppets in his collection, he was left with his favourite female puppet which he finally decided to use as firewood for cooking some leaves. But the puppet called on magical powers to spit flames at the puppeteer, and in agonizing pain and remorse, he was forced to plunge into a well where he drowned. It is not known whether the tale was written by a male or female though it has inspired one of Britain's foremost feminist novelists, Angela Carter, to base her short story, 'The Loves of Lady Purple'[123] on it. What is significant about the Japanese tale is that the protest could only have been articulated by a puppet, just as the three puppet *jôruri* plays staged in the Kanazawa theatre in 1614 collectively articulated the story of female self sacrifice through puppets, though if irony was intended by the use of puppets in any of these performances, it went unnoticed. In an ambience in which males and females were not accustomed to believing that they had any individual rights,[124] the rule of custom and social expectation was supreme, and any modern Western value judgements must be cautiously applied. Indeed, apart from the memorial sites erected in Yahagi in homage to Lady Jôruri, there seems to have been a total absence of male remorse for the sacrifices exacted from women for the preservation of society and the image of the male puppeteer drowned in a well through the power of a female puppet is a graphic reversal of the more familiar image of a woman drowning in a river either for her own sins or for those of the community. A rare image too perhaps prompted by the puppet world's knowledge that the Edo authorities were less likely to clamp down on puppets than on actors bent on the same satirical course. One could speculate endlessly on this subject but the hard fact remained that the authorities had nothing to fear as theatre only continued to romanticize the theme of female sacrifice and, in some cases, provoke more actual suicides.[125] Shogunal authoritarian control remained supreme as shown in the story of the forty-seven *rônin*. The retainers were from one point of view justified in avenging their master's death. The latter had broken the Shogun's regulation regarding the raising of a sword in his palace, and so just as the master was ordered to commit *seppuku*, so were the forty seven *rônin* even though they were acting out of loyalty to him by tracking down and killing his assailant. It was imperative that Shogunal authority be considered inviolable.

The Puppet Theatre, Healing and Shamanism

Lady Jôruri, like so many of the women who fell victim both to the faithlessness of men and the repression of the Shogunate, drowned herself in a river. An ancient Japanese healing ritual connects interestingly here: in this ritual, dolls (*ningyô*) are cast into running water so that they are cleansed and purified and, with them, the souls of their owners. This practice still takes place in the Awashima Jinja Shrine at Kada, Wakayama, in Wakayama Prefecture.[126] According to legend, this shrine was founded by Empress Jingô in the third century when on her way home from a battle in Korea, her ship was overwhelmed by a fierce storm in Kataura Bay. Being a shamanic diviner, she implored the help of gods which guided her ship to Tamoga-shima Island where she set up an altar to the god of medicine. It was in the 4th century when the shrine was moved by Emperor Nintoku to Wakayama. This custom of transferring sins on to objects and then floating them down rivers, was derived from an ancient Chinese purification ceremony held along a river during the third lunar month in which courtiers exorcised their impurities and disposed of them through scapegoats in the flow of the water. At the Awashima shrine today, women can be seen stroking their sins into dolls which they believe will be purified when cast into the flowing water, while at the same time cleansing and freeing their owners from their sins. Similarly, there is little doubt that the strong emphasis in Yahagi on the drowning of Lady Jôruri in the River Otogawa is to reinforce her role as community and national scapegoat.

The Jôruri story is of course unique: not only did it begin the puppet theatre but it became part of the puppet theatre repertoire.[127] And the fact that in a historical documentation of her story, she straddled the two worlds of theatre and prostitution, meant that it faithfully recorded the strange fusion of brothel and theatre in Edo times which was seen as two sides of the same coin. Lastly, a final comment on the association of water with 'marginal' women, like Lady Jôruri, connected with healing and purification.

It is interesting that women who provided sexual services were euphemistically called *mizushobai*, 'the water trade'.[128] The allusive image of water should be taken in its literal and metaphorical sense: one thinks straightaway of the *kawamono* or 'river bed people' among whom were prostitutes, and also of the indispensability and power of water associated with prostitution. This is paradoxical because it highlights at once through the 'water' connection the insignificance and significance of prostitutes: though consigned to the bottom of the hierarchical scale in Confucian society, their indispensability to the ordering of the state could not be underrated. It was well known that during periods of great political and social disorder, the function of women who sold their sexual services was inestimable: such was the situation during the Wei, Tsin, and the Southern and Northern dynasties (265–589AD) for example,[129] and ironically this also coincided with the enforced drowning of baby girls. Drowning was also a punishment associated with loss of chastity or its preservation as in the case of the wife of Chih Chi Liang of the state of Chi. He was killed in the fierce war between the states of Chi and Lu and his young, beautiful, and clever wife was ruthlessly pursued to be the concubine of the Duke of Chuang. The story maintains that she travelled to the Great Wall where she found her husband's corpse among the debris and mourned and wept for ten days, winning much sympathy. The intensity of her grief and tears even caused part of the wall to collapse. It was inevitable that she then drowned herself in the Tzu river and so preserved her chastity, merging indistinguishably into water – the great receiver, absolutionist, purifier, and giver of life with which the 'Female' is associated.[130]

At this point it is worth looking at early references to water and its strange power in connection with the lowly and subservient as delineated in the ancient Daoist classic *Tao Te Ching*. In Daoism water, as the 'emblem of the unassertive', and the 'low ground', as the home of water, became dominant images. Water is meant as the model to the ten thousand things. And it is by absorbing the spirit of water that the whole of creation lives. Another name for this life force is the 'Mysterious Female'. So Chapter 8 of the *Tao Te Ching* begins with a hymn to Water:

The highest good is like that of water. The goodness of water is that it benefits the ten thousand creatures; yet itself does not scramble, but is content with the places that all men disdain. It is this that makes water so near to the Way.[131]

And Chapter 78 asserts clearly:

Nothing under heaven is softer or more yielding than water; but when it attacks things hard and resistant there is not one of them that can prevail. For they can find no way of altering it. That the yielding conquers the resistant and the soft conquers the hard is a fact known by all men, yet utilised by none.[132]

The power of insignificant things, symbolised by water, is an idea which is central to Daoism and one which Chikamatsu endorses in *Tethered Steed and the Eight Provinces of Kantô*:

Water is not a drill for stone but its drops falling from Mt. Tai bore through rocks.[133]

There is no doubt that Chikamatsu lent his weight to the voice of protest, however indirect, against the tyrannical role of *giri* (duty) enjoined by the *Bakufu*. Taking as an example his famous *Sonezaki Shinjū* ('The Love Suicides at Sonezaki'), it would be difficult to dispute that his sympathies lay with the ill-starred lovers who were clearly proponents of *ninjō* (emotion) as against *giri* (duty). He also wrote a *jōruri* play, dated 1590, based on the story of Lady Jōruri and was one of the earliest writers to focus on her heartbreak and suicide while some versions of her tale merely ended with her night of love with Yoshitsune. It is clear that Chikamatsu did not sanction the repressive military control which required a sacrifice such as hers, and judging from the number of his plays about the force of private passion, one cannot imagine him condoning the inhuman strictures of State control for the supposedly higher good of society. But nor was he advocating the flouting of rules. His particular genius enabled him to take the spectator at once inside and outside the Edo framework of control and place him squarely on the side of his protagonists trapped in the conflict between their private passions and unrelenting social mores. He creates a tension which produces an immensely compassionate world view, arrived at in a curiously detached and manipulative way so that one gets the feeling that the supreme puppeteer of his puppet plays is really none other than Chikamatsu Monzaemon himself.

In general there was little criticism of draconian military control so that the jōruri puppet theatre can be seen as an inevitable artistic portrayal of a ruthless system of manipulation of every aspect of society and individual life, justified by its defenders as necessary in a time of famine and disease. Rigorous control intended to rationalise or curb the scale of such disasters was not of course enough, and it was not surprising that people turned to the supernatural. Hence the proliferation of Healing Buddha temples and the popularity of the Jōruri story so strongly connected with the Healing Buddha.

The Puppet Theatre, Control and Exorcism

Within the puppet theatre itself, the strictures of control found expression in the measures introduced in the 18th century to regulate and reform the manipulation of puppets. When in 1734 Yoshida Bunzaburo (?–1760) of the Takemoto-za (where puppet recitation was born and developed), evolved the idea of using three puppeteers to manipulate one puppet,[134] it was a revolution in two senses: firstly, it was so aesthetically unusual that it brought the puppet art to the level of sophistication it enjoys today. Until then the puppeteer was hidden from the audience; now, dressed in black and hooded except for the main manipulator, the three puppeteers appeared with the puppets in a bid to manifest the control unashamedly. But even more than that, it reflected the almost inhuman, social control which the individual was subjected to in real life and of which the three-man control of the puppet was symbolic in a very real and tangible form. Until this time, each puppet was handled by one man only; there was now a trinity of control to the extent of sanctifying the art of control. Three puppeteers, the *omo-tsukai* who manipulates the puppet's head and right arm, the *hidarite-tsukai* who works the left arm, and the *ashi-tsukai* who only moves the legs, function as one in total harmony of mind and body to create a unique form of control. It is as though the three draw one breath and produce a forcefulness and eloquence derived from deliberate, centralized and co-ordinated control. It is said that the training of the puppeteers to accomplish such a magnificent network of ordering takes the following respective years: eight years for the one handling the legs; eight for the one controlling the left arm, and forever for the central puppeteer controlling the head and right arm. It would have been impossible for a less regimented and controlled society to have produced such a uniquely regulated system of puppet manipulation. In other words the logistics of puppet control or manipulation as perfected in the art of bunraku, formerly called *jôruri ningyô* after Lady Jôruri, can be traced to the regulation of Edo society itself. The ramifications of its control system stretched from prescribing the exact size of a peasant's hut to the strict sanctioning of every warrior's marriage contract. In an almost eerie manner, the way a chief puppeteer controls a female puppet (see Plate 3) mirrors exactly the way women were controlled by Edo society: from under the obi of the puppet, he inserts his left hand into her hollow chest in order to get at the grip for the head which is situated in the centre of the shoulder board. Attached to this grip are different cords connected with the interior of the puppet's head. So by pulling or releasing these cords the puppeteer can manipulate the ears, eyes, eyebrows, mouth and even the nose of the female doll. A woman's heroism lay in her total submission to the three obediences demanded by Confucianism: 'The Great Learning for Women' (*Onna Daigaku*) emphasised the highest importance attached to a female obeying her father as a child, her husband as a wife and her eldest son as a widow.[135] The puppet art and its related ceremonies and rituals represented one of the finest artistic flowerings of an extraordinarily regulated society.

There is of course a world of difference between puppet theatre as a form of art for entertainment and ritual puppetry used to drive away disease or to ensure a good catch in order to sustain the fish industry for example. And yet somewhere in the middle, there is the perception of the puppet as a means of communication between heaven and earth. For example, in the Zhou dynasty (1066–256B.C.), in the Fujian province, wooden (or clay) funeral figures of the deceased were considered to be the first puppets of China.[136] They were effigies of the deceased's relatives which were placed in the tomb to be of service to him. As part of the funeral rites, the presiding shaman was supposed to have manipulated these jointed figures so that they seemed to be possessed by the spirit of the dead. A strong belief was generated that these figures or puppets had the capacity of attracting spirits as well as influencing them.[137] And this idea of puppets as repositories of spirits soon spread across Asia and was certainly dominant in Japan. So the Emperor was regarded as the 'puppet' of the Sun goddess Amaterasu through whom she could manifest her spirit and make her wishes known.[138] A puppet was therefore regarded with some awe as an object in which a spirit could be persuaded to reside and in any case it possessed indefinable powers of communicating with spirits. And so evolved the idea that by staging huge carnivalesque affairs called *furyû* in which puppets dance and perform on giant floats to the accompaniment of deafening drum beats and music for exorcism, as well as other colourful wild displays of juggling and clowning and other pageantries, these festivals could stave off diseases and epidemics. This was certainly the raison d'être of the famous 9th century Gion festival, associated with the Yasaka shrine and staged when Kyoto was struck by an epidemic.[139] It has since then continued as a mark of thanksgiving for deliverance from trouble which has inspired many other carnivals and pageants used to entertain mortals and immortals and believed to be instrumental in warding off illness and obtaining blessings. On April 14th 2000, I saw for myself the spectacular use of puppet performances on giant floats at the Takayama Matsuri in Takayama (a city enfolded in the mountains of Gifu prefecture) in a wonderful spirit of carnival and celebration which also served as a gigantic placatory offering to ward off diseases. Closed, the floats could represent multi-tiered, highly ornate castles, but when the wings were open, hidden manipulators (sometimes children) by pulling strings, could transport us to a battle scene or turn puppet warriors into alluring women, a technique which Kabuki actors have learned in order to transform themselves into new characters on stage. Within a confined space at the top of a multi-tiered float, puppets seemed to be transformed before our very eyes either by spirits which had entered into them or a host of spirits summoned by the strange medley of sounds and rhythms to be part of the performance. The animated puppets symbolize the spirits to such a degree that it is difficult not to regard them with awe even after the performance when the spirits leave the habitations to which they have been invited. An awe-filled sense of otherness clings to them so strongly that a broken puppet is not just thrown away but ceremoniously buried in a cemetery for puppets.[140] They are such an important constituent of the human negotiation with the world of spirits that questions such as why do actors on stage move like puppets almost seem redundant: it is part of the grammar of human-spirit communication. There is a sense of returning to the primal necessity of contacting spirits in the only viable way that humans believe spirits can understand. And this way is inextricably bound up with puppets and the way they move and their power to influence spirits. And of course the way puppets move (if we remove the intervention of spirits for a moment) is determined by the way they are manipulated. But the logistics of the mechanism of such movements disappear in the superstitious belief in the efficacy of such movements and that they are in a large part motivated by spirits. No wonder then that not only are the three main national theatre arts of Japan, Noh and Kabuki, puppet related, and the third, Bunraku, an unadulterated puppet art, but a quarter of all folk performing arts in Japan have a puppet inspiration.[141] Such is the awe in which puppets are held in the theatrical performing arts in the East that in some way or other they have permeated into the human stage either in the philosophy or choreography of movement itself.[142]

At another festival of *butaigei* or *tairaigei* (this term means a variation of a stage art where the familiar takes on a new twist) at Nôgô village in the Hida prefecture on April 13th, 2000 (this takes place annually on this date at the Hakusan shrine), the puppet factor was also used to exorcise spirits, avert disease and promote health for the people in this community. Sixteen families in this village are delegated the task of putting on these presentations (ten are delegated to perform Noh and six Kyôgen) and they are proud to make it known to visitors that they have in their collection late medieval masks as well as a playbook from 1598. What came across clearly to me as I sat with the locals and visitors on the grass in front of the stage was the intimacy of the occasion: this stylized ritual in which actors stalked the stage like giant puppets represented in effect a simple negotiation with the other world to protect this community by promoting health and averting epidemics. So concerned was I to observe and record the puppet-like nature of the stage movements that I must have been the only one who did not, and could not, participate in the efficacy of the ritual. The Noh presentation of *Takasago* was pure celebration: it was an invocation of blessing for the community through the double images of the Takasago and Sumiyoshi pines standing both for marital bliss and the power of poetry. But the special message of this *butaigei* festival came across in the folk Noh performance of *Rashômon* (The Rashô Gate)[143] in which the subject touched on the exorcism of evil spirits, and where this sharp coincidence of style and subject matter, directed at expelling evil spirits, conveyed the essence of folk performing arts which have never lost their umbilical link with the spiritual world. I felt somewhat ashamed with my camera and note pad analysing and recording a magic ritual in which the entire community participated so naturally as part of the whole business of living and must have done so from the beginning of time when there was no insuperable division between the world of man and that of spirits. Lost in these thoughts, I only came to when a gentle tap on my shoulder from one of the organizers reminded me that if I wanted to catch the only train that evening to take me back to Nagayo and Osaka, it was time to leave and he was prepared to drive me to the station.

There does not exist any documentation establishing a direct link between Lady Jôruri as archetypal medium/healer and the general use of puppets in negotiating good health for a community. But that an entire network of indirect links exists between certain theatrical arts and healing is irrefutable. In the case of *jôruri ningyô*, the word *jôruri* means 'the pure world of the Healing Buddha'. This name *jôruri*, which was given to our heroine, connotes 'healing' in its fullest sense and is in fact the starting point of the '*Jôruri*' story. Lady Jôruri is the unmistakable manifestation of the healing powers of the Healing Buddha – the answer to the prayers of a childless couple. And if the puppet art has been given her name, *jôruri ningyô*, the implication is that it must in some way participate in the activity of healing either literally, or metaphorically, or a combination of both. Noh drama, which has a strong shamanic origin, for example, has been called 'Healing without medicine'.[144] According to one, Kobori Enshu, mental and bodily health were considered one of the fifteen virtues of Noh both for the performer and spectator. He added: 'Dancing (i.e. Noh dancing) is especially known, by its circulation of the blood to keep off the disease of old age.'[145]

Umewaka Minoru, who transmitted Noh drama to the West through Ernest Fenollosa, Ezra Pound and William Butler Yeats, conceived of the Noh as an art which worked in pure spirit, and for that reason it was higher than other arts. He felt that an actor inevitably revealed his character in his performance and for that reason he insisted that his sons should be moral, pure and true in their daily lives, otherwise they could not become the greatest actors. He spoke of how the Shogun would require Noh actors to sign articles to the effect that they would not visit houses of pleasure or go to the theatre in order to maintain clean living and purity in their lives for the sake of their art.[146] As to the therapeutic effects of Noh dancing to enhance good blood circulation, I have devoted Chapter 3 to discussing this in relation to *T'ai Chi Ch'uan*, an ancient Chinese form of callisthenics based on puppet movements, which underpins Chinese theatre. It has been proved that apart from the exorcising function of puppets and puppet movements, there is a strong correlation between the way a string puppet moves and the art of maintaining good health. So having proclaimed its fundamental correlation with rigorous discipline, clean moral living and good health, the fourteenth century Noh, "which only works in pure spirit" became the prime example for the later, more popular arts of Kabuki and *jôruri ningyô* which paradoxically reached their heyday when they were inseparable from the pleasure quarter.

Awaji Island, Puppets and the Art of Survival
Awaji Island, which lies between the main islands of Honshu and Shikoku, and is fairly close to the port of Kobe, is known as the cradle of Japanese puppet theatre.[147] It may or may not be a coincidence that the healing or medical profession was singularly important in the Awaji puppet world in the early sixties. At that time the principal leader of the puppet troupe was a woman whose stage name was Ichimura Rokunoji. In real life she was called Toyada Hisae and she came from Kyûshû. She had met her husband, an Awaji puppeteer, when he was on a touring expedition to Kyûshû. After marriage she threw herself so thoroughly into her husband's occupation that on his death she was more than able to assume

his stage name and carry on his profession. There is such a scarcity of documents relating precisely how women or the wives of early puppeteers were involved in what began as a man's job. So the case of Ichimura Rokunojo in Awaji provides strong clear evidence of how this process of absorbing females into early puppetry must have begun: male puppeteers used their wives as assistants and they generally became so proficient that they were capable of acting as puppeteers and musicians. In Ôe Masafusa's account of the wandering *kairaishi* or puppet performers, he avers that the women among these wanderers also served as prostitutes. Ichiura Rokunojo's involvement with puppetry and healing was of course extremely above board and respectable. She rose to prominence when her son, a doctor, also acted as her business manager. The leader of one of the other three troupes on the island then was also a doctor and so was the principal adminsitrator of puppetry in Awaji as well as the ear, nose, and throat specialist, Matsutani Tatsutsuku, who was not just a devotee and patron of puppet theatre but was himself a skilful amateur puppeteer.[148] One cannot ascribe this strange intermingling of healing and puppetry to chance and business coincidences.

There is of course the deep seated belief among the islanders that the good health of a community is completely dependent on the performance of puppetry. This belief finds expression in a story about Hyakudayu, the man who founded the Awaji puppet tradition.[149] He was not a native of Awaji Island but was exiled there by his master, Dokumbo, a highly skilful puppeteer and temple priest at the shrine of Ebisu, which is part of the large Shinto establishment of Settsu Nishnomiya, in what is now the town of Nishinomiya. Ebisu is one of the gods of good fortune connected with the seabream industry of the Inland sea. From a text dated 1638, we are told that Dokumbo daily staged a puppet performance invoking the blessing of Ebisu for a profitable fishing season. The story goes that the disciple, Hyakudayu, was in disgrace because after learning the secrets of puppetry from his master, he performed for gain in rival temples and was consequently banished from Nishinomiya. But after Dokumbo's death, long spells of bad weather and a series of fishing disasters occurred and so Hyakadayu hit on the idea of making a doll in the likeness of his former master performing puppetry to appease the deity Ebisu. The disasters ceased and the efficacy of averting disasters through the practice of puppetry was recognized. The people of Awaji learned this art of survival from Hyakudayu. So puppet plays involving the appeasement of Ebisu became crucial for the purpose of protecting homes, farms and fishing boats. Today the mere staging of the Ebisu puppet successfully catching a big fish is sufficient to ensure success and prosperity in the fishing industry and so secure prosperity, health and good fortune for the islanders. With only a slight twist, the almost clock-work performance of the puppet play *Kesei Awa no Naruto* ('The Infant Pilgrim') eight times a day, every week, at Awaji's main puppet theatre, 'Awaji Ningyô Jôruri Kan' in Fukura, is exemplifying the same old superstitious reverence connecting puppetry with successful business enterprise. The play concerns a samurai in the service of the Lord of Awa (part of Shikoku). He now lives in Osaka with his wife, having sacrificed everything, including his infant daughter and his wife's happiness in order to devote his life to retrieving his lord's stolen sword. The twenty-eight minute scene chosen for presentation only focuses on the union between mother and long-lost daughter and the mother's agony as she makes a quick decision to send her daughter away with all the money she can spare her, without revealing her identity. For many reasons the subsequent scene where the father unwittingly robs his child and then kills her is never portrayed to the large number of visitors to the show. It would seem that even for a modern audience, male accountability for domestic tragedy is played down while the female still has to accept full responsibility for self sacrifice. It would also, I imagine, be difficult to apportion any blame to a Lord of Awa since it was he who protected Awaji puppetry until the end of the 19th century. As a foreign visitor in April 2000, after watching the 'unalterable' *Awa Kesei no Naruto* twice, I asked if there could be a change of programme. In deference to my great interest in puppets, *Hidakagawa* ('The Hidaka River') was staged though the puppeteers I spoke to felt that Lady Jôruri had little relevance to puppetry apart from giving her name to their theatre.[150]

Jôruri Ningyô and its Debt to Lady Jôruri

A great deal of ceremony, spiritual dignity and a sense of humility, surround the performance of *jôruri ningyô*, just as they do in Noh drama. I would like now to examine the preliminary ceremony leading up to the *tozai* incantations to see if there are any grounds for viewing the puppet art as a semi-sacred healing ritual in secular dress. Backstage each performer carries out simple purification rites. After putting on *tabi* (white socks), the narrator is handed the long waist band which is wrapped firmly around the abdomen to support the muscles and so aid voice control. But before he puts it on, he lifts it above his head, and bows to it as though in prayer and supplication to the waistband to grant him the additional strength for the performance. The stiff vestlike *kataginu* is then placed over his shoulders with the long wide bands hanging down in front. The bands are similarly lifted above his eyes and once again he bows to them. He then puts on the *hakama* (broad trousers) and then seats himself on the small revolving stage. Finally he receives the *futokoro* which resembles a long, narrow, sand-filled pillow. This, too, is reverently saluted before it is passed through the sleeve and placed inside the front of his kimono above the waistband. It is this which keeps the costume in place while the narrator tells the story accompanied by a wide range of emotions and sometimes extremely vigorous movements. The small stage is then revolved and the narrator and his shamisen accompanist, with bowed heads, are revealed to the audience. When all these preliminaries have been discharged, the oldest puppeteer in the troupe appears on stage with a black hood to make the announcement called *tozai* meaning 'east – west'. It has never been specified that this is simply an approximate indication of the full breadth of the auditorium the performance is meant to cover. That indeed would be far too literal an interpretation for a multi-dimensional art which transcends so many different boundaries. Let us look at the way the *tozai* announcement is made: '*Tozai!* I hereby announce the performers for today. The narrator is ..., and his accompanist on the shamisen is .... *Tozai!*' Even if one were unaware of the ceremony of humility behind the stage, it is difficult not to submit to the incantatory mesmerizing effect of *Tozai* cries as they ring out from the hooded figure on stage. 'East' and 'West' are also the locations of the two different paradises of Buddha: the one in the 'East' is associated with the Healing Buddha or the 'Medicine Master'; and the one in the 'West' is the Western Paradise of Amida. So the puppet art is situated in the pilgrim's progress from the Eastern Paradise of Healing to the Western Paradise of future happiness: in other words between the 'now' of healing and relief in this world and the 'afterwards' of salvation in the next. It is an extremely solemn and optimistic declaration which turns the ensuing entertainment, engaging all our emotions of pity and revulsion, laughter and sorrow, into something resembling a mammoth healing therapeutic ritual. So because *Jôruri Ningyô* takes its alpha from the Eastern Paradise of the Healing Buddha, it provides in an even more striking way than the 14th century Noh, an example of 'Healing without medicine.'

All this while the narrator and his accompanist maintain their deep bow as though in support of this declaration and it is only after the second *Tozai* that they raise their heads to face the audience. And then follows a piece of ceremony which significantly represents the sanctification of the text in its performance through the office of the story teller. It is tantamount to saying that the storytelling is even more important than the text which is considered sacred. In no other form of theatre is the art of story telling so exalted and singled out. In Noh drama the story telling is passed between the main character played by the *shite* (main) actor, the *waki* (secondary actor) and the chorus; in *jôruri ningyô* the story-teller is more important than all the characters on stage: he is given his own pulpit as it were, for it is his narration or story telling that will open the eyes of the spectator to new vistas of understanding. The importance of the narrator's role underlines the function of narration here, a narration which must be understood in close relation to its Latin root *gnarus* meaning 'knowing'. For it is in knowing and understanding that healing can begin. This puppet art began with a piece of story telling, the story of a woman, Lady Jôruri, who loved deeply, healed her lover and then was forced by circumstances to kill herself. The essential theme is that of the redemption of the warrior through female sacrifice. Indeed, this is the central theme of *Bunraku* itself presented at each performance with reverence and ceremony so that as the narrator picks up the text or libretto from the bookstand, lifts it above his head with both hands, and bows – the consecration as it were – he expresses respect for the author, calling on the power of the written word to support the dramatic presentation, offers a prayer that the performance will justify the written work; and gives thanks to the spectators for being present, humbly hoping that they will give him their attention.[151] Audience participation or interaction with the puppets is a crucial element requiring sanctification for it is this which will animate the entire show and provide the healing. The narrator then replaces the book on the stand, opens it to the title page, and the oldest puppeteer intones his final *tozai* which fades into the introductory music of the shamisen player. It is said that the great humility generated by so much bowing, from the first moment behind the scenes until the final *tozai*, helps the narrator to regulate his breath and maintain control as well as prepare the audience for an entertainment which goes beyond entertainment and becomes a ritual for the healing of body, mind and spirit. The introductory cries of *tozai*, like those of the muezzin calling the faithful to prayer in the Muslim world, have the power to break through barriers of real time and can take the audience to the threshold of the healing process.

And here we come back to Lady Ono no O-Tsû, who, as described above, is the most likely 'inventor' of the story of Lady Jôruri – a story which she used to heal the Shogun, Oda Nobunaga. For him, the story and the way it was narrated provided consolation. Maybe it was meant as a moral lesson for the ailing lord whose brutalities in pursuit of power had left the nation bewildered; maybe the nurse's tale was meant to suggest that the war-worn, disease-ravaged country, like the insomniac leader himself, was in need of healing. Apparently he found both the story and the way it was narrated consoling. Was it meant as a moral lesson for the war-obsessed ailing Shogun whose brutalities to gain power left the nation bewildered? Was the nurse's tale meant to suggest that the war-torn disease-ravaged country, like the ailing insomniac leader, was also in need of healing? History does not record any change of heart on his part and it is quite likely that the allegorical point about a story of healing within the context of unrest was purposely overlooked because that would have gone dangerously close to criticism of harsh existing powers. But there is ample evidence (barring inaccuracy of dates) that the Lady Jôruri story as narrated by Ono no O-Tsû became immensely popular, and it eventually spearheaded a remarkable puppet theatre. It certainly has more significance than being merely similar in style to a nurse's or attendant's tale called *o-togi-zôshi*, a genre of story telling with attached Buddhistic morals which was popular in the late 15th century. And even the fact that Ono no O-Tsû, this supposed first storyteller, could have been a fictitious character fabricating a story about another fictitious character, is immaterial: Chikamatsu Monzaemon, the greatest playwright of the puppet world whose playtexts are often on the book stand of *jôruri* narrators, which are reverently lifted above their heads and bowed to, in the way described above, was adamant that there was no division between truth and fiction.[152] The people of Yahagi, as attested by the seventeen memorial sites which I have discussed, are clearly of the same mind as the great dramatist. Since the early 16th century, as recorded in the *Munenaga Shuki* document, they have treated Lady Jôruri as though she were a real person, and, perhaps over-studiously collected artefacts and preserved them in temples to bolster her reality against the strong wall of dissent about her identity that has grown up in the puppet theatres in Osaka and Awaji-shima. And so in deference to her unappeased spirit, her story must be told for it contains the seed of story telling itself. For towering even above the solid castle of Okazaki, with which she and Shogun Ieyasu Tokugawa are associated, is the beckoning, irrepressible phantom of Lady Jôruri herself, controversially real or fictitious, prostitute, Buddhist saint, and healer, all rolled into one, in short, an icon, which the puppet world can ignore but cannot really dispense with, without dislocating its very foundations. For the story of Lady Jôruri, whose name has been struck off the official register, is, as I have tried to show, the puppet theatre's foundation, compounded out of story-telling, superstition, folk belief, female devotion, warrior supremacy and sacrifice. Her tale is not just that of an abandoned woman forsaken in the conflict of civil war, but encapsulates the interaction of the elusive human element with the indomitable flow of social, political and historical currents which mingled to create the most refined and sophisticated puppet theatre in the world during the Edo era of reunification.

Notes and References

1. In 1805, Uemura Bunrakuken came to Osaka from Awaji Island and formed a puppet troupe. Although it was a successful venture, the troupe did not have a permanent home until 1811 on the grounds of the Naniwa Shrine in Bakuromachi, Osaka. In 1871, it established itself in another part of Osaka, and performed there under the name *Bunraku-za*.
2. Otozuru was a *kusemai* (unconventional dance) performer belonging to the Kaga group from Nara, who taught her art to Kan-ami (1333–1384) – the father of Noh drama. It was his incorporation of this popular song form into Noh drama which both revolutionised its structure and produced its characteristic blend of musical styles
3. The Kabuki art originated in 1603 in the sensational songs and dances of Okuni, an entertainer/prostitute and priestess of the Izumo shrine who performed on the dried-up bed of the river Kamo in Kyoto.
4. See p. 129 for a discussion of this festival at the Awashima Shrine.
5. See Barbara Ruch's 'The Other Side of Culture in Medieval Japan' in *The Cambridge History of Japan, Medieval Japan,* Vol. 3, eds. John W. Hall et al., Cambridge: Cambridge University Press, 1990.
6. Charles J. Dunn, *The Early Japanese Puppet Drama*, p. 109. London: Luzac and Co., 1966. See also F.J. Daniels, *Selections from Japanese Literature*, p. 46, London 1958 and M.W. De Visser, *Ancient Buddhism in Japan,* p. 534, Paris, 1928–35.
7. See the magazine, *Yakushiji,* issued by the Yakushi-ji Temple, Head Temple of the Hosso Sect in Nara, trs. Shinji Takahashi and Penny Totsui. Tokyo: Asukaen Co. Ltd., April 2000.
8. *Heike Monogatari* ('The Tale of the Heike'), Vols.1 & 2, translated by Hiroshi Kitagawa and Bruce T. Tsuchida, Tokyo: University of Tokyo Press, 1975. This 13th century epic was based on historical facts and regarded as one of the greatest prose classics of Japanese literature.
9. Giô was an extraordinarily gifted *shirabyôshi* dancer (*shirabyôshi* means 'white-beat', a reference to the accompaniment to the dances which used a 'plain ordinary beat' like that called *shirabyôshi* in Buddhist chanting). She became the favourite courtesan of Kiyomori, the powerful 12th century Heike priest/premier. The longest canto in the opening section of the Heike story is given to her tale.
10. At the height of Kiyomori's power, it was said of him that he held in his palm both heaven and earth. His brother-in-law once proudly declared: 'Unless a man is a Heike, he is not a human-being.' See Hiroshi Kitagawa's translation of *Heike Monogatari,* op.cit., p. 16.
11. Kenreimon-in, daughter of Kiyomori, was married to Emperor Takaura (1168–80) and gave birth to Antoku who later became the crown prince and heir

with a heart-rending description of her son's suicide to her father-in-law, Go Shirakawa Hô-ô, who, like his daughter-in-law, had taken holy orders.

12. Wakatsuki Yasuji maintains that there are really forty versions of the story ranging from the moveable-type Saga-bon text to Chikamatsu Monzaemon's 1690 version. Thirteen of them have been reprinted in Yasuji's *Kinsei shoki kokugeki no kenkyû* (Studies in Japanese Drama of the early modern [17th century] period), p. 181f, 1944. See also Dunn op.cit.1966, p. 37.

13. My summary of this tale is based on Charles J. Dunn's translation of the version edited by Suwara Kyuba in 1906 and reprinted by Takano Tatsuyuki in *Nihon Kayôshûsei* ('Collection of Japanese songs') 1928 vol.5, p. 422. See also Dunn's *The Early Japanese Puppet Drama*, op. cit., pp. 31–34.

14. Fanny Hagin Mayer in *Ancient Tales in Modern Japan: an Anthology of Japanese Folk Tales*, Bloomington, Indiana: Indiana University Press, 1984, xiii, makes a distinction between a legend and a folk tale. The former is a brief statement of an incident said to have occurred at a specific place while the latter is set in a certain unnamed place where a complete story occurs.

15. The temple Hôrai-ji (Temple of Hôrai) shares the same name as the mountain which is in the Aichi prefecture. *Hôraiji* is known as *Peng Lai Shan* in Chinese (*Shan* meaning 'mountain') and believed to be the home of divine beings like Yang Kuei Fei who was incarnated as the beautiful mistress of Emperor Tang Ming Huang. On this mountain grows a herb of immortality. See Masako Graham, *The Yang Kuei Fei Legend in Japanese Literature* Vol 6, p. 6, New York: The Edwin Mellen Press Ltd., 1998. Both Yang Kuei Fei (whom I have labelled the 'Chinese Birdwoman') and Lady Jôruri are therefore associated with *Horaiji* and there is a jôruri play entitled *Nihon Hôrai-san* ('Mount Hôrai of Japan'). See Dunn op.cit., p. 72.

16. It is interesting that in both East and West seminal figures associated with puppets or marionettes are said to have been born of immaculate conception: Lady Jôruri, Marshal Tian and the Virgin Mary.

17. *Kaimami* or 'peeping through a fence' is a device patterned on the famous *kaimami* scene from *Ise Monogatari* ('The Tales of Ise'). See *Dan* 1 in which the hero, having an estate in the village of Kasuga near the old capital of Nara, went hawking and peeped through a fence at two very elegant sisters living in that village. One of Chikamatsu Monzaemon's historical plays *Tôryû Oguri Hangan* performed at the Takemoto-za in Osaka in 1714 was a modernisation of the narrative patterned on the scene as described above. See H.J.Harris (tr.) *The Tales of Ise*, Tokyo: Charles E. Tuttle Company Inc., 1972, p. 75. This opening *kaimami* or 'Peeping Tom' presentation of the initial scene in *Jôruri Monogatari* enhances the erotic nature of its subject as well illustrated in Lucy Bailey's production of Tennessee William's *Baby Doll* at the Lyttleton Theatre in London in March 2000. The scene opens in darkness with the sound of a drill and we gradually see a small slide projection of a woman in a cot and as the stage lights turn up, the picture enlarges to depict a man in the adjoining room drilling a hole through the

bedroom wall to obtain a view of the same subject seductively curled up in a child's cot. The sensuality of this optical view speaks for itself.

18. Yoshitsune, like Prince Genji – the hero of Murasaki Shikibu's *Genji Monogatari* ('The Tale of Genji'), completed by 1008 – excelled in the art of love. Prince Genji's affair with Lady Yûgao is recounted in chapter 4, pp 54–80, in Arthur Waley's translation of Lady Murasaki's *Genji Monogatari* 'The Tale of Genji', London: George Allen & Unwin, 1975. Lady Yûgao lives in the house next to that of Prince Genji's old nurse. He spies her through an opening in the fence (*hajitomi*) and notices that this barrier is completely covered with *yûgao* or 'moonflowers'. The scene continues with one of her maids plucking a moonflower, placing it on a fan, and presenting this floral offering to the prince. Symbolically, this presages the tragic death of Lady Yûgao as her name also means 'moonflower'. Zeami's Noh play *Yûgao* is based on this episode.

19. See Ichiro Hori's article 'Mysterious Visitors from the Harvest to the New Year' in *Studies in Japanese Folklore*, ed. Richard M. Dorsan, Series No. 17, Bloomington: Indiana University Press,1963, pp. 76–77. Great emphasis was placed on the appearance of 'mysterious visitors' at harvest time or at the turn of the year. They were regarded as 'Life-Givers' sent to instil new life power in rice seeds and in human-beings to ensure vigorous germination in Spring. Ancient Japanese peasant philosophers tried to explain the interrelationship between the four seasons of the year and the cycle of growth and decay of the rice plant. Visitors of eminence like deities are called *marebito*. Yoshitsune was deified after his death.

20. See Wakatsuki Yasuji, *Kinsei shoki kokugeki no kenkyû*, 'Studies in Japanese drama of the early modern period (17th century)', 1944, p. 593.

21. In addition to the long version, there is a medium version which ends with Yoshitsune's flight from Lady Jôruri's room and this consists of fifteen sections, while a short version is made up of eight or nine sections. Such a version is in the possession of the actor family Nakamura, dated 1775. See C.J. Dunn op.cit. p. 593.

22. The 1522 original document *Munenaga Shuki* ('The Handbook of Munenaga') in two volumes is unavailable but there is a reprint of it in Hanawa Tokinoichi (ed.), '*Gunsho ruijû* ('Complete Collection of Japanese Literary Works'), v.326, Nikki-bu 7, published in 1986 by the Onko Gakkai, Tokyo. There are only two holdings for it: Ritsumeikan University in Kyoto and Sugiyama Jogakuen University in Nagoya.

23. See *Jôrurihime koseki junrei zue* ('The map for the pilgrimage to the memorial places of Lady Jôruri') by Ishida Mosaku in his book *Jôrurihime no koseki to densetu* ('The Memorials and Legends of Lady Jôruri'), Okazaki: Shibundo, September 1969. This map is also reprinted on p. 26 of the *Bulletin of the Society for the Study of Okazaki Local History,* Vol. 6, Okazaki: Society for the Study of Okazaki Local History, 1978. The engraver of the map is Horikan aka Suzuki Kanjirô.

24. In early Indian art, Buddha is represented by the imprint of his feet. See *The Crossroads of Asia: Transformation in Image and Symbol in the Art of Ancient Afghanistan and Pakistan*, ed., Elizabeth Errington and Joe Cribb with Maggie Claringbull, Cambridge: the Ancient India and Iran Trust, Brooklands House, 1992, p. 124. See also *Songs on the Buddha's Footprints*, tr., Philippi in *Nihonbunka-Kenkyusho-Kiyô*, Tokyo: Kokugakuin University, No.2, March 1958, p. 153. In these songs, composed in the 8th century, Buddha is portrayed as a great healer and a *marabito* – a Shinto term referring to a *kami* (spirit) who visits villages from a far-off place during the time of harvest.

25. *Jûgoya* as with *Yôhiki* (Emperor Tang Ming Huang's celebrated mistress), were popular names used by prostitutes in the 17th century. See James L. McClain *Kanazawa: A seventeenth century Japanese Castle Town*, New Haven and London: Yale University Press, 1982, p. 64.

26. There has been much controversy over the mislabelling of memorial 10 as the grave of Lady Jôruri's maid, Jûgoya. Scholars like Takeda Isamu in his article *Jôrurihime no kenkyû* ('A Study of Lady Jôruri') in the *Bulletin of the Society for the Study of Okazaki Local History*, op. cit., Vol. 3, 1974, pp. 12–28, are convinced that memorial site 10 assigned to Uba Reizi no Haka (Jûgoya's Buddhist name) is indeed the real tomb of Lady Jôruri for three reasons: as a maid, Jûgoya cannot be permitted to have two tombs; as shown on the map, memorial 10 is placed on a higher level than memorial 8 which is correctly labelled as Jûgoya's tomb: the proximity of memorial 10 to memorial 9 (which marks the Kômyôin Temple regarded as central to the Lady Jôruri cult) is sufficient proof that it must be the real tomb of Lady Jôruri. The seriousness with which this whole issue of status and siting of tombs is taken apropos mistress and maid indicates the great concern to establish them as real persons.

27. See 'The Double-Grave System' by Takayashi Mogami in *Studies in Japanese Folklore*, op.cit., pp. 167–180. The Japanese term for the burial grave is *umebaka* while *mairi-baka* is used for the memorial tomb. However in some locations such as Yahagi, the word *haka* is used for both. Hence memorial 14 is called *Jôrurihime no haka*. Again the fact that she has been given two tombs represents the strenuous efforts of the Yahagi community to present her as more than a fictitious character.

28. See Donald H. Shively, *Shinju Ten no Amijima* ('The Love Suicide at Amijima'), *A Study of a Japanese Domestic Tragedy*, Cambridge Massachusetts: Harvard University Press, 1953, p. 25.

29. See Takeda Isamu's article, 'A Study of Lady Jôruri', op. cit. in Note 26.

30. In some versions (see ibid.) Lady Jôruri gave birth to a baby girl called Yoshinoe; in others a son called Senyumaru.

31. Takeda Isamu points out that after the statue of Buddha had been moved into the Rurikô-san-Anjei Temple, Lady Jôruri's father, Kanetaka Chôja, took possession of it. The writer also places the story a generation earlier than most other versions with Lady Jôruri's mother presented as the owner of a lucrative inn left to her by her parents and her father a courtier from the Minamoto family and

therefore involved in the bitter inter-clan dispute with the Tairas. According to this story, which involves some genealogical tinkering to elevate him, the father, to the level of his daughter's lover, Kanetaka falls in love with the future mother while hiding in her inn during a period of exile and flight to Yahagi. They marry and after some time, the Healing Buddha answers their supplications for a child with Lady Jôruri. Again, in this version, it is the father and not the mother who pursues his daughter to Fukiage where she has gone in search of her lover Yoshitsune. Having failed to persuade her to give him up, Kanetaka disinherits her and she is forced to take the tonsure. Her mother intervenes by building a hermitage for her and together they take shelter, reciting the sûtras till Lady Jôruri's death (by this account) on 12th March 1177, her mother dying some five months later. Kanetaka dies in 1185. The strongly Buddhist focus in this version is meant to remove any association Lady Jôruri might have had with prostitution, a connection which Takeda Isamu is anxious to refute, even to the point of denying the existence of any licensed brothel quarters in Yahagi in Lady Jôruri's time. Referring to earlier editions of the tale, he is adamant that Lady Jôruri was not referred to as a *yujô* (prostitute) but as a *yukun* (mistress).

32. See Hall, John W. et.al .*The Cambridge History of Japan, Early Modern Japan*, Vol. 4, Cambridge: CUP 1991, p. 383. The Zôjôji temple is known as the *Bodaiji* (a temple affiliated to a particular family) of the Tokugawa Shogunal line and contains the graves of some of the most important family members. Prayers are offered here for the successful passage of the souls of the deceased into the realm of the Buddha. The term *bodai* (Skt: *bodhi*) originally referred to the state of enlightenment.

33. See also C. Andrew Gerstle 'Heroic Honor: Chikamatsu and the Samurai Ideal' in *Harvard Journal of Asiatic Studies*, Vol. 57, No.2 (December 1997) p. 314.

34. Self-sacrifice as a means of servicing the system was still in force as late as 1944. The following is an extract from a letter which a twenty-three year old *kamikaze* pilot wrote to his father: *The living embodiment of all wonderful things out of our past is the Imperial Family which, too, is the crystallization of the splendour and beauty of Japan and its people. It is an honour to be able to give my life in defence of these beautiful and lofty things. (Sunday Times Weekly Review 23/11/75).*

35. See Barbara Ruch's 'The Other Side of Culture in Medieval Japan' in *The Cambridge History of Japan*, editors John Hall, Marius Jansen, Madoka Kansai and Denis Twitchett, Vol.3, op.cit. p. 505.

36. Helen Craig McCullough (tr), *Yoshitsune, A Fifteenth Century Japanese Chronicle*, California: Stanford University Press 1966, p. 36.

37. See Shingyo Norikazu's article, *Jôruri Gozen Monogatari to Yahagi no hanmei* ('The Tales of Lady Jôruri and the Prosperity of Yahagi') in 'Chapter 2: Muromachi Feudal Government and Okazaki Area' in *The History of Okazaki City: Medieval Age*, Vol.2, Okazaki: Okazaki City, March 1989, pp. 489–521.

38. See Conrad Totman, *Tokugawa Ieyasu Shogun*, California: California Heian International Inc., 1983, p. 30.

39. See *Cambridge History of Japan*, Vol.4, op.cit., p. 37. In 1431, 1440, 1450, 1459, 1491–1500 and 1540, disease and famine were widespread in Japan. See also Joseph Kitagawa, *Religion in Japanese History*, New York and London: Columbia University Press, 1966, p. 172. He refers to the ten great famines which took place in 1619, 1642, 1675, 1680, 1732, 1783, 1787, 1836, and 1837. Among the poor the practices of abortion (*makibi*, literally 'thinning out') and of abandoning children became common.
40. See Ôc Masafusa, *Karaishi-ki* ('Account of Karaishi') c.1070 in *Gunsho ruijû* ('Collection of LiteraryTexts'), ed. Hanawa Hokinoichi, vol.9, 1928, pp. 324–5.
41. See Tanabe Hisao, *Nihon no ongaku* ('Music of Japan'), 1954. Dunn cites this in *The Early Japanese Puppet Drama*, op. cit., p. 18.
42. Fujiwara Akihira, *Shin-sarugaku-ki* ('New Account of sarugaku') c.1070 in *Gunsho ruijû*, op.cit.vol.9, pp. 340–351. It is in an entry in Minamoto Shitaga's dictionary, *Wamyo-ruishi-sho* ('Notes on Japanese names in subject order'), early 10th century, reprinted in 1954, ed. Masamune Atsuo, that we find the first name for 'puppets' in Japan given as *kugutsu*. See *Dainihon-shiiryô* ('Source Materials of Japanese History'), Series 12, vol.14, 1910, p. 715. Note that the term *sarugaku*, referring to all kinds of popular entertainment including songs, dances, acrobatics and magic, was brought to Japan in the 8th century from China where it had had a long history after its arrival from Central Asia. See P.G. O'Neill, *Early Nô Drama: Its Background, Character and Development 1300–1450*, London: Lund Humphries 1958. p. 4.
43. See Dunn, op.cit., p. 17.
44. ibid., p. 23. See also Tsunda Ichiro, *Ningyô geki no seititsu ni kan suru kenkyu* ('Studies relating to the development of the Puppet Theatre'), Osaka: Kuroya Shuppan, 1964, p. 352.
45. Dunn in ibid., cautions against too much weight being placed on the absence of references since many documents and records have been destroyed throughout the history of Japan.
46. Ibid., pp. 23–25.
47. I have used Dunn's translation in ibid., pp. 21–23.
48. In ibid., p. 65, Dunn refers to the possible derivation of the word *kugutsu* from *kugu* but considers it erroneous. According to Origuchi Shinobu, *kugutsu* originally referred to a kind of basket called *kugu* carried by the early sea people (*amozoku*) to collect seaweed and shellfish. This is cited by Jane Marie Law in *Puppets of Nostalgia: the Life, Death and Rebirth of the Japanese Awaji Ningyô Tradition*, Princeton, New Jersey: Princeton University Press, 1997, p. 95.
49. This idea is clearly enunciated in Donald Harper, 'The Sexual Arts of Ancient China as described in a manuscript of the second century BC' in *Harvard Journal of Asiatic Studies*, Vol.47, No.2, Cambridge, Massachusetts, December, 1987, p. 571.
50. Cited in ibid.
51. In Chinese mythology the 'Fifteenth Night' is especially connected with the union of the sexes or that of the sun and moon signifying the male and female

elements respectively. This concept is expressed through the enforced separation and reunion of the archer Shen Yi and his wife Chang Ee. Having stolen the elixir of immortality from her husband (who is associated with the sun), Chang Ee flies to the moon leaving her husband on earth. Out of pity for them the gods decree that once a month, on the fifteenth night, husband and wife can meet for sexual intercourse. To be noted is the use of the number 12 in the stipulated 12 meetings a year, suggesting an endlessly renewing ceremony of sex. Another Chinese ritual connected with the fifteenth night during Chinese New Year is the custom for virgin girls to throw oranges into a river in the hope of procuring a good husband. The story of Chang Ee and the moon can be found in *World Mythology*, ed. Roy Willis, London: Simon and Schuster Ltd., 1993, p. 95.

52. See James L. McClain, 1982, p. 64. Other provocative names adopted were *Yôkihi* (the celebrated mistress of Emperor Tang Ming Huang) and *Rifujin* (Lady Li, consort of the Han Emperor Wu Ti).

53. Donald H. Shively, *The Love Suicide at Amijima (Shinju Ten no Amijima): a Study of a Japanese Domestic Tragedy,* Harvard University Press, Cambridge, Massachusetts, 1953, p. 22.

54. Saeki Kaisho, the head priest of the Jôruriji (Jôruri Temple) in Nishi-o, Kamo-cho, Soraku-gun, Kyoto prefecture, was adamant that his temple had no connection with the Lady Jôruri story despite the name and gave me a pamphlet disclaiming any association. However when I showed him the map of the memorial sites erected in homage to Lady Jôruri he was impressed and made a photocopy for his records.

55. See Daisetz T. Suzuki, *Zen and Japanese Culture*, Bollingen Series LXIV, Princeton: Princeton University Press 1959, p. 121.

56. An English translation of the Noh play *Sotoba Komachi* can be found in Arthur Waley, *The Nô Plays of Japan*, London: George Allen and Unwin Ltd., 1965, pp. 148–160.

57. Ono Takeo in *Yoshiwara, Shimbara*, Tokyo: Kyoikusha, 1978, p. 32, maintains that from at least the 12th century, there was licensing of prostitutes.

58. See Joseph M. Kitagawa, 1966, p. 24.

59. Ibid., p. 26.

60. See Martin Hurlimann and Francis King, *Japan*, London: Thames and Hudson, 1970, p. 49.

61. Cited by Joseph Kitagawa, 1966, p. 35.

62. Ibid.

63. Ibid., p. 38. In 783, to foster and symbolise the rapprochement between Buddhism and Shintoism, the *kami* Hachiman was named *Daijizaiten-bosatsu*, thus equating him with a Buddhist *Bodhisattva*.

64. See Martin Collicut, Marius Jansen and Isao Kumakara, *Cultural Atlas of Japan*, Oxford: Maidon Press Ltd., 1988, p. 83.

65. See footnote 24.

66. This information was published at the back of the magazine entitled *Yakushiji*, op. cit.

67. I was there on April 8th 2000 and witnessed for myself the open door through which visitors and pilgrims were able to have a glimpse of the Healing Buddha.
68. See Charles Dunn, 1966, p. 10. A fairly full version of this work can be found in *Mukashi mukashi monogatari* ('Tales of Olden Times'). Quoted in *Kindai Nihon Bungaku Taikei* ('Collection of Japanese Literature, 1600–1850'), 1926–30, vol.2, p. 17.
69. Ibid., p. 8. Dunn quotes from Sôchô, *Sôchô Nikki* ('Sôchô's Diary'), p. 1265.
70. See *Yodarekake* ('The Bib') 1648, in *Edo Jidai Bungei Shiryô* ('Source materials of Literature in the Edo period 1600–1850'), vol.4, 1916.
71. *Shikidô Ôkagami* ('Great Mirror of the Way of Love'), 1678, in *Zoku-Enseki Jisshu* ('Enseki's Second Collection of ten items'), vol.2, 1909, pp. 403–558.
72. Ono no O-Tsû has also been associated with the wife of Toyotomi Hideyoshi. See *18th Century Japan: Culture and Society*, ed. C. Andrew Gerstle, Richmond, Surrey: Curzon Press, 2000, p. 51.
73. See Charles J Dunn, 1966, op.cit. p. 15.
74. See Donald Keene, 'Fujimoto Kizan and the Great Mirror of Love', in *Appreciations of Japanese Culture*, Tokyo: Kodansha, 1971, pp.245–249.
75. See Donald Harper, 'The Sexual Arts of Ancient China as described in a manuscript of the second century BC' op.cit., p. 539.
76. *Ishimpô* was authored by Tamba Yasuyori, completed c. 984 and circulated in manuscript form until the 19th century. Ishihara Akira et al., *Ishimpô: kandai – nijûhachi, bônai* (Tokyo: Shibundo, 1970) is an annotated Japanese translation of chapter 28 with illustrations and appendices. This book is the basis for an English translation of chapter 28 by Ishihara and Howard S. Levy in *The Tao of Sex*, New York: Harper and Row, 1970.
77. See Nancy R. Rosenberger, *Japanese Sense of Self*, Cambridge: Cambridge University Press, 1992, p. 75. See also Arthur Waley, *The Nine Songs: A Study of Shamanism in Ancient China*, London: George Allen and Unwin Ltd., 1955, pp. 9 & 14. Shamans were spirit-intermediaries and magic healers. One of their methods of healing was to go to the underworld and find out how the powers of death could be propitiated. In this connection, for example, when Yoshitsune fell ill and was close to death, Lady Jôruri assumed the function of a shaman and was summoned to his aid. The way Lady Jôruri encounters Yoshitsune, the brevity of their love affair, his disappearance and her vain wait for his return parallel the typical form of the 'Nine Songs' in which the Spirit invariably proves fickle after the rapturous meeting with the Shaman and she is left destitute and forlorn.
78. This incident is mentioned in *Yoshitsune (Gikeiki)*, an anonymous 15th century work which is the oldest extant collection of stories concerning his boyhood and fugitive years. See McCullough, 1966, p. 226.
79. *Cambridge History of Japan*, Vol.3, op.cit. p. 524.
80. Ibid, Vol.4, p. 748. See also 'A Note on Prostitution in Chikamatsu's Plays' in Donald Keene (tr.), *Major Plays of Chikamatsu*, New York and London: Columbia University Press, 1961, p. 474. Prostitutes were divided into *age-jorô* (women of considerable culture) and *mise-jorô* (common prostitutes), ranked in a

complicated hierarchy. Below these came lower levels of prostitute called, picturesquely, *tides, reflections* and *moons* – the names derived from the Noh play *Matsukaze*: *The moon is one, the reflections two, the swelling tides...* A *moon* received one piece of silver for her services, a *reflection* two pieces, and a *tide* three.
81. An *asobime* is a low ranking prostitute similar in status to a *yûjo*.
82. *Cambridge History of Japan,* Vol. 4, op. cit., p. 742.
83. The ordinary male citizen of a town is called a *chônin*.
84. See Joseph Kitagawa, 1966, p. 153.
85. See *18th Century Japan*, op.cit., p. 4.
86 *Cambridge History of Japan,* op.cit., Vol.4, p. 741.
87. The term *bakufu* (taken from two Chinese characters) means 'tent-government' or the 'field headquarters of a general in war'. In other words it refers to the military government of Japan. During the Edo period the Tokugawa family ruled the land and thus the government was known as the Tokugawa *bakufu*. Earlier *bakufu* was established by the Minamoto family (Kamakura *bakufu*, 1185–1333) and the Ashikaga family (Muromachi *bakufu*, 1333–1573).
88. See Donald Keene, 'Fujimoto Kizan and the Great Mirror of Love', op.cit., p. 242.
89. See Michael Mackintyre, *The Shogun Inheritance*, London: William Collins, Sons and Co., Ltd, 1981, p. 125.
90. See Donald Keene, 'Fujimoto Kizan and the Great Mirror of Love', op.cit., p. 244.
91. Ibid.
92. Ibid., p. 245 and see also Daisetz T Suzuki, *Zen and Japanese Culture*, op.cit. p. 121.
93. Ibid., p. 248
94. See Harold Hakwon Sunoo, *China of Confucius: a Critical Interpretation*, Virginia Beach, VA: Heritage Research House, Inc., 1985, p. 179.
95. Ibid.
96. G.B. Sansom, *Japan: A Short Cultural History*, rev.ed., New York: Appleton-Century Crofts, 1962, p. 410.
97. See H.G. Creel, *Chinese Thought,* op. cit., p. 34.
98. See Arthur Waley, *The Way and its Power: The Tao Te Ching and its place in Chinese Thought*, London: Unwin Hyman Ltd., 1987, p. 23. As an example, Waley cites the word now written 'heart' plus 'blood' which originally meant to draw blood from a sacrificial animal. If it bled freely, this meant that the ancestors accepted the sacrifice.
99. Ibid., pp. 17–18.
100. See D.T. Suzuki, *Zen and Japanese Culture,* op.cit., p. 70. This 17th century work was started by Nabeshima Naoshige, the feudal lord of Saga in the island of Kyûshû. It states that no great work has ever been accomplished without piercing the ordinary level of consciousness. Hence the readiness for the samurai to sacrifice his life at any moment should the need arise. The samurai's fearlessness

of death is at one with the heart of Zen doctrine which teaches indifference to life and death.

101. This is a reference to *Kanadehon Chushingura* ('The League of the Forty-seven *Rônin*'), one of the most famous classical plays, first staged at the Takemotoza Theatre on August 14th, 1748. It was written by Izumo Takeda, proprietor of the Takemotoza, and two others and was based on the famous vendetta of the 47 *Rônin* ('Retainers') of Ako which took place in 1701. Fictitious names were used by the playwrights for the persons involved in the incident and it was moved back in time to the Ashikaga Era.

102. See *Cambridge History of Japan*, vol.4, op.cit., p. 749.

103. See Charles Dunn and Bunzô Torigoe (eds. and trs.), *The Actors' Analects (Yakusha Rongo)*, Tokyo: University of Tokyo Press 1969, pp. 51 & 62. Offstage, *onnagata* ('female impersonators') in Kabuki carried on behaving with the utmost femininity: some continued to walk and sit like women, wearing women's clothes and dressing their hair in feminine coiffures. Famous *onnagata* like Segawa Kikunojo (1741–1773) (also known as *Roko*) became greatly influential in ladies' fashion and his name came to be used as a brand name for products ranging from incense and hair-oil to ornaments and clothes. Courtesans who were the original models for the development for the *onnagata* style in the 17th century were in real life imitating *onnagata* in the 18th century. See Andrew Gerstle (ed.) *18th Century Japan*, op.cit. p. 38.

104. See *Razan Sensei Bunshu*, quoted in *Dainihon Shiryô*, series 112 (Tokyo: Tokyo Teikoku Daigaku, 1901), vol.1, pp. 260–61. This is cited in *Cambridge History of Japan*, vol.4, op.cit., p. 750 .

105. This quotation is cited in Martin Hurlimann's *Japan*, op.cit., p. 75.

106. Ibid., p. 753.

107. After the death of Yoshitomo (Yoshitsune's father) in 1160, the Minamotos vanished from the scene and Kiyomori (the Taira head of a united family) became the most powerful man in Japan. Tokiwa, Yoshitsune's mother, became Kiyomori's concubine for a while but he soon tired of her. Yoritomo (Yoshitsune's elder brother) was banished to Izu while Yoshitsune (boyhood name: Ushiwaka) was sent to a temple (Kurama-dera) for religious training.

108. see Tsuneyoshi Matsuno, *Wives of the Samurai: their Eventful Lives during the Period of Civil Wars*, New York, Los Angeles, Chicago: Vantage Press, 1989, pp. 1–3.

109. The story of Okiku is recorded in Tanabe Seiko, *Oan to Okiku*, Shusei-sha, 1977. See ibid., p. 56 in which Tsuneyoshi Matsuno retells Okiku's story. Oan and Okiku were women who lived their lives at the bottom of society through civil wars initiated by men and survived to tell their stories which have been recorded.

110. See Helen Craig McCullough (tr.), op.cit., p. 31. Fifty or sixty out of the 240 plays in the current Noh repertory are based on hero legends. There are over 30 extant Noh plays about Yoshitsune and these constitute the largest single category of Noh plays.

111. Ibid., p. 30. During or shortly after the lifetime of Hôgan Yoshitsune (*Hôgan* was the title given to a secondary officer in the police and judicial office charged with maintaining peace and order in Miyako – Kyoto), a new expression *hôgan biiki* which means 'sympathy for the hôgan' and by extension 'sympathy for the underdog' entered the Japanese language. The sympathy for the tragic hero was responsible for the growth and popularity of the Yoshitsune legend. See also Ivan Morris, *The Nobility of Failure: Tragic Heroes in the History of Japan*, New York: Holt, Rinehart and Wiston, 1975, pp. 67–105.
112. See Dunn, 1966, pp. 7–8. Except for the year, dates have not been adjusted to European time. Months and days have been left in their original lunar calendar form.
113. Ibid., p. 8.
114. Ibid., pp. 8–9.
115. Ibid., p. 9.
116. Ibid., p. 29. See for example, Kuroki Kanzô, *Jôruishi* ('History of Jôruri') 1943, p. 46.
117. Ibid., p. 29. *Ushiwaka-maru-jûnidan* is translated as 'The Story of Ushiwakamaru (Yoshitsune's boyhood name) in twelve parts'. Amida, the Japanese form of the Sanskrit *Amithaba*, is the name of a Buddha who dwells in a Paradise in the West and is regarded as the protector of mankind.
118. See Charles Dunn's translation of this play from Yokoyama Shigeru's text in *Kojôruri-shohon-shu*, vol.2, p. 45 f. as Appendix 11 in ibid., pp. 113–134.
119. For a fuller version of this story see ibid., pp. 42–43.
120. For a further exposition of this term which refers to the element of self-sacrifice in conjunction with women, see Nicola Liscutin's thesis, *The Social Grammar of Otherness: Sekkyô-bushi Texts, Performers and Sociohistorical Context*, PhD., University of Cambridge, 1996, p. 124. The term is applicable to women who, out of selfless love, surrender everything to save the hero and help him with his task. Such women, and Lady Jôruri falls into this category, are willing to offer their special knowledge, powers and bodies to rescue the hero.
121. The term *sekkyô-bushi* refers to sermon ballads which were used to simplify and illustrate a Buddhist concept as well as to entertain. It is an oral narrative performed with musical accompaniment by itinerant mendicant chanters from the 16th century or earlier. Around the turn of the 17th century it developed into a popular form of puppet theatre but disappeared as a theatrical form during the 1720s and has only survived as a story-telling art form in rural areas.
122. The story about the *sekkyô-bushi* puppeteer is recounted by Shinoda Jun'ichi in *Chikamatsu no Sekai*, Tokyo: Heibonsha, 1991. Shinoda has taken the tale from *Shokoku inga monogatari* ('Tales of karmic retribution from various provinces') written in 1707. An abbreviated version of the text is provided by Shinoda.
123. Angela Carter's re-working of this Japanese tale is included in *Fireworks*, London: Virago Press, 1988.
124. See Eric A. Feldman, *The Ritual of Rights in Japan*, Cambridge: Cambridge University Press, 2000, pp. 17–19: *Having no idea of rights, the Japanese*

naturally had no word to express the idea and their difficulty in grasping its meaning is well illustrated by their difficulty in choosing a suitable word.

125. See the introduction by Donald Keene (tr.) to *Major Plays of Chikamatsu*, op.cit. p. 17. Chikamatsu's 1703 play, based on a contemporary actual case of double suicide, started a trend for love suicides as evident from a publication of the following year: *The Great Mirror of Love Suicides*. In 1722, as the number of suicides onstage and off multiplied, the government banned plays with the word *shinju* ('love suicides') in the title.

126. See Jono David's article, 'Shrine of the Living Dolls' in *South China Morning Post*, Jan 26th, 2000, p. 18.

127. In contemporary records of the earliest repertory of the puppet theatre, it is stated that the story of Lady Jôruri was first performed in Kyoto in the Keicho period (1596–1614). It is also recorded clearly in *Sanko kikigaki* (a local history of the Kanazawa area) that *Ushiwakamaru-jûnidan* ('The Story of Ushiwaka in Twelve Parts'), which is another name for the Lady Jôruri story, was first performed as a puppet play in 1614. See Dunn, 1966, p. 29.

128. See Sumiko Iwao, *The Japanese Woman: Traditional Image and Changing Reality*, New York: The Free Press, A Division of Macmillan Inc., 1993, p. 106.

129. See Harold Hakwon Sunoo, 1985, p. 171.

130. Ibid., pp. 182–3.

131. See Arthur Waley (tr.), *The Way and its Power: The Tao Te Ching and its Place in Chinese Thought*, op.cit., p. 151.

132. Ibid., p. 238.

133. *Chikamatsu jôrurishu* 11, p. 357. My quotation is taken from C. Andrew Gerstle, *Chikamatsu and the Heroic Ideal*, op.cit., p. 318.

134. See Tsuruo Ando, *Bunraku: the Puppet Theatre*, New York & Tokyo: Walker/Weatherhill, 1970, p. 132. In 1734, in the production of *The Tale of Ashiya Doman Ouchi*, Bunzaburo evolved the idea of using three puppeteers to manipulate one puppet.

135. See the *Onna Daigaku*, usually ascribed to Kaibara Ekken in Sakai, *Kaibara Ekken and Onna Daigaku* in Cultural Nippon, VII (no.4, 1939), pp. 43–56. For example, in this treatise written by a distinguished Confucian scholar of the late 17th century which formed part of the curriculum of the *terakoya* (temple schools for the primary education of the common people) though it was originally written with the samurai in mind, the following admonition is given to a woman: *approach your husband as you would Heaven itself, for it is certain that if you offend him Heaven's punishment will be yours...The great life-long duty of a woman is obedience.* This quotation is taken from Richard Storry, *The Way of the Samurai*, London: Orbis Books, 1978, p. 124.

136. According to Jiang Shangli, in an article entitled 'Chinese Puppetry' in *China Today*, Beijing, Vol. XLV No.6, June 1996, p. 68, the emergence of the puppet is closely linked with the custom of burying slaves with their deceased masters. Pottery figurines took the place of slaves in the late Shang dynasty (6th–11th century BC) and later, wooden figures with moveable joints – the precursors

of puppets – were excavated in 1979 from ancient tombs in Laixi County, Shandong province.
137. See Vibeke Bordahl (ed.), *The Eternal Storyteller: Oral Literature in Modern China*, Richmond, Surrey: Curzon Press, 1999, p. 128: the idea is advanced that the string puppets were originally fashioned to look and move like human beings so that they could serve as repositories for spirits fooled into entering them instead of humans. According to this theory, marionettes were regarded as polluted and potentially dangerous.
138. See Joseph M. Kitagawa, op.cit. 1966, p. 19.
139. See Barbara E. Thornbury, *The Folk Performing Arts: Traditional Culture in Contemporary Japan*, New York: State University of New York Press, 1977, p. 17.
140. See Jane Marie Law, op.cit., p. 202.
141. See Barbara Thornbury, op.cit. p. 88.
142. See Chapter Five: 'The Image of the String Puppet: Its Indian Origin and Relevance to Zen Buddhism, Noh Drama and Chinese Theatre', in which I discuss the philosophy of puppet iconography and its impact on the movements of actors in many puppet-based, Eastern theatrical forms.
143. See a summary of this fifth group, 'Demon Noh' play in P.G. O'Neill, *A Guide to Nô*, op.cit., pp. 140–141. In the second act of this exorcistic piece, Tsuna, the *Nochi-Waki* ('secondary actor') triumphantly vanquishes the Devil played by the *shite* (main actor).
144. See Ezra Pound and Ernest Fenollosa, *The Classic Noh Theatre of Japan*, op. cit., p. 29.
145. Ibid. Cf. Emperor Yu's 'Great Dances' in 2300 BC which he made compulsory for his subjects in order to improve their blood circulation and so avert disease. See Note 32 in Chapter 3.
146. Ibid. Noh actors used to go to the theatre in disguise.
147. See A.C. Scott, *The Puppet Theatre of Japan*, Tokyo: Charles E.Tuttle Co., 1963, p. 11.
148. Ibid., pp. 11–13
149. A.C. Scott gives a succinct account of the role played by the Shinto priest, Hyakudayu, in founding the Awaji school of puppetry in ibid., p. 15. For a detailed account see Jane Marie Law, op.cit., pp. 151–63.
150. Since my visit I have received a letter from its Director, Umazume Masaru, assuring me of his interest in my research and offering to be of any assistance.
151. All the foregoing rituals of a Bunraku performance I personally observed during my stay in Osaka in Spring 2000. See also Tsuruo Ando, op.cit., pp. 80–92.

152. See *Naniwa Miyage* ('Souvenir of Naniwa'), written by Hozumi Koretsura, published in 1738, ed. Ueda Kazutoshi, Tokyo: Yuhokan, 1904. (Naniwa was the old name for Osaka). At the beginning of this work there is a reference to the aesthetic theory, strongly supported by Chikamatsu Monzaemon himself, that truth and falsehood are thinly divided.

1. Two female dancers dressed to resemble the mythical bird (*nok isi*) at a *Manora* rehearsal in the village of Plaiyuan, Nakhon Sri Thammarat, Thailand, April 1997.

2. The 'Angel' in Hagoromo ('Feather Robe') played by Kongô Hisanori, makes a costume change *(monogi)* in full view of the audience. This ceremonial robing by stage attendants in the presence of witnesses is to emphasise the contractual nature of the restoration of her feathers without which she cannot return to Heaven. Matsuyama, Shikoku, 1998.

3. A moment during a performance of Hanji Chikamatsu's *Keisei Awa no Naruto* ('The Infant Pilgrim') at Awaji Ningyô Jôruri Kan ('The Awaji Puppet Theatre') in Fukura, Awaji Island. Mother and daughter are 'manipulated' by black-hooded puppeteers. April 2000.

4. The Puppet god, Xianggong or Marshal Tian, dancing on the *T'ai Chi* symbol and 8 trigrams as part of a rite of exorcism. Singapore, 25th September 1999.

5. The same puppet god performing a dance in front of the stage as a postlude to the 5 day performance of *Mu Lien Saves His Mother.* Quanzhou, August 1994.

6. One of the twenty-four angels at the top of the East Pagoda, Yakushiji Temple ('Healing Buddha' Temple) Nara, playing a flute in praise of Buddha.

Courtesy of the Yakushiji Temple

7. A puppet-based folk art performance of Kirijô's Noh play Rashômon ('The Rashô Gate') at which one of the servants of Minamoto no Yorimitsu defeats the devil played by the shite (main actor). 13th April 2000 at the Hakusan shrine, Nôgô village, Hida prefecture.

8. One of the most famous memorial sites in homage to Lady Jôruri. Yahagi, April 2000.

9. Puppet cases in the National Museum of Ethnology in Osaka. The middle case shows string puppets from Rajasthan, believed to be the earliest examples of string puppetry.

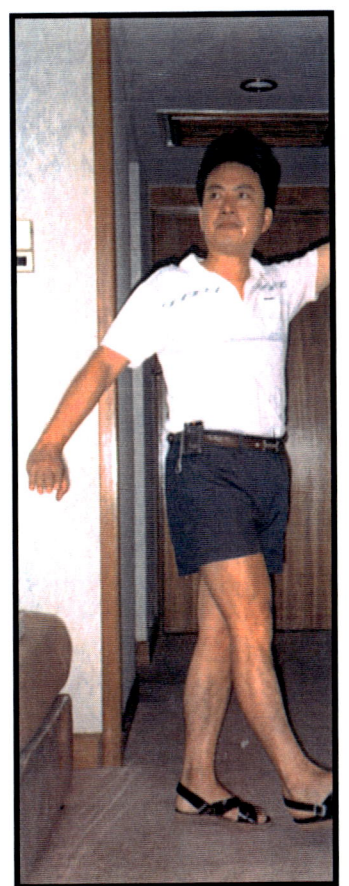

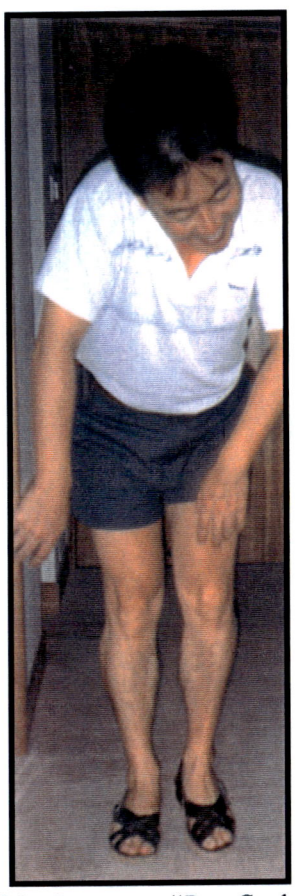

10. Hsieh Yong Chien, a teacher of the *Li-yuan-xi* ('Pear Garden Theatre') in Quanzhou, demonstrating string-puppet derived movements adopted by actors. 1994.
(*Figures read from left to right.*)

Figure 1: *Xianggogn Mo* ('Xianggong or Marshal Tian pattern')
Figure 2: *Shiu Xing* ('The actor is about to set forth')

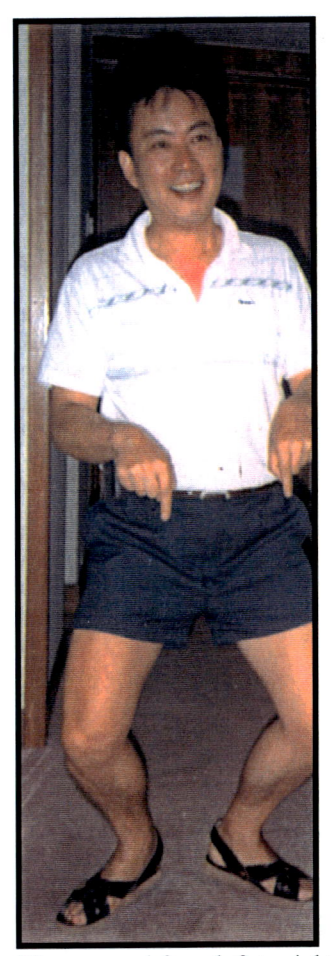

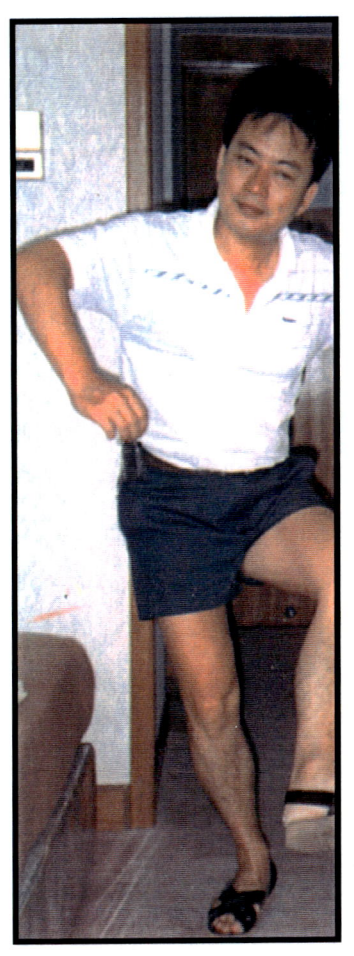

(Figures read from left to right.)
Figures 3 and 4: Shiu Xing ('The actor is about to set forth')

(Figures read from left to right.)
Figures 5 and 6: *Jia Li Luo Xian* ('Gathering up the strings')

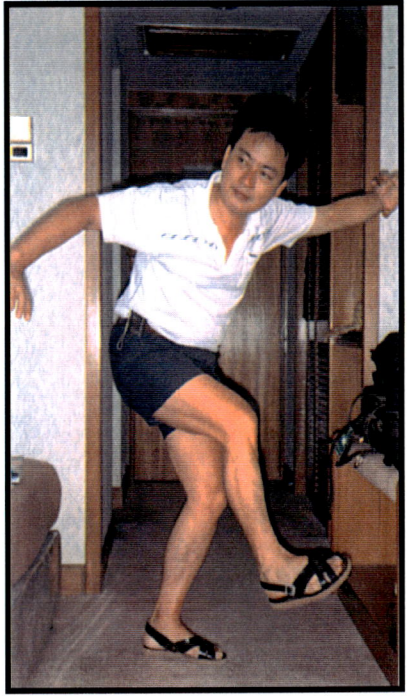

(Figures read from left to right)
Figures 7 and 8: Jia Li Luo Xian ('Gathering up the strings')

A MAP FOR A PILGRIMAGE TO THE MEMORIAL SITES IN YAHAGI & OKAZAKI CONNECTED WITH LADY JŌRURI

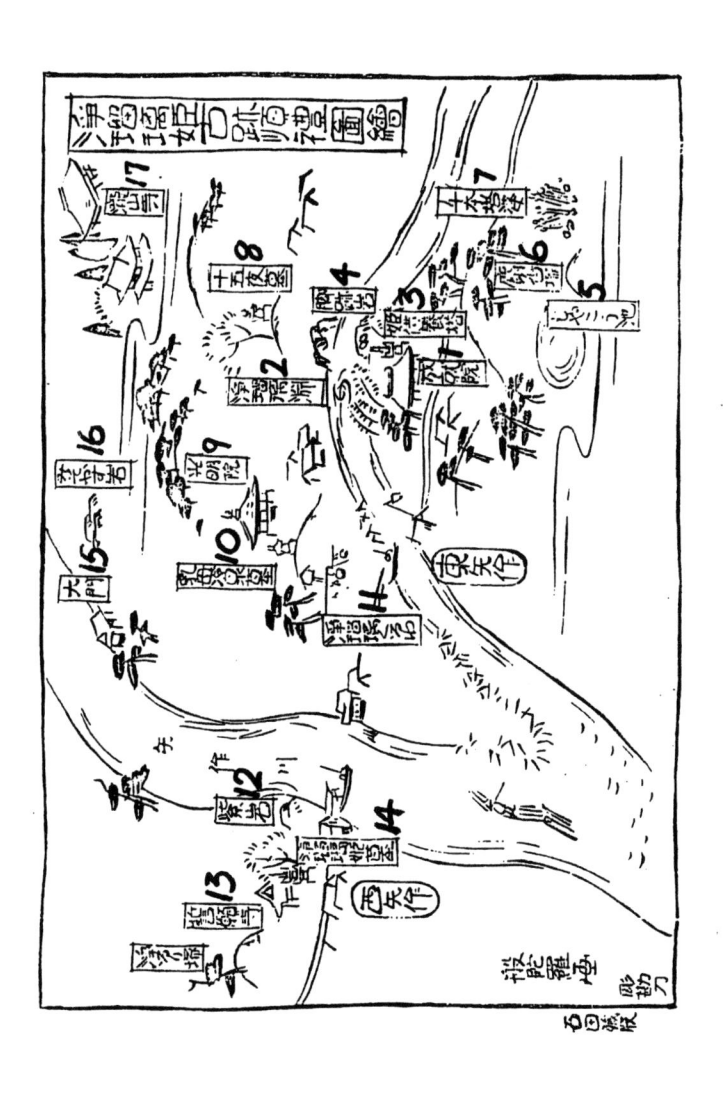

1 Jōjuin 2 Jōruri Ga Fuchi 3 Hime Kuyōtō 4 Hime No Ashiatoiwa 5 Jakō Ike 6 Jakō Dsuka 7 Senbon Toba 8 Jugoya No Haka
9 Kōmyōin 10 Uba Reizei No Haka 11 Jōruri Kuruwa 12 Murusaki Iwa Ishi 13 Seiganji 14 Jōruri Hime No Haka 15 Dai Mon
16 Misokasu Iwa 17 Takisanji   (See Chapter 4, pp. 92-4)

Chapter Five: The Image of the String Puppet, its Indian Origin and Relevance to Zen Buddhism, Noh Drama and Chinese Theatre

Once upon a time in Rajasthan, in the north of India, there lived a carpenter called Sevakram who could make the most beautiful dolls. These were so utterly captivating that one could wish that they would come to life. Shiva (later called the god of puppets and movement) and his wife Parvati were passing by and they were so impressed by Sevakram's dolls that Shiva allowed her to persuade him to bring them to life. They began to dance animatedly and Sevakram's heart was full to bursting. But then abruptly they stopped and Sevakram's anguish knew no bounds. Taking pity on him, a voice from Heaven instructed: "Sevakram, if you want these dolls to move, insert strings through their limbs and manipulate the former and these figures will once again commence their dance." Sevakram set to work immediately and made many such dolls which he animated with life by pulling their strings.[1]

Parvati once made a puppet which was so beautiful and perfect that she hid it from her husband for fear that he might covet it and take it from her. Secretly she carried this puppet to the Himalaya mountains and thought that her beloved puppet was safe. However, Shiva discovered her hideout, and seeing the beauty of the puppet, fell so desperately in love with it that he brought it to life.[2]

An ancient legend asserts that the first Rajasthan puppeteer was spewed out of the mouth of Brahma, the Creator. So for this reason most Rajasthan puppeteers are devoted to their art and trace their ancestry from the court actors and dancers known as 'bhats', a name derived from Bharata, the legendary founder of the arts of music, dance and theatre. Their puppets are called 'kathputli' and these are manipulated with only one or two strings.[3]

Three slightly different Rajasthan stories accounting for the origin of puppets in India[4] and also for the blurred transition from doll to puppet. What is common to these accounts is the idea that puppets are the products of divine intervention, wholly associated with gods, and that when they move they take on an independent existence almost synonymous with a miraculous creation. The second story, focusing on a conflict over a treasured toy, echoes Titania's and Oberon's quarrel over a changeling boy in *A Midsummer Night's Dream*. However, the fact that these three are 'Rajasthan' legends and that 'string' puppetry is strongly associated with Rajasthan, with Shiva Nataraja – 'Lord of the Dance' and 'God of Puppets' – and with part of the *trimurti* consisting of Shiva, Brahma (Creator), also known as 'Sutradhara' (the 'Holder of Strings'), and Vishnu (Preserver), provides a clear indication of the crucial importance of this part of India to the history and development of string puppetry.

Rajasthan and the Indus Valley Civilisation

Rajasthan is the one region where the highly organised and ancient five thousand year old Indus valley civilisation spread and was kept intact whereas it was utterly destroyed in the Indus basin. There is evidence that marionettes existed in the Indus Valley civilisation and Rajasthan enjoys the reputation of having had the earliest known puppets in India. These are believed to have been string puppets (see Plate 9). It was during this period (3000–2000 BC), that the idea of a puppet as a means of amusement was added to its previously ritualistic role and since as many string-manipulated toys (clearly precursors of dramatic puppets) have been found in Rajasthan as figures with moveable limbs have been discovered in the tombs of ancient Egypt – toys crafted for the delight of children long before the time of Moses – many scholars regard the proto-Dravidians as the true builders of the Indus Valley civilisation and puppets as part of the Dravidian legacy.[5]

Puppet Culture as fostered by the Dravidians and Babylonians

When the fair-skinned Aryan invaders settled in the upper valley of the Indus between 3000–1500 BC, they were in contact with dark-skinned Dravidians whose advanced culture was related to the Chaldeans or Babylonians, and associated with a special class of magicians. This connection is strongly supported by excavations in Harappa, one of the two main cities of the Indus Valley civilisation. Originally a Semitic people, the Chaldeans first came from Arabia along the coast to the Persian Gulf, settled in the vicinity of Ur (Ur of the Chaldees, Genesis xi.28), and at a very early date began to encroach on other Semitic Babylonians. A thorough amalgamation of the Chaldeans and Babylonians occurred during the sudden rise of the Babylonian empire under Nebuchadnezzar and it is important to bear in mind that Babylonia was an important part of ancient Mesopotamia (in ancient Greek 'the land of two rivers', the Tigris and Euphrates). It was in Mesopotamia that the world's first cities arose between 4000 and 3000 BC and the idea of a god king came from *Sumer*, the ancient name for Southern Babylonia: each Sumerian city had a king whose power was believed to emanate from the gods. Their concept of kingship, and love of idols and moveable figures were disseminated eastwards and Mesopotamian patterns were repeated by the Dravidian race, occupying the oldest geological formation in India. The Dravidians have been called the aborigines of the Deccan and from there they appear to have spread over part of northern India. It is not difficult to see a connection between the Dravidian and Babylonian/Chaldean love and veneration of idols – effigies of divinities and even today, the veneration of idols, a practice known as *puja,* continues on the southeast slope of the Deccan where ogresses like Kali and Durga (one of the forms of Parvati, Shiva's wife) are shown piety.[6]

Puppets in Ancient Egypt, Babylonia and the Indus Valley Civilisation

The Dravidians in the Indus Valley could lay claim to the opulent Egyptian heritage of carved wooden figures moveable by strings and so enrich their own veneration of dolls and effigies. According to Herodotus, at the festival of Osiris, women carried wooden images of the god, each with an exceptionally large phallus which was moved up and down by means of a string and resembling primitive marionettes.[7] The period from 1600 to 1200 BC in the Near East has a complicated history of military and diplomatic strategy necessary for powerful empires struggling for control, and a balance of military powers had to be maintained, for example, between Egypt and Mesopotamia of which Babylonia was a part. Rich cultural exchange became an important part of the pattern and in this climate of mutual survival, the Babylonian love of moveable effigies or puppets could easily have been inspired or strengthened by the Egyptian veneration of the same kind of figures. There is in existence a piece of 14th-century BC cuneiform (the cuneiform script came from Southern Babylonia) from Armana in Egypt revealing correspondence between the 'Great Kings' of the area, showing that they frequently sent envoys and presents, and even married each others daughters.[8] In this climate of exchange, the veneration of puppets was a strong bond linking Egypt, Mesopotamia and the Indus Valley civilisation and although there is no evidence of the existence of puppet stages in Egypt, it seems likely that puppets played an important part in religious ritual, a role that was central to their Indian origin. Here, the image of the string puppet assumes literally astronomical importance, seen as synonymous with destiny's control of humans, represented by the image of Brahma as a puppeteer controlling mankind with three strings.[9] The metaphor of 'control' is one that has run through my exploration of Eastern puppet theatre and nowhere is it seen more clearly than in its Indian origins.

Shiva, Parvati and Puppets

The origin of the god Shiva is closely associated with Rudra, the 'prince of demons' (Bhudapati), a savage figure and the god of the dead (also called Pasupati, Lord of the Animals). After the Vedic age (circa 2000 BC), Shiva, who also bears the title of 'prince of demons', 'Bhudapati', assumes a role of first

The Image of the String Puppet

importance. If one scrutinises his name which in spite of his reputation means 'the favourable', or 'the benevolent', since he is meant to propitiate a dangerous deity associated with death and pestilence, we can understand why he has been specifically chosen to be the 'god of puppets'. Puppets in India, as in other parts of the East, are intended both to entertain and to heal, often taking on an exorcistic role. In this context, performances of puppet plays generally take place today during religious festivals.

During the Spring Festival of Mahashivarati which celebrates the birth of Shiva, all-night puppet performances are organised outside temples dedicated to him. The main theme of these performances is extracted either from the great Hindu epic *Ramayana* or sometimes from the equally important *Mahabharata* which actually makes a reference to puppets.[10] As evident in two of the Rajasthan legends recounted at the beginning of this chapter, Parvati, wife of Shiva, enjoys a very special relationship with puppetry. This is further endorsed by an anecdote popular in Kerala, southern India, whose original inhabitants are believed to have been the puppet-loving Dravidians. As part of certain temple festivals, a section of the *Ramayana* epic is performed and, customarily, between the episode of Ravana's death and Rama's crowning, there is a night's interval, meant for the cleansing of any sins accruing from an encounter with evil as symbolised by Ravana. (This is a reference to Ravana's abduction of Sita, the wife of Rama, to his kingdom in Lanka and the doubts which hung over her chastity even after her release from captivity.) It is believed in Kerala that Parvati was absent on the day set aside for the re-enactment of the killing of Ravana by Rama, and for this reason Shiva recreated the entire tale through a puppet performance for the benefit of his wife. Since then puppet shows have traditionally been performed exclusively either outside a temple of Shiva or Parvati in Kerala.[11]

Apart from being the 'God of Puppets', Shiva is even better known as 'Lord of the Dance'. Indeed, Hindus believe that dance was created by him. The Aryans who brought their Sanskrit language to India sometime between 3000 and 1500 BC considered the entire earth as a dancing ground and their chief deity

Indra was supposed to have been a great dancer. Dance is mentioned throughout Vedic literature not only as part of ritual but as an extremely popular and esteemed form of recreation. For example, during the Mahvrata supplication ceremony for rain to water the crops, maidens, holding pitchers of water on their heads, danced round a sacred fire[12] and in the *Vishnudharmottara*, it is stated that the prerequisite for being a good painter, sculptor, or carver, is to have a thorough grasp of dance.[13] So Shiva's Dance is seen as a recurring phenomenon, placed at the centre of life, sustaining the universe and imparting order and purpose to its activities. To a discerning Hindu, the iconographic representation of the 'Dancing Shiva' constitutes the whole Indian philosophy of life. By that token, since he is both 'Lord of the Dance and of Puppets', the image of the string puppet as intermediary between the needs of humans and the deities who can meet their demands, takes on an aura of semi-divinity and influences the movements of human actors which in some instances are unmistakably puppet-like. In the South Indian Dance Drama, Kathakali, for example, the actors look and move like giant marionettes[14] and, throughout India, the puppet is so revered, that its ancient name *gombe* is adopted as a surname by some Brahmin priests.[15]

Tandava: Shiva's Dance and Exorcism

Shiva's dance is known as *tandava* and it is said that he performed 108 types of the form. This number, as has been seen in the section on the impact of the string puppet image on Chinese theatre and *T'ai Chi* (see **chapter 3**), **has a** special significance since the world of evil is thought to contain 108 influences and there is a strong belief that the carefully choreographed or prescribed set of movements or forms as laid out in *T'ai Chi,* can counteract or exorcise evil forces. A similar belief may lie behind the form of *tandava*, which, apart from meaning 'dance', also refers to one of the two modes of rendering classical dance: that which is expansive, masculine and robust, while the other mode, *lasya,* refers to that which is tender and feminine. Possibly because the *tandava* has been associated with Shiva, the entire structure of dance as presented in the *Natyashastra* (the treatise on dance, music and drama composed by the scholar-ascetic Bharata Muni in the 2nd century BC) is founded on it. So, in the chapter devoted to the fundamentals of dance conceived in the *tandava* mode, there are rules governing the basic vocabulary of dance: for example, a *karana* is described as a unit of dance, comprising co-ordination of a basic stance, decorative hand gestures, and movement of the legs or feet and Bharata Muni carefully enumerates 108 *karanas* and specifies how and where each is to be rendered. It is a testimony to the respect in which Shiva is held and to his association with dance that a huge monument in the form of the Temple of Nataraja at Chidambaram in Tamil Nadu has been erected with carvings of the 108 types of *karanas* on the walls near the four gate-towers. These sculptures are in the form of stone tablets with a female dancer in a *karana* attitude at the centre of each, arranged one above the other so as to give the impression of pillars projecting from the walls. The temple seems to be a hymn to the exorcistic power of Shiva as manifested in the art of dance – a power which he extends to the puppet art of which he is also the Chief Deity.[16]

String Puppets and the Measuring String: Connections and Influences
Since there are many forms of puppet performance –'shadow' (a strong contender for first place in antiquity in the history of puppets), 'hand', 'glove', 'rod' and a combination of these forms, the question naturally arises as to why the 'string' puppet should have assumed so important a role in the chronicles of Eastern theatre. There is no clear answer to this question but there is a great deal of available evidence accounting for the special prominence of this particular type of puppet performance in India, both through the kind of story which opened this chapter and through the history of the development of Indian human theatre. A particularly significant connection is provided by the *soota* or *sutra*, the measuring thread used to delineate the exact measurements required in the construction of a theatre house.

It was Bharata Muni, the author of the treatise on dance, music and drama described above, who spelt out the importance of the *soota*. In ancient India there were of course no theatre houses to serve as precedents and the idea of a stage put up in a temple courtyard and under a kind of sacred protection was a later development. Bharata himself was in no doubt that a theatre house needed protection. Shortly after he'd composed his treatise, the *Natyashastra*, he was asked to prepare and produce his first play. He decided to dramatise the traditional story 'The Churning of the Nectar' (see Chapter 1), a play which encapsulated the conflict between the gods and demons and led to the demons' defeat. In one of those moments in Indian history when myth and fact blur, it is related that the defeated demons complained to Brahma, the Creator God, who ruled that drama's sole purpose was to show acts and feelings impartially and was never meant to uphold the cause of the gods against the demons. For a while the demons were pacified but Bharata was far from certain that a permanent solution had been reached. He felt that drama by its very nature would always create a disturbance and therefore the only means of control was to protect the theatre house during every show. At a fundamental level the *soota* became the source and symbol of that protection since it was the tool by which the theatre house was measured and therefore responsible for the proportions and strengths of the building in which the drama was performed. Bharata even specified how and by whom the *soota* should be made and if the thread were to break at any point during the construction it was expected that a calamity would occur. So the word *soota* became associated with the means of obtaining special protective powers as well as extending its etymological meaning to create a closer connection with the art of poetic drama itself. For example *soota* can also mean a hereditary bard, perhaps as an indication of his crucial benedictory role in society, while the word *sutradhara* (*sootadhara*) came to mean producer or manager of Indian drama and was later applied to a company's chief actor. In one of the inscriptions on a temple called Pattadkal (near Badami in Karnatak) it is written that the *sutradhara* was the architect, a further extension of the meaning to imply control for a word originally meaning 'measuring string'.[17]

The Image of the String Puppet

Although puppets are not directly mentioned in the *Natyashastra*, the treatise does allude to the producer/director of a human performance as *sutradhara* which in this context translates as 'a holder of strings' and clearly refers to a tradition already in place before the 2nd century BC when the treatise was written. While there is no other written evidence to support the theory, it seems likely that the term came from some very early marionette theatre. Indeed scholars have long maintained that the puppet theatre reached great heights of popularity long before the human theatre crystallised and that the superiority of the string manipulated marionette which has a far greater flexibility of head and body movement over other types of puppet has never been in doubt.[18] In any case, the connection between the string-manipulated puppet and the use of the *soota* as a measuring thread for the protection of the theatre house has turned the image of the string puppet into an important icon in East Asian theatrical history and the *sutradhara* ('holder of strings') into a God/Destiny figure.

This interpretation is further upheld by the Hindu religion which perceives Brahma the Creator as the supreme *Sutradhara* with the world as his stage and human beings as the puppets he manipulates. Humans in turn have imitated their Creator and created puppets and in many societies the puppeteer is an important agent of reform establishing a rapport with the spectators through his puppets. Good invariably triumphs over Evil and the puppets epitomise the religion and philosophy of the people. Moreover puppets are believed to possess spiritual powers and puppet shows are performed to cure diseases and ensure rain for agricultural communities. In *Srimad Bhagavata*, God is compared to a puppeteer who with three strings – *Sattva, Rajas* and *Tamas* – manipulates all mankind.[19] Such a comparison has no doubt helped the string puppet to enjoy its ascendancy over other forms in terms of age and prestige.

Puppets, *Puttalika,* or 'Little Son'

The Sanskrit-based word for 'puppet' is *puttalika* or *puttika* meaning 'little son'. As the etymology suggests, Indian puppets are considered living beings, in sharp contrast to the English derivation of the word 'puppet' from 'pupa' meaning 'doll' in Italian. Though the doll can be animated, it is essentially an inanimate object whereas Indian puppeteers take the etymological meaning of *puttalika* so seriously that they usually keep the box containing puppets in their bedrooms. These treasured figures are often worshipped before they are placed in a box and when a puppet can no longer be used it is taken to a river and, to the chanting of a mantra, ceremoniously committed to the water.[20] Again, the idea of the puppet as intermediary between humans and gods is confirmed and again the dance is crucial. The two seminal activities of dance and puppet movement merge so that they seem almost indistinguishable from life itself. Both activities are regarded with extraordinary respect and merge with the unquestionable veneration of Shiva.

The Role of the *Sutradhara* ('Holder of the Strings')

The importance of the role of the *sutradhara* or 'holder of strings' can best be seen in the temple dance dramas of the Brahmin village of Kuchipudi situated on the estuary of the river Krishna. Known also as the 'conductor', the *sutradhara*, who assumes this role, wears make-up and costume and carrying a short curved stick of authority known as the *kutilaka,* conducts the music, speaks lines in dialogue with the principal characters while cracking jokes and witticisms very much in the manner of a Malay *dalang* or 'shadow puppeteer'[21] and so provides the only humour in this presentation.

The singular role of the *sutradhara* in an *Ankia Nat* performance (this is a new and distinct genre of theatre in Assam) in which dancing and singing dominate, testifies to the special regard with which this personage, named after the puppeteer of string puppets, is held in India. Such performances take place in a thatched hall of prayer; a rectangular area in the centre is prescribed for the all-night presentation while spectators sit on the floor on all sides. The *sutradhara* begins with a musical prelude and then proceeds to dominate the stage. He first recites a traditional prayer in Sanskrit and at the end intones a request begging for forgiveness of any faults in the presentation and also exhorting the spectators to abstain from evil and follow the path of goodness. This is meant to indicate that the *sutradhara* is more than master of ceremonies and has become an integral part of the presentation: in him are joined the roles of producer, director, compère, principal singer, dancer, actor and commentator, manipulating the mood and responses of the spectators and interjecting moral instruction at the appropriate moment. All the participants are celibate monks who have been trained in the arts of dance and singing as part of their religious discipline.[22] Seen in this light it is not difficult to see the *sutradhara* as a reflection of God and the image of the string puppet as distinctly extra-terrestrial. It is little wonder then that this image has left its imprint on Zen Buddhism, Noh drama and Chinese theatre.

The String Puppet and Zen Buddhism

Bodhidharma, the first patriarch of Zen[23] Buddhism in China[24] (where Zen is regarded as the Chinese way of responding to Indian thought) arrived there in 520 AD and was given his celebrated interview with Emperor Wu of the Liang dynasty, one of the greatest patrons of Buddhism. To the emperor's question, 'What is the holy ultimate truth?', the Indian priest replied, 'It is emptiness itself and there is nothing holy.' This incident was duly recorded in the famous Rinzai Zen classic *Hekigan-shû* ('Blue rock collection') as its first case.[25] It took another six centuries from Bodhidharma's confrontation with the Chinese Emperor before Zen Buddhism (of the Rinzai[26] variety) reached Japan through the offices of the Rinzai Zen priest Eisai (1141–1215), who is generally regarded as the first to introduce Zen into Japan. And it was another Rinzai priest, Gettan Sôkô (1316–1389) who provided Zeami, one of the founders of Noh drama, with the idea of a string puppet, tied to a cart, which became a crucial image of control in his seminal treatise on Noh acting. Gettan Sôkô had said:

When we come to face death, our life might be likened to a puppet on a cart (decorated for a great festival). As soon as one string is cut, the creature crumbles and fades.[27]

and it was this idea which so impressed Zeami that it became a dominating image in his own acting treatise. This analogy of the human being to a string-controlled puppet is also, as we have seen, an ancient Hindu mythological concept and therefore not only peculiar to Zen Buddhism which originated in India. Indeed, it is possible that Zen Buddhism derived its idea of man being compared to a puppet from Hindu philosophy. But what is different is the emphasis: Zen Buddhism starts off with the idea of the human manipulated 'string' puppet but crucially changes the centre of control from the 'conscious' to the 'unconscious' or to use Zen terminology, from the 'ego-consciousness' (*ushin no shin*) to the state of 'no mind' (*mu-shin*) in Japanese or (*wu-hsin*) in Chinese. In fact, the entire training of a Zen monk consists in locating the source from which all activities rise, the alpha of our self-nature, which is the 'unconscious' and enlightenment is realising and being in touch with this "rockbed of one's being".[28]

The Unconscious and the 'True Heart'

The difficulty in coming to terms with or understanding the idea of the 'Unconscious', which Bodhidharma, the father of Chinese Zen Buddhism, calls "the true mind",[29] is that there is no satisfactory translation of the word for 'mind' which is represented by the Chinese character *hsin*. It means more than a compendium of 'heart', 'thought' and 'mind' because it connotes the centre or raison d'être of existence and is one of the most significant terms in Chinese philosophy.[30] For example, there is a statement in the Sanskrit *Vajrachedika* – 'The Diamond Sutra', which has exerted great influence on the study of *Zen* : "*Na kvacit pratisthitam cittam utpādayitavyam.*" In Chinese, this runs: "*Ying wu so chu êrh shêng ch'i hsin*" which freely translated, reads: '*Let your mind take its rise without fixing it anywhere.*' *Citta* is rendered generally as 'thought' but more frequently translated as 'mind' or 'heart'.[31] *Hsin*, as I have indicated, can only be roughly translated as a condensation of 'heart', 'soul' and 'mind', but the idea of *hsin* as free, unattached state, bespeaking independence and perfect mastery of oneself, does not come across clearly. In the pattern of *Zen* thinking which seeks by stripping away to get to the heart of the matter, the 'true' heart becomes known as the state of 'no mind' (*mu-shin*), the perfect circle whose centre is nowhere fixed and therefore limitless. In other words it is a spiritual attitude a person assumes towards all stimuli and therefore constitutes the very ground of his existence.

By 'thought not being fixed' is meant, 'psychologically that consciousness rises from an unconscious source', to quote D.T Suzuki, 'because according to Buddhism, there is no such psychological or metaphysical entity as that which is known as the ego-soul, and which is generally regarded as making up the basis of an individual being, and which is therefore the point of fixation for all its mental activities.'[32] The state of 'no-mindedness', whose range is infinity and is an apt location for a Zen master, is in fact the starting point of true creativity. This is applicable to all activities of man: from being just a 'string puppet' dancing within a circle whose radius is fixed by the full length of the string attached to the pole in the centre, he must turn himself into a puppet in the hands of the 'Unconscious' whose circumference knows no limits. So though the state of 'no-mindedness' may seem to convey a negative process, it is in fact the positive starting point of creativity.

In the Zen configuration of the empire of the 'true' heart, the 'Unconscious' must replace the 'Conscious' as the ultimate controller. Metaphysically speaking, again according to Suzuki, this sums up the philosophy of sunyata ('emptiness') which is closely related to the idea of 'ego-lessness' (*muga*) and 'no-mindedness' (*mushin*). So the 'mind', which is free from any point of fixation is like a 'cloud which floats away in the sky with no screws or nails attached to it.' For this reason Zen Buddhist monks are called 'cloud-water people because they drift like clouds and flow like water'.[33] The equation is therefore clear: Emptiness is no-mindedness; no-mindedness is ego-lessness, and this strict chain of identification constitutes the grammar of 'unconsciousness'. Freed from ego-consciousness which interferes with a free display of proficiency, the single-minded performer is invincible. There is a Chinese saying that when someone is totally single-minded he becomes so invincible that even gods and demons will flee from him. In the East, unlike the West, ego-lessness describes an active condition, the springboard for decision and achievement.

'Ego-lessness', the Marionette and Swordsmanship

It is not difficult to understand why the 'string-controlled' puppet or marionette, inert till brought to life by the puppeteer, has been chosen as a symbol of 'ego-lessness.' And in the following quotation from Yagyû Tajima no Kami Munenori (1571–1646), one of the greatest swordsmen in the history of the art who studied under the famous Zen master Takuan (1573–1645) and incorporated a great deal of Zen teaching into his triple treatise on swordsmanship, the connection is clear:

> *Emptiness is one-mindedness, one-mindedness is no-mindedness,*
> *and it is no-mindedness that achieves wonders.*
> *Have nothing left in your mind, keep it thoroughly cleansed of its*
> *contents, and then the mirror will reflect the images in their isness.*
> *You are said to have mastered the art where the technique works*
> *through your body and limbs as if independent of your conscious mind.*
> *Turn yourself into a doll made of wood: it has no ego, it thinks nothing;*
> *and let your body and limbs work themselves out in accordance with*
> *the discipline they have undergone. That is the way to win.*[34]

To be labelled 'wooden', from the Western point of view, is far from being a compliment. However, within the Zen frame of perception, to be 'wooden' in the sense of being impervious to all distractions is the prerequisite for any meaningful form of creativity. Our consciousness is generally too full of clutter and over-responsive to stimuli from outside[35] which prevents it from functioning properly. Yagyû Tajima no Kami, in addition to using the image of the 'wooden' doll, also compares the state of *mushin* (no-mind) to the 'wooden horse' facing the flowers and birds. This horse is utterly unmoved because it has no mind, no sentiency.[36] If a performer cannot be like a 'wooden doll' or a 'wooden horse', but responds to all kinds of stimuli, he will be committed to his distractions and not be master of himself. The best way to cope with distractions is to clear the mind of all clutter and turn the consciousness into a puppet in the hands of the unconscious.

The ego-lessness of the puppet and the corresponding ego-less state of mind the puppet master must maintain as the crucial condition for the success of his performance, render his art similar to that of swordsmanship. Takano Shigeyoshi, one of the greatest swordsmen of modern Japan, in an essay published in *Bungei Shunju* ('Literary Annals'), feels that when the marionette master puts his mind wholly into the puppet performance, his state of mind approximates to that of the swordsman's. He sees no distinction between himself and the doll he manipulates. The fact that a swordsman confronts an opponent who could kill him makes no difference because both the puppeteer and the swordsman operate in a state of ego-lessness and maximum concentration and in that attitude of mind, the marionette master becomes the marionette and the swordsman his opponent.[37]

Yagyû Tajima no Kami, writing about the similarities between the art of the marionette master and that of the swordsman in the beginning of the seventeenth century, clarifies the remarkable analogy by insisting that the perfect swordsman should perceive himself as a marionette in the hands of a master manipulator. He feels that it is crucially important to see the marionette as something which does not move of itself. In this respect, the marionette is similar to the swordsman's sword and even the swordsman himself, which by not moving of their own volition are free from all ego-centred motives. What should really control the swordsman's behaviour is not his analytical feelings but his

'Unconscious'. And because of this the swordsman feels that his sword is controlled by some agent unknown to him and yet not unrelated to him. It would seem that all the technique he has consciously acquired comes into play as if directed by the source of his 'Unconsciousness' which in terms of Zhuang Zi, is 'the integration of pure spirit' (*ch'un ch'i*).[38] If the true swordsman is a partial realisation of 'the perfect man', one can understand why in the feudal days of Japan a "master of the sword" was often called an *oshô* ('master' or 'teacher') which is the title commonly given to a Buddhist priest and the hall in which swordsmanship is practised is called *dôjô*, a place devoted to religious exercises.[39] When one takes into consideration the spiritual dimension of swordsmanship, it is not difficult to understand the sense of divinity which surrounds the art of the string puppet, so clearly identified with swordsmanship within the ambience of Zen Buddhism.

'An Art Tied to the Heart by Strings'

> *Birth and death, coming and going,*
> *A marionette on a stage;*
> *Break the string and in that moment*
> *It falls and is broken.*   (Gettan Sôkô, 1316?–1389)[40]

Puppets can move in many different ways, almost like a living thing. Puppets however can't move by themselves; They are controlled by the strings held by the manipulator. Cut the strings, and the puppet drops to the floor. The way a player performs his various movements in the Noh may be compared to a puppet. The player must seek an equivalent to the puppet's strings in his heart, which he should never reveal to the audience or anyone else. In exposing his heart to an outsider as he performs, the effect is the same as the public catching sight of a puppet's strings. I could never repeat this too often. The heart is the centre for all the connecting

> *strings enabling the player to orchestrate his movement and synthesise his artistry. If the player follows this advice, his Noh will be truly alive. Nor, moreover, should he keep this notion in mind only on stage...Day and Night, when seated, lying or walking – he should never forget that the Noh has to be tied to the heart.*[41]

The above quotation comparing Noh acting with the way a string puppet is manipulated is taken from the section entitled *Banno kanisshin no koto* ('Ten thousand Noh aspects connected to the Heart') in *Kakyô* or 'Mirror of the Flower', which is considered to be Zeami's most influential treatise on Noh acting. What is important for this scrutiny of the 'string puppet' image is that Zeami compares the strategy of Noh movements with the way string puppets are manipulated. The writer, Tanizaki Jun'ichiro, has compared puppets to Noh actors, and by that token, Noh actors are likened to puppets.[42] Tanizaki puts this analogy into the mouth of one of his characters and is chiefly concerned with the value of ancient costumes. Zeami's comparison runs far deeper: using the 'string puppet image in the heart' to locate precisely the centre of control in Noh drama,[43] it seems to underpin his entire concept of Noh acting, and it is clear that he is referring to a paranormal level of control. The Noh actor is meant to set up in his 'heart' a system of regulation comparable to that maintained by the manipulator of a string-puppet. This is of course recognising the taxing role of the puppeteer who has the task of 'animating' or giving an *anima* ('soul') to the puppet. Hence the energy which the performer is meant to generate is called *ki* (in Japanese) or *ch'i* (in Chinese) meaning 'breath'. And furthermore Zeami transfers the analogy of puppet control from a 'conscious' to an 'unconscious' level. Behind all this lies the concept of the two different kinds of 'heart' he has in mind: the 'physical' heart, and the 'true' heart,[44] and he is adamant that it is this 'inner' activity (he even distinguishes several levels of inwardness, the last, indefinable), and most significantly, the 'unconscious', 'true' heart that controls 'outer' movement in

Noh acting. So using the image of controlling 'strings', he insists that Noh is 'an art tied to the 'heart' by strings.'

'Move the Heart Ten; Move the Body Seven'

In trying to understand Zeami's writings or teachings about the art of Noh acting, it is important to be aware that he only uses the 'conscious' level of acquiring technique as a starting point (though insisting that daily practice is crucial), and then shifts into the 'Unconscious' control of the 'true' heart which he regards as the 'real' source of motivating the meaningful and powerful movements in his art. 'The Noh that succeeds through the Heart' is 'a Noh that surpasses technique, a Noh that transcends outward manifestation.'[45] There is no doubt that the understanding of the workings of Noh strategy involves an unsparing process of elimination, a rigorous journey into the interior or in the words of Zeami:

> *It is said: Forgetting the theatre, watch our art, forgetting our art, watch the actor, forgetting the actor, watch the 'heart', forgetting the 'heart', understand our art.*[46]

This level of understanding may not be always attainable but as far as the strategy of Noh acting goes, it is the 'heart' (as 'controller/puppeteer') regulating the movements of the Noh actor (the 'controlled puppet' as it were), which determines what is seen by the audience. With this double image of 'puppeteer/puppet' in mind, Zeami formulated his golden rule for movement on the Noh stage:

"What is felt in the Heart is Ten; What appears in Movement Seven."[47]

This accounts for the great restraint in visible Noh movements and has led to the widespread belief that there is perhaps very little inner activity on the part of the Noh actor. On the contrary, as Zeami demonstrates in his ratio, there is far greater inner concentration than outward expression (10:7) in the art of a Noh actor and this accounts for the unique effectiveness of restraint he aimed to achieve in the Noh. Testimony to this inner 'force' is provided by a 1989 NHK experiment in which a pace maker was attached to an actor performing the *rambyôshi*[48] dance in the Noh play *Dôjôji*. Though his outer movements were relatively minimal, his heart rate soared above 200 beats per minute exceeding that of an athlete running at top speed.[49] This is also a good example of Zeami using the principle of opposites – maximum inner concentration pitted against minimal outer movement – to create a tension which is effective theatre.

The Theory of *Riken* ('Detached Eye') and Shiva's 'Third Eye'

In addition to his golden rule for Noh movement, Zeami also developed the theory of *Riken no ken* or the 'Detached Eye' in which he asserted the importance for the Noh actor of stepping out of himself, detaching his 'heart' as it were, or using a 'third eye' to scrutinise his performance from the view point of a spectator. This theory not only helps to account for the paradoxical mix of subjectivity and objectivity in Noh acting but is also reminiscent of the 'third eye' on the forehead of the Hindu God of puppets and movement, Lord Shiva.[50] Indeed, in the Hindu context, in which Lord Shiva merges in his person both universal human and puppet movement, it is impossible to separate the way a puppet moves from 'Cosmic' movement and difficult not to concede an element of divinity to it. Similarly, when we watch a Noh actor move so restrainedly and 'inhumanly' on stage, as if controlled by strings tied to the 'heart', and if we cast our minds back to Zeami's operational metaphor of the highly controlled 'string puppet', there is a distinct similarity between the actor's movements and those of a giant marionette which are equally awe-inspiring and touched by 'divinity'.

'The Feelings of One's Heart Show in One's Face'

Not only did Zeami emphasise the phenomenal power of the 'heart' to produce recognisable visible effects in his 'Mirror of the Flower' treatise, but he even expressed this same idea through the roles of the two sisters, Matsukaze and Murasame, in his masterpiece *Matsukaze*. Confiding their grief to the priest who seeks shelter in their hut for the night, they say: 'The feelings of one's heart show truly in one's face.' This is supposed to be a paraphrase of a famous saying by the

Chinese sophist and humourist, Ch'un Yu-k'un: 'When there is anything within, it manifests itself without.[51] Even on a narrative level in this superb Noh play, the main character, Matsukaze, is driven by the strength of her heartfelt, undying love for her aristocratic lover, Lord Yukihira, and it is this which propels her back to earth to relive her love for him. In other words, the power of the heart – which is the seat of love – is unbounded, and by extension, the power of the 'true' heart which is the 'Unconscious' or 'Emptiness' is equally omnipotent and inexpressible. It is from this 'Emptiness' or 'Nothingness' that all visible forms in creation have arisen, an idea expressed in the saying: *skiki-soku-zeku-zeshiki* ('Emptiness is form, form no other than Emptiness'), quoted by Zeami in his treatise *Yûgaku shûdô fûken* or ('Disciplines for the Joy of Art') and practically lifted verbatim from a mantra in an Indian Buddhist 'Heart sûtra' called *Hanna Shingyô* or *Prajna Paramitahrdaya*.[52] Again, as in *Matsukaze*, Zeami puts this strong expression of the power of the 'Unconscious' into the mouth of another character, Yamamba, in the Noh play of her name.[53] Through the chorus, which in Noh convention sometimes speaks for the main character, Zeami not only suggests that the 'Unconscious'('Nothingness' or 'Emptiness') is the source of everything visible but that all forms will eventually dissolve into nothingness and so begin the eternal cycle of existence and non-existence. Though *Yamamba* ('The Old Woman of the Hills') was composed by Zeami, the story on which it is based is supposed to have been written by the noted Rinzai Zen abbot of the Daitokuji Temple – Ikkyû (1394–1481),[54] and we can deduce that this idea of identifying 'emptiness' with 'form' was favoured by Rinzai Zen Buddhism.

Inner Directives for Tuning the Spirit: 'In Shinra the Sun Shines at Midnight'

There will always be difficulties in understanding the meaning of *kokoro* ('heart') and the part it plays in the way a Noh actor moves and what exactly takes place in his psyche as he receives these secret messages or impulses from his heart and then has to translate them into outward physical movements. The process of

The Image of the String Puppet

transmuting something so indefinable and abstract into stage practice is a paradox of which Zeami is very much aware and which he refers to as the ninth level of artistry, *myôkafu*, in his treatise *Kyûi* ('Notes on the Nine Levels'), using the term *myô* to indicate something wonderful but ultimately inexplicable.[55] So when in a Noh performance we witness the supreme artistry of a master performer we have to accept that even he will not be able to put into words how the miracle has occurred and while 'It came from the Unconscious' may not seem a wholly satisfactory answer to the analytical Western mind, there is no other explanation. It would seem that the Hindu concept of Brahma/Creator, the Supreme Being, as the 'Master Holder of Strings' is not inappropriate here, and the Western concept of divine inspiration approximates to the control of the 'Unconscious', described as best as we can by the image of the string puppet.

The Secret Strings

Although neither actor nor audience will ever be able to explain this mystery (*myô*), there are in existence secret choreographic manuals called *katazuke* containing closely guarded instructions, with regard to a whole complex of minute movements, belonging to the various schools of Noh,[56] which are meant to assist the Noh actor in generating and then converting 'spiritual' impulses into actual 'physical' movements charged with power. There are many internal ways of tuning the spirit so that the result can be visibly observed through the intensity of a physical stance.

In the Noh play, *Matsukaze,* for example, when the central character Matsukaze holds in her arms the robe which her lover gave to her as a keepsake, one can surmise what the actor must be imagining in order to invest his action with the appropriate intensity. Is the robe meant merely as a symbolic representation of her lover and is it sufficient for the actor playing the heroine to regard it as such? How is he meant to embrace the precious keepsake? And one must not forget that he has to project emotion through thick layers of costuming and a wooden mask. Since these inner directives must remain secret, we cannot know what internal acrobatics the actor has to perform. But in a genre as outwardly chaste and severe as that of Noh drama, which is dependent on the principle of opposites or the 'unexpected', to produce the inner tension reflected in the actor's outward comportment, the secret instructions may turn out to be remarkably tangible. We get a hint of how this might work in a moment from the Noh play *Yoroboshi* or 'The Priest with a Faltering Tread' written by Motomasa, Zeami's son who died young. Though unnoticed by the audience, the *shite* (main actor) playing the blind priest uses a white stick to tap out on the floor of the Noh stage the Chinese character for 'heart', *hsin* or *kokoro*[57] and through this direct and simple action is able to exteriorize the interior philosophy which underlies the whole art. Conversely an action that would seem crude if performed too literally has to be performed 'from inside'. In *Sanemori*, for example the old Heike general, Sanemori, has to dye his white hair black in order to lead the Heike contingent into battle with the Genji and later, appearing as a ghost and engaged in conversation with the 'priest', imagines seeing his own decapitated head at the *shosaki* (front of the stage). He is obviously overwhelmed with emotion recalling how he was killed in battle and his severed head washed in the river till the black dye ran into the water in the enemy's attempt to ascertain his true identity but has to convey this deep feeling of the heart despite the wooden mask and heavy costume. In the Umewaka (one of the leading Noh families) *katazuke* the word *kokoro* features frequently in its instructions to the actor playing Sanemori who is told to draw his movements from an internalised essential feeling. Again, we cannot know the details of these secret instructions but we know that there is a paradox that the actor has to solve through the heart (*kokoro*). Paradoxes abound because the impression is that all the outward physical aspects of the Noh seem to be governed by something spiritual and internal. And interestingly, it is deep inner meditation that leads to intense corporeal awareness. But these at best are only hints of an intriguing transaction between inner and outer movements. The supreme control of the *kokoro* in generating powerful physical movements is however unchallengeable in Noh drama.

Swordsmanship and Noh Acting

In an earlier section on the importance of the 'string puppet' image to Zen Buddhism I referred to the former's relevance to the art of swordsmanship. There are in fact striking similarities between the art of swordsmanship and that of the Noh player. The grandson of Zenchiku (Zeami's son-in-law) – Konparu Zenho (1454–c.1529) – went so far as to say that the way of the swordsman and the way of the Noh player are identical.[58] Not surprisingly, both these arts make use of the 'puppeteer controlling puppet' image to illuminate the crucial importance of inner control. The master swordsman Musashi Miyamoto (d.1645) in his *Gorinshô* ('Book of Five Rings') elaborates on his concept of heart (*kokoro*) which is identical to the way the *kokoro* is perceived in the strategy of physical movements for the Noh actor:

> *The heart should be ample and direct...It should enjoy a state of constant fluidity...when the body is static, the heart should not be and, when the body is moving fast, the heart should not...Be more careful about the state of your heart than you are about the state of your body.*[59]

The same principle of tension and opposition underpins Noh performance. Zeami puts it in this way:

> *For the chant, the dance and various sorts of gestures that will be employed, the actor's heart' or spirit should be as delicately attuned as possible, but, at the same time, his physical stance should be as relaxed and broad as possible.*[60]

He here extends the principle of opposites to body and feet movements: violent foot movements and gentle body movements. When the body is moving very fast the heart should be functioning in an opposite way.[61] He seemed fascinated by the intricate mechanism of inner control, the exact amount of pressure to be applied to each 'string' in order for the Noh actor to regulate his body in the best possible way to achieve full command of his outer movements. Some of his aspirations were clearly unattainable simply because the sky was his limit: where is the goal if one has oneself the task of going far beyond techniques and forms? Zeami likens this goal to 'a bird that opens its wings and trusts itself to the movements of the winds.' He labels this the 'Skill of Movement beyond Consciousness' which he puts above the 'Skill of Self-Conscious Movement.'[62] This strong tendency to go deep beneath the surface and set in motion a network of intensive activity is a Zen trait which he uses to indicate his strategy of controlling movements on the Noh stage. In *Sarugaku Dangi* ('Reflections on Art'), Zeami compares a gifted performer to an impressive waterbird, floating effortlessly on the surface, but underneath working energetically.[63]

Zeami and Zen Buddhism

Since the discovery of some valuable 15th century documents from the Fugan (sometimes pronounced Hogan) temple in the area known as Kansai,[64] by the eminent Noh scholar Omote Akira in March 1959, Zeami's strong connections with Zen Buddhism (apart from evidences in his plays and treatises) have been conclusively established. It was at this same temple that the young Zeami studied Zen under the master of the Sôtô School – Shikyo Chigen (13??–1423).[65] But as an adult he became the pupil of Giyo Hoshu (1361–1424), a Rinzai[66] School Zen Master of the Tofuku temple. Not only is his funeral dated in these documents but it is also recorded that in 1423 under the name of Shio Zenmon, at the age of sixty, he joined the priesthood of the Sôtô sect. But it is in the letter (which has survived) written to his son-in-law, Zenchiku, which provides strongest evidences of his unusually strong Zen leanings. He reminded his son-in-law how important it was to avoid vaingloriousness at all costs and repeated what he had been taught by the second head priest of the Fugan temple. And this was that in the Buddhist law the true learning of Buddhist doctrine comes only after the doctrines have been memorised and indeed the whole process of becoming a priest, can only be accomplished after some kind of enlightenment. Zeami adds:

Always remember that repetition and practice to polish technique after the technique has been mastered is the most important part of the learning process. Never allow yourself to neglect daily practice to gain an even deeper insight into the principles and techniques of the art.'[67]

But what is vitally important and lost in most English translations is the inclusion of exclusively Zen terms such as *shiusi, sangaku, tokuho* and *inka* all rooted in Zen and part of the vocabulary of Zen learning. This has led the scholar Kosai Tsutomu to comment that Zeami's approach to training his son-in-law seemed more akin to the schooling of a Zen sage than to the training of a dramatic successor.[68] I have quoted this letter at some length because not only is it drenched in Zen exhortations of constant discipline and repetition (certainly adopted in Noh training) but it also refers to the back-breaking task of mastering techniques constituting almost a formula for the development of true skills. Zeami was never too abstract to forget the necessity of starting with the acquisition of basic techniques. The knowledge of the skill has to be there and through constant and repetitive practice, the process slides into the unconscious like a 'bird with outstretched wings trusting itself to the winds.'

Zeami and Rinzai Zen
Zeami's 'string puppet' quotation in his *Kakyô* treatise is from a saying of a priest of the Rinzai School of Zen and we have seen how influential this has been in determining his strategy of aligning visible Noh movements with strong inner directives, cues from the *kokoro* to tune the spirit before appearing on stage. Zeami began with the Zen Sôto School and though he studied under a Rinzai master for a while, it was to the Sôto School that he returned in his later years. Nevertheless, the Rinzai School not only gave him the 'string puppet' image but fostered his tendency to look inwards and see into another dimension.

There is a level of acting which Zeami called 'the art of the flower of tranquility' and he expressed it as a 'silver ball filled with snow' or as it is sometimes translated, 'snow piled on a silver dish.' Whichever translation we follow there is a sense of penetrating coldness which is used to indicate the truth beneath the surface. This is supposed to be taken from a very well known Zen idea expressed in Section 13 of the *Pi yen lu* or 'Blue Cliff Records' (*Hekiganroku*) which is regarded as a classic of the Rinzai sect. Zeami felt very drawn to this image of coldness and called the Noh which is performed from the heart 'chilled Noh' (*hietaru kyoku)* The seventh level of attainment which Zeami called the 'art of strength and delicacy' is also expressed in an ambience of coldness: 'The metal hammer strikes; the precious sword glints coldly.' This again is a Zen notion taken from the *Hekiganroku*. So all these references testify to his Rinzai Zen leanings and strong obsession to pierce beneath the surface into the heart of Noh in several senses of the word. What is paradoxical is the association of the apparent coldness or the melancholy quality of Noh movements with the full activation of the heart.

Just as the strings of the puppet must remain invisible to the spectator, Zeami, like the swordsman Musashi Miyamoto, insisted that the 'strings' of his strategy must be kept 'invisible' or secret. This perhaps accounts for the fact that the art of the Noh actor is still shrouded in secrecy. We on the outside observe the various devices in force to reduce the ego such as the strict rituals of procedure and courtesy before a performance, the many-layered costuming to reduce the self-body as it were, the reverential placement of the sacred wooden mask to eliminate facial expression, and the fact that the theme of ego-lessness very often extends to the main subjects of Noh plays. Frequently, these are women who are totally self-effacing or who love so devotedly that self is no consideration at all, e.g. Matsukaze or the 'Wife' ('Daughter of Ki no Aritsune') in *Izutsu* (she is even nameless). But the actual process of 'transubstantiation' still remains a little elusive. However we have had great help in understanding the way a Noh actor tunes into his Unconsciousness or to use Zeami's phrase, activates his heart ten while moving his body seven, from the writings of the late, great actor, Kanze Hisao (1925–1978).

Kanze Hisao and the String Puppet Image

Not only was Kanze Hisao regarded highly in Noh circles in Japan but he took pains to cultivate the friendship of Western 'body' practitioners like Jean Louis Barrault, the great theatre and mime director. They both appeared at a memorable practical workshop shortly before Kanze's death in 1978 to illuminate the inner mechanics of body control. For this reason Kanze has come closest to letting outsiders have a glimpse of what takes place inside the 'consciousness', and, even more importantly, the 'unconsciousness' of the Noh actor. Kanze in the following quotations reveals how hard the Noh actor has to work inside to produce the strong though abbreviated movements shown outwardly. In articulating how the actor balances the tension between conscious and unconscious activities, he also uses the metaphor of string control, the actor on stage like an ego-less puppet 'joined to the heart by strings', which Zeami himself uses in *Kakyô*. In Kanze's mind, when the Noh actor subjects himself to the control of his 'Unconscious' on stage, he is engulfed by such a sense of the infinite that 'he has to fight for his very existence' by using deliberate though minimal movements fully motivated and supported from within, by his *heart*. As one of the greatest Noh actors in the 20th century, Kanze Hisao put into practice Zeami's cardinal laws concerning the strategy of Noh acting and remarkably illuminating about the intricate mechanics of inner control, particularly in delineating that vital relationship between the actor and his controlling Source – the Unconscious or what Zeami called the 'true heart'. If we have at the back of our mind the 'string puppet/puppeteer image', it is as though the 'string puppet' (identifiable with the Noh actor) is taking us inside its/his psyche and expressing how much and how hard it/he has to work within the stage space, or perhaps even against it, 'when the strings are pulled' to produce movements for the delight of the audience. As another Noh actor once put it :

When you bring your hand holding a fan forward and point to the front, you have to feel that your fan strikes something and it cannot go further forward beyond that.[69]

This sentiment is strongly reiterated by Kanze Hisao :

The Noh actor has got to feel always this kind of resistance in some way.[70]

The 'resistance' Kanze alludes to presupposes a powerfully-charged space against which the Noh actor has to contend in order to establish his existence on the stage. So indirectly one has an inking of the absolute power, strength and purpose of Noh movements born from a confrontational tension between opposites.

The Noh Mask and Movement

One contributory factor to the generation of this power is the wooden mask which only permits vision from one eyehole and is linked to the single-mindedness of the Unconscious. Kanze certainly saw the mask as an empowering agent:

> *A Noh actor resembles a soul drifting between this world and the next. He therefore needs something in which he can believe in order to give him the power of confidence to transmit feeling into the character he is representing. That thing is the mask.*[71]

The final preparation for moving on stage begins in the *Kagami no ma* ('Mirror room') when the Noh actor composes himself after being costumed and concentrates in front of the mirror. His face is fitted to the mask and Kanze said of the mask that *it allows something of the true self of the actor to well up from his innermost being.*[72] And further:

> *As for the use of the mask, the slight change of the angle creates different effects on it. Thus you cannot move even one centimetre without vital reason.*[73]

It is clear from the last sentence that the mask serves as the one tangible device for ensuring the Noh actor's awareness of the minutest shift of movement on stage and the evolvement of the 'true self'. In Kanze's mind this 'true self' is closely identified with the 'Unconscious' which the Noh actor, having relinquished his ego, must tap:

The Image of the String Puppet

Standing on the Noh stage, I always wish to let my feelings communicate with the eternal and infinite space continuously and calmly.[74]

To stand still in the middle of the stage, I feel pulled by something invisible infinitely from all directions and that I am balancing these forces.[75]

What is it to feel standing in the middle of the Noh stage, the universal space which has a high ceiling like a well shaft. It is nothing but to reduce the uncertainty in the theatrical space to its limitation as much as possible by the actor's own inner power. In other words, he needs something welling up from the depth of his heart. In order to do so he has to reduce his individual personality as an actor to the ego-less state.[76]

I want to be there on the stage with a high ceiling like a well shaft, transcending myself as a human being. I want that space to be changed by myself as an actor. In order to do so the actor has to feel as if his existence has taken root in the stage itself very firmly. Then by even standing in a stationary position he can create a new universe.[77]

And finally in the four following quotations Kanze transports us into the heart of the inner mechanism of control in terms of the 'string puppet' image as used by Zeami. One sees the 'puppet/actor', as it were, submitting to the pull of strings and adjusting to the finest degree of regulated control but at the same time, forging dents or carving patterns in the stage space with deliberate, powerful movements or with no visible movements, through this breathtaking balancing act within.

I am pulled from all directions by invisible strings. If one of these strings were cut off, I would not be able to balance myself and would fall down.[78]

The Noh actor exists powerfully in the centre of the limitless space.[79]

I have to fight for my existence within the vast space.[80]

Objectively, I am sitting on the stage motionlessly but my heart is moving actively and dancing around the stage.[81]

The Noh actor's objective perception of himself is paramount: not only must he step out of himself and appraise his image but he must merge with the spectator's view of him. He is as it were defined by the collective eyes of the audience because like a 'puppet', he cannot see himself. As Zeami said:

You have to keep it in your mind that your eyes cannot see your eyes. Thus in order to see yourself you have to see yourself from the auditorium and from behind, left and right.[82]

The actor is situated as it were in the nexus of a multitude of eye lines. Kanze emphasises the extra sensitive skin perception of a blind person compared to one who sees normally and so the partially 'blind' masked Noh actor (rendered thus by the visually restrictive mask) 'feels strongly the invisible energy which comes from the audience.' So in other words the actor's energy – the vital breath translated into movement – (*ki*) in Japanese and (*ch'i*) in Chinese – is the product of conscious and unconscious activity of which the audience is a part.[83] There is no doubt that the energy of movement in Noh is 'tied to the heart by strings' in all senses of the string puppet image. The Noh theatre is a clearly documented example of a theatrical form underpinned by string puppet imagery. Zeami's seminal treatise encapsulated in a key section from the saying of a Rinzai priest provides that documentation. The situation is very different in China where no official treatise on the nature of acting has survived. Nonetheless the connection between puppet movements and the movements of Chinese acting is equally striking.

The String Puppet and Chinese Theatre

In the reign of Emperor Chu Mu Wang, sometime in the 10th century BC, a famous puppeteer by the name of Yang Shih was summoned to the palace to stage a performance before the Emperor. The puppets moved in a way so captivating and life-like that the Emperor was enthralled. And then he suddenly became furious because he was utterly convinced that one of the performing puppets was winking lasciviously at his favourite concubine. He stopped the show and ordering the puppeteer Yang Shih to be brought to him, insisted that the presumptuous performer should be summarily executed. Yang Shih bowed in fear and begged if he could be permitted to be the executioner as the supposed offender was none other than his own beloved son.[84] He then went to the back of the stage and brought out the culprit and before the startled eyes of the entire court, dismantled it and revealed that it was composed of nothing more than wood and strings. The astonished Emperor immediately ordered that Yang Shih should be rewarded with a purse of gold and declared: "You have created a great art form."[85]

In most stories of origins there is an element of improbability and therefore of scholastic scepticism as to its accuracy. By this token the above story has to be taken with a pinch of salt but this does not invalidate its central thrust which is that as far back as three thousand years ago, the puppet theatre won the royal seal of approval as a great form of entertainment. And there are of course arguments that the 'offending' puppet in question might not have belonged to the 'string' variety. There are many different types of puppets ranging from glove, rod, hand and shadow, to those which are simply mechanical toys fitted with their own special operating devices. But as in India, the 'string' puppet is believed to be the earliest type found in China.

Puppets and Mortuary Figures

A large wooden figure was unearthed in the Shandong Province in the spring of 1979, in a tomb belonging to the Western Han dynasty (about 107 BC). It is believed to be the earliest extant Chinese puppet, over 2,000 years old, and holes have been found in its abdomen and legs which could have been used for attaching strings.[86] But on the other hand it is possible that this puppet was operated by another type of device. However the fact that it was found in a tomb strongly affirms the strong connection between puppets and mortuary figures and its particular operational device should not affect the general function of puppets as far as the deceased is concerned. In the early period of China's history, during the Shang dynasty (16th–11th century BC), slaves and captives of war were buried with their masters in order to provide the latter with their services in the next world. Eventually wooden or clay figurines with moveable parts (called *yong*) were used as substitutes and the presiding shamans at these funeral services would activate or animate them in order to give the impression that they were possessed by the spirit of the dead. There is one theory that the 'animated' mortuary figure or puppet is a sign that the spirit of the dead has really entered into it and is being conducted by the shaman safely into another world. What is clear to the spectators is that the coming to life of the mortuary figure signifies possession by the spirit of the dead and hence the awe which an animated form evokes, whether it is a mortuary figure or a puppet. So from this one can see how closely the puppet or marionette theatre is connected with the ritual of spirit invocation and possession. A puppet in motion inculcates awe and generates its own magic, a fact which helps to explain the aura of supernatural power with which puppet movement is invested. Indeed the etymology of the word 'puppet'– in Chinese *k'uei lei* or *ka le* – reinforces its intermediary function between the living and the dead. The first word *k'uei* consists of two components representing 'man' and 'spirit' (or 'demon'), and the second word *lei* means 'ugly, withered and foul'; so the two words taken together, *k'uei lei*, suggests an 'intermediary figure' (probably deformed) which can be entrusted with important transactions between humans and the spirit world. Puppets are thus regarded as effective agents of exorcism extraordinarily empowered to control and dispel evil spirits. So they are certainly regarded as more than mere figures of entertainment, though this aspect also enters into it, and as the Min-nan demotic version of *k'uei lei*, as *ka li* (meaning 'auspicious ritual') indicates, they are crucial ambassadors or negotiators between man and the spirit world.

Puppets and Early Chinese Folk Religion

To understand this, one has to dig into early Chinese folk religion which envisaged the world filled with multitudes of spirits with propensities for doing good and evil. It is possible for these spirits to take possession of human beings but the former could be persuaded to inhabit objects and this is where puppets, which are made roughly to resemble human beings, are useful in that spirits can be fooled into regarding them as alternative habitations. So because of their great propensity to attract spirits, puppets are locked away or dismantled by separating their heads from the rest of their bodies. In fact, such is the awe in which puppets are held that stories (both true and exaggerated) circulate about self-animating puppets and so increasing their aura of magic and supernatural power.

Another strong theory is that puppets originated from the great 'Exorcism' ceremonies which were held just before New Year and also at funeral services of important personages to exorcise demons, pestilence and evil spirits. As early as the Zhou and Han dynasties (1066 BC to 220 AD), an official exorcist figure called the *fangxiangshi*, wearing a bear skin and probably a mask with four golden eyes, would wield a lance and battle with a host of evil spirits and demons. This is a good example of the officialising of a folk superstition. In his retinue were one hundred and twenty 'masked' boys representing little spirit warriors who could vanquish and devour evil spirits and demons of pestilence. It is believed that the young masked attendants were eventually replaced by puppets. In fact, the term *k'uei lei* used for puppets has also been employed to refer to masked actors.[87]

From this it can be seen that puppets are strongly connected with exorcism. In any collection of puppets there are in principle thirty-six heads and seventy-two different body parts. Altogether there are one hundred and eight pieces and so a collection of puppets refers to, or represents, the 108 evil influences in heaven and earth (72 *te soah* or murderous influences of earth and 36 *t'ien kang* or celestial evil influences) and the ability of 'animated puppets' to counteract them.[88] In other words to animate a puppet is in effect to invoke the spirit of the character which the puppet represents and to take possession of it. If one recalls the 108 *karanas* or dance units built into the temple of Shiva – the Hindu 'Lord of Dance and of Puppets' – the 108 spikes on the prick-balls of Chinese 'youth' mediums known as *tang-ki*[89] and the 108 movements in the art of T'ai Chi Ch'uan (see Chapter 3), one realises how widespread belief in the power of this number and its ability to counteract the 108 malign spirits, through puppets and certain choreographed movements, is.

Quanzhou and the String Puppet
The string puppet has been particularly associated with the city of Quanzhou in the south-east province of Fujian from as early as the eighth century. This is because a young boy, Tian, the only one who could play the jade flute belonging to Emperor Tang Ming Huang and was consequently promoted to the post of 'Top Imperial Scholar', and 'Chief Leader' of Ming Huang's actors and puppeteers, came from Quanzhou (see Chapter 2). He became known as *Hsiang kung yeh* ('The Reverend Lord Minister') and also as *T'ien tu-yuan shuai chiu-tien feng-huo yuan*, 'Marshal Tian of the Court of Wind and Fire in the Nine Heavens'. It is important to emphasise the function of the wind in carrying all messages to heaven and that of fire as all writs and letters addressed to the gods are invariably burnt after recital. The fact that Marshal Tian is associated with the power of fire to reduce all requests to ashes and that of the wind to carry supplications to the heavenly Emperor is an indication of his importance. He was considered able to have instant access to the Supreme Being and not only did he promote an exciting

The Image of the String Puppet

interchange between human theatrical and puppet movements because of his royally endowed position as the leader of these two genres in the eighth century but an iconic string puppet was made in his likeness which was, and still is, raised up at the back of the puppet stage to preside over every puppet performance. And this string puppet figure referred to reverentially as 'Marshal Tian' (the title 'Marshal' emphasising his role as 'Warrior Guardian', the whole process of encountering evil spirits perceived as a 'battle') has acquired such tremendous powers of exorcism over the centuries that he has become a dominant theatrical force particularly outside Quanzhou, which has to bend somewhat to the anti-superstition policy prevalent in Beijing. However, it is to Quanzhou we must turn as the origin of 'string puppet' power. There is no doubt that in this historic city the 'string puppet' is synonymous with Quanzhou puppetry where it is known as *k'uei lei xian de kua chi lai* ('puppets suspended from strings') and puppet plays are sometimes referred to as *xian hsi,* 'string plays'. The Quanzhou puppet theatre is the only one in China which can boast of having its own music: three hundred songs and ancient tunes played to the accompaniment of cymbals, gongs and a special foot-pressed drum.

But outside Quanzhou, in Singapore for example, where there are no political restrictions to religious practices, and where there is a thriving Chinese community consisting of descendants of immigrants from Fujian province during the great Diaspora to various parts of South-East Asia at the turn of the twentieth century, the reign of Marshal Tian, the 'King of the String Puppets', is unquestionable in Chinese theatrical practice and religious observances. It is impossible to separate Chinese theatre from religious ritual and Marshal Tian, the string puppet 'deity', features centrally in the interweaving of puppet show, actor performance and propitiatory ceremony. For although in Chinese history, Emperor Tang Ming Huang is officially associated with the string puppet through his own comparison of himself to one in a famous poem (see Chapter 2) and as the royal patron of Marshal Tian, in Singapore, it is Marshal Tian himself, or rather his 'spirit' animating the body of the string puppet (see Plate 4) who is considered the most potent figure both in religious practice and Chinese theatre. The dancing puppet figure of Marshal Tian on the sacred diagram is considered so magically potent that this performance takes place without being observed by spectators. Indeed quite a few puppet performances are staged for their exorcistic rather than entertainment value and so there is no need for an audience.

Even in China, despite political restrictions, the Quanzhou Puppet Theatre, which has inherited the legacy of string puppetry from the time of Emperor Ming Huang, is still active. Some of the puppet heads in their possession are fine examples of carving and engraving in the Tang and Sung dynasties. The number of strings to each puppet ranges from sixteen to thirty and this gives an idea of the intricacy and degree of control exerted by the puppeteer over each puppet. And perhaps it is this regulative power which strings maintain over the puppet that endorses string puppetry's claim of superiority over other types of puppets. But apart from the parallel between the spirit possessed animated puppet (movement being a sign of spiritual possession) and the human actor perhaps incarnating a god on stage, and the historical connection between puppet and human actor movements as fostered by Marshal Tian in the eighth century, there is still another persuasive reason why the exorcistically charged movements of puppets should be the model for actors. And this has to do with the exceptional quality of puppet movements which in themselves compel imitation. It has been said that because puppets are incapable of changing their facial expressions, the puppeteer is forced to use their movements to convey every nuance of emotion, while the restrictive size of the puppet stage forces movements and gestures to be distilled to their essence. For these reasons puppet movements per se have attracted great admiration and the art of puppetry has been identified with the art of movement itself. Chinese actors and puppeteers however find it difficult to explain why puppet movements take such a pre-eminent role in Chinese theatrical circles apart from reiterating almost by rote that it was Marshal Tian who imposed the definitive puppet-like characteristics on human actor movements. 'He taught actors how to move', or 'the gods prefer puppet movements to those of actors' were the replies I frequently received when I asked Quanzhou puppeteers to account for the striking similarities between puppet and stage actor movements. 'Only Marshal Tian of the "Court of Wind and Fire in the Nine Heavens" has influence over, and direct access to, the Heavenly Emperor', was another explanation. All these statements were uttered with such conviction that although they may be criticised in the West as somewhat fictional or figurative replies, unbased on actual data, they point to the fact that puppets occupy first place in Chinese theatrical thought and boy and adult actors are down-graded accordingly. Another proof of the string puppet's pre-eminence lies in a detail: the way an actor playing a male role and one playing a female have to take opposite directions when going upstage after addressing the audience from frontstage. This has its root in string puppet theatre where such a move is designed to prevent the accidental crossing of strings which would almost certainly happen if puppets were moved in the same direction. Even a mistake on the human stage is labelled *fan hsien*, meaning 'the strings have twisted'. Indeed in the Sung dynasty (960–1279AD) the puppet and human theatres were so close that puppeteers often appeared as actors in a variety of stage performances, and there was even one famous actor known as '*Lu of the Golden Strings*'.[90] Once again the human theatre acknowledges the presiding inspiration of the string puppet theatre.

'Pear Garden Theatre' Movements, Marshal Tian and String Puppets

I would like to end this section by discussing eight photos illustrating the undeniable affinity between some of the movements of Quanzhou's *Li Yuan Hsi* ('Pear Garden Theatre')[91] and the *K'uei Lei Hsi* ('Puppet Theatre') known also as 'Quanzhou Municipal Marionette Troupe.' I believe that these photos demonstrate the fundamental sense of 'strings' shown in the movements of Chinese actors in the Marshal Tian tradition (see Plate 10):

(1) *Xianggong Mo*: The step or stance identified with *Xianggong* (The Reverend Lord Minister) or Marshal Tian (Fig.1). The puppet movement from which this is derived is called *Chu Chang Liang Xiang*. Translated freely, this is an instruction

for the puppet to be brought to the stage and 'manifest its presence' or 'to emanate radiance and light.' In 'human' theatrical terms this is the movement to send out the *ch'i* ('breath') or that special quality of charisma which approximates to divinity or something extraordinary. That this stance or gesture to manifest the crucial creative impulse is called after the 'Puppet King' is the clearest acknowledgement of the debt of actors to puppets. The essence of a striking stage movement has its origin in the puppet.

(2) *Jia Li Luo Xian*: 'In accordance with excellent rules of propriety, the actor is about to embark on a step and he is to gear himself by 'gathering up the strings'. The puppet movement from which this step derives is referred to as *Tiao Ye Huo De Ding Xing* which literally means 'jump and arrive in a modified stance'. But because the 'string' image derivation is so unmistakable, I am showing through four photos (Figs.5, 6, 7, 8) how the actor begins and turns just like a string puppet.

(3) *Hu Zhi Tan Jing*: 'The tiger looks down into a well.' This is a quite majestic looking pose as suggested by the tiger simile. The puppet stance which has inspired this pose for the human stage is called *Tan Shi Xia Fang*. This translates roughly as 'to look down and regard something with respect.'

(4) *Mao Zhi Xi Lian*: 'The cat washes its face.' This step is reminiscent of the way a cat washes its face but its puppet derivation – *Sheng Qi Huo Ji Dong Shi De Dong Zhuo* – is a movement to express anger and the whole process of arousing excitement.

(5) *Kai Shan:* 'Opening a mountain' – This is a pattern of movement reserved for someone of exalted status. (In Min-nan demotic this is called *Kuah Pan,* 'the pattern of a high lord.') Its puppet counterpart is *Pai Chang Shi De Jia Shi* which translated freely means a 'gesture pattern of presenting yourself'.

(6) *Shiu Xing (Sheng, Dan, Chou)*: This step indicates that the actor/character is about to set forth and can be used by the three role types – 'male', 'female' and 'clown'. (Figs. 2, 3, 4) This is derived from the puppet style of indicating that 'the character is setting out': *Xing Dang Ke Bu*. And just like puppets, Pear Garden actors and actresses focus primarily on movements.[92]

There is no doubt that the ethos of the string puppet has inspired many movements in the Pear Garden Theatre. Emperor Ming Huang's poem in which he compares himself to a string puppet and the human dilemma when a string is broken poignantly indicates what a meaningful image the string puppet is for capturing the human condition. After the tragic loss of his beloved concubine, Yang Kuei Fei, it was as though one of his strings had snapped and as he put it: 'the show is over, and we're back once more in the dream like life.' So aptly, he has been responsible for focusing attention on the 'string' puppet. And if we regard Emperor Ming Huang's 'Pear Garden' as the fountain head of Chinese Theatre, it is difficult not to acknowledge Marshal Tian – the 'String Puppet King' he set up – as the patron saint of both puppet and human theatres wherever there is a thriving Chinese community for whom theatre, ritual and life are inextricable.

In the stomach of this omnipotent marionette are encased the kernels of five kinds of grain (emblems of his power), a pair of scissors and a traditional carpenter's measure. The last two take us back full circle to the *soota* or *sutra* ('string'), mentioned near the beginning of this chapter, with which the Indian architect used to measure out the proportions of a theatrical stage in order to keep out disturbances. The importance of the 'string' and 'stringholder' as part of a control system in theatre both literal and metaphysical, with mortals being controlled by gods, demons and destiny is certainly a seminal strand of thought in Asia, leading to the rise of puppet-inspired theatres in which movements (either hand, or a combination of hand and body) compel attention. The Kathakali of Kerala, the Japanese Noh theatre and the classical Pear Garden Theatre of Quanzhou in Southern China are all examples of the influence of puppet movement and theory on the human stage in many parts of Asia, an influence which has spread further through the writing and thought of a few western critics and practitioners, themselves influenced by the power of the Asian string puppet. In my concluding chapter I would like to look more closely at the way puppets and the Puppet Theatre have been viewed in the West.

Notes and References

1. M.L. Varadpande, *Invitation to Indian Theatre*, New Delhi, Arnold Heinemann Publishers India Ltd., 1987, p. 63.
2. See Richard Pischel's address entitled 'The Home of the Puppet Play', on assuming the office of Rector of the Konigliche Vereinigte Friedrichs-Universitat, Halle-Wittenberg, on 12th July 1900. Hereford: Stephen Austin and Sons, 1900, p. 6.
3. See Michael R. Malkin, *Traditional and Folk Puppets of the World*, South Brunswick & New York: A.S. Barnes & Co., 1977, p. 74.
4. Scholars are still divided over the question of the first home of puppets. Richard Pischel in *Der Heimat des Puppenspiels*, translated as 'The Home of the Puppet Play' (Halle, 1900) (see Note 2 above,) advanced the idea that 'the puppet play is in reality everywhere the most ancient form of dramatic representation' and that in India, 'we must look for its home.' This view was disputed by Professor William Ridgeway in *The Dramas and Dramatic Dances of Non-European Races* (1915) whose view was that 'if there has been any borrowing, India rather than Europe has been the borrower.' Ridgeway's view is supported by George Speaight in *The History of the English Puppet Theatre*, London: George G. Harrap & Co., Ltd., 1955, p. 273.
5. Savitry Shivalingappa, *Marionettes and their Role in Society*, Teheran: Asian Cultural Documentation Centre for UNESCO, September 1975, p. 10.
6. See *New Larousse Encyclopedia of Mythology*, op. cit., p. 325. See also *Encyclopedia Brittanica* (11th edition), London and New York: Encyclopedia Brittanica Co., Ltd., 1910–11, pp. 804–5, which states that the names 'Chaldean' and 'Babylonian' were practically synonymous. 'Chaldean' is applied in the *Old Testament* to the Babylonians (Dan. iii 8, v.30,). The term is also used as a name for a special class of magicians.
7. See Max von Boehn, *Dolls and Puppets*, London: George G. Harrap and Company Ltd., 1932, p. 252.
8. See *The Guiness Encyclopedia*, ed., Ian Crofton, London: Guiness Publishing Ltd., 1990, p. 364.
9. *Marionettes and their Role in Society*, op. cit, p. 5.
10. *Dolls and Puppets*, op. cit., p. 299. See also *Invitation to Indian Theatre*, op. cit., p. 17. Both string as well as shadow puppets are mentioned in the *Mahabharata*. A man controlled by destiny is compared to a wooden doll, string-manipulated by the puppeteer. The final form of the *Mahabharata* was fixed around 400AD. The *Ramayana* was compiled after the *Mahabharata* though the events related in it precede those recounted in the *Mahabharata* by about 150 years.
11. See *Marionettes and their Role in Society*, op. cit., p. 15.
12. See Mohan Khokar, *Traditions of Indian Classical Dance*, New Delhi: Clarion Books, 1979, p. 24.
13. Ibid., p. 26.

14. The puppet-loving Dravidians were the original inhabitants of Kerala and it is therefore not surprising that the performers of Kathakali – a dance drama of Kerala – move in a way remarkably similar to that of marionettes. See K. Baratha Iyer, *Kathakali:The Sacred Dance Drama of Malabar*, London: Luzac & Co., Ltd., 1935, p. 4.
15. See Malkin, 1977, p. 83. The learned Brahmins of the south formed a separate class who used the word for 'puppet' – *gombe* – as a family name, viz., *Gombe* Anantatchar. See also J. Tillkasiri, *The Puppet Theatre of Asia*, Ceylon: Department of Cultural Affairs, 1969, p. 21.
16. See Khokar, 1979, p. 18.
17. Adya Rangacharya, *The Indian Theatre*, New Delhi: National Book Trust, 1971, pp. 11–13.
18. Jiwan Pani, *Living Dolls: Story of Indian Puppets*, New Delhi: Publications Division, Ministry of Information and Broadcasting, Government of India, 1986, p. 4.
19. Ibid.
20. Ibid.
21. See P.L. Amin Sweeney, *The Ramayana and the Malay Shadow Play*, Kuala Lumpur: The National University of Malaysia Press, 1972, p. 53.
22. See Khokar, 1979, pp. 215–16.
23. The term *Zen* (*ch'an* in Chinese) is an abbreviated form of *zenna* or *ch'anna*, which is the Chinese rendering of *dhyāna* or *jhāna* meaning 'meditation'. From this fact alone, according to D.T. Suzuki, 'Zen has a great deal to do with this practice which has been carried on from the early days of the Buddha, indeed from the beginning of Indian culture.' See D.T. Suzuki, *Essays in Zen Buddhism*, First Series, London: Rider and Co., 1950, pp. 79–80.
24. Although Bodhidharma was considered to be the first Zen patriarch in China, he was placed as the 28th Zen patriarch in India in a line stemming directly from Sâkyamuni, the Buddha. Hui-Neng (637–713), the sixth patriarch after Bodhidharma, was the real Chinese founder of Zen and after him, Zen was split into several schools, the two main ones being the Sôtô (Tsao-tung) and the Rinzai (Lin-chi), which are still in existence in China and Japan. Traditionally (though the historicity of this incident has been questioned), Zen was supposed to have been transmitted by the Buddha to his foremost disciple Mahâkâsyapa. When the great teacher held out a flower to his congregation, Mahâkâsyapa smiled in a great moment of understanding.
25. *Hekigan-shû* meaning 'Blue Rock Records' is the combined work of Hsueh-t'ou Chung-hsien (980–1052), Secchô Jûken (in Japanese) and Yuan-wu Fo-kuo (1062–1135), Yengo Bukkwa (in Japanese). Secchô selected one hundred cases from the history of Zen of which Bodhiddharma's meeting with Emperor Wu was the first, and wrote a commentary on each of them in verse form. See *Iwanami Bukkyô Jiten* ('Iwanami's Dictionary of Buddhism'), ed. Nakamura Hajime, Tokyo: Iwanami, 1989, p. 27.

26. Rinzai (Lin-chi, d. 867) was the founder of the Rinzai sect. The Rinzai and Sôtô schools of Buddhism were the two most powerful sects in Japan between the 12th and 19th century.
27. This is taken from J. Thomas Rimer and Yamazaki Masakazu (trs.), *On the Art of the Nô Drama: The Major Treatises of Zeami,* Princeton, N.J.: Princeton University Press, 1984, p. 97.
28. See D.T. Suzuki, *Essays in Zen Buddhism,* Third Series, 1953, p. 108.
29. Ibid., p. 27.
30. Ibid., p. 114.
31. Ibid., p. 111 & 114.
32. Ibid., pp. 114–115.
33. Alan Watts in foreword to Gia-fu Feng, *T'ai Chi – A Way of Centering and I Ching,* London: Collier – Macmillan, 1970.
34. See the section on 'Zen and Swordsmanship' in Daisetz T. Suzuki, *Zen and Japanese Culture,* New York: Princeton University Press, 1959, p. 165.
35. See the story of the 'wooden' cockerel and the 'impassive' cat, both impervious to outside distractions but invincible against adversaries in ibid., p. 439; and pp. 428–435. The story of Heinrich von Kleist's impassive but invincible bear is recorded in Idris Parry, *Hand to Mouth and Other Essays,* Manchester: Carcanet New Press, 1981, pp. 17–18.
36. See D.T. Suzuki, *Zen and Japanese Culture,* Bollingen Series LX1V, op. cit., p. 148.
37. Ibid., pp. 205–206. When 'Ki-no-Aritsune's Daughter', the ego-less wife in the Noh play *Izutsu,* looks into the well, she does not see herself but her husband's image: she (the subject) has merged with the object of her desire.
38. Ibid., p. 438.
39. Ibid., p. 128. Its original Sanskrit name, *bodhimandala,* means the place of enlightenment. The name was borrowed from Zen Buddhism.
40. Poh Sim Plowright, *The Classical Nô Theatre of Japan,* Cambridge: Chadwyck-Healey, 1991, p. 110.
41. This quotation is taken from *Banno kanisshin no koto* ('Ten thousand Noh aspects connected to the heart') in Zeami's treatise *Kakyô.* See Nose Asaji, *Zeami jûrokubu-shû hyôshaku* (Zeami's sixteen treatises) Vol. 2, Tokyo, 1940, pp. 379–380. The English translation is by Naohiko Umewaka.
42. See Barbara Thornbury, *Folk Performing Arts: Traditional Culture in Contemporary Japan,* New York: State University of New York Press, 1997, p. 141.
43. Zeami's son-in-law, Konparu Zenchiku, said in his treatise, *Rokurin Ichiro Hichu* ('The Secrets of the Six Circles and a Sword') that it is the heart which provides the source of control in Noh theatre. He is also adamant that if there is feeling within, it will show outside. This treatise was completed in August 1465 when Zenchiku was 61 years old. and the gist of his statement can be found in the Kansei period version, Tokyo 1969, p. 23.

44. D.T Suzuki differentiates two kinds of heart – the 'physical' heart which is subject to changes of emotion and the 'true' heart which is immoveable. See his *Zen and Japanese Culture*, op.cit., p. 185.
45. Rimer, 1984, p. 101.
46. Arthur Waley (tr.) *The Nô Plays of Japan*, London: George Allen and Unwin,, 1921, p. 44.
47. Rimer, 1984, p. 75.
48. This dance is only performed in *Dôjôji* and is considered unique in that it is accompanied solely by the *ko-tsuzumi* ('small hand drum') with the flute occasionally joining in for a few seconds.
49. The Noh actor who featured in the experiment was Naohiko Umewaka and a film was made of it entitled 'The Universe Within' by NHK in 1989.
50. See *World Mythology*, op.cit., p. 80.
51. See *Matsukaze* in *Japanese Noh Drama, Ten Plays*, Vol. 111, Tokyo: Nippon Gakujutsu Shinkôkai (The Japan Society for the Promotion of Scientific Research), 1960, p. 46.
52. Rimer, 1984, p. 46.
53. See *Yamamba* in *Japanese Noh Drama, Ten Plays*, Vol. 11, op.cit., p. 175.
54. The following poem with a strong string puppet image, reminiscent of Gettan Sôkô's saying, has been ascribed to Ikkyû:
> The puller of strings is himself the chief actor
> As earth and water unite at the will of fire and air.
> When the play on the stage has ended
> The setting suddenly is empty again.

See Donald Keene, *Nô and Bunraku: Two Forms of Japanese Theatre*, New York: CUP, Morningside Edition, 1990, p. 133.
55. Zeami's treatise *Kyûi* begins with the ninth level and the phrase 'In Shinra the sun shines at midnight' can occur in a slightly different way as quoted by Zen priests of that period. See *On the Art of the Nô Drama*, op. cit., p. 120, where the metaphor is put thus: 'In Silla, in the dead of night, the sun shines brightly.'
56. The five 'main actor' schools of Noh drama are : Kanze, Hôshô, Konparu, Kongô and Kita. The last school dates from the early years of the 17th century.
57. See Naohiko Umewaka, 'The Inner world of the Nô: The Influence of Ritual and Metaphysics on the Choreography in the Nô theatre' in *Contemporary Theatre Review*, Vol. 1, London: Harwood Academic Publishers, 1992, p. 35.
58. This is also the view of the Noh actor Naohiko Umewaka (see above) whose father Naoyoshi Unewaka was a fine swordsman as well as a great Noh actor. See ibid., p. 29. See also Omote Akira and Ito Masayoshi (eds.), *Konparu Zenho, Konparu Kodensho Shusei*, Tokyo:Wanya, 1969, p. 407.
59. Musashi Miyamoto, *Gorinshô (Book of Five Rings)*, Tokyo: Iwanami, 1985, p. 43.
60. Rimer, 1984, p. 92.
61. Ibid., pp. 75–76.
62. Ibid., pp. 79–80.

63. Ibid., p. 206.
64. This area now referred to as Kansai, used to be known as Yamato comprising Kyoto and Nara. The four Noh schools, viz. Kanze, Hôshô, Kongô and Komparu came from this area.
65. Dôgen (1200–1253) was the founder of the Sôtô School of Zen Buddhism. This sect subscribed to the theories of *Yin/Yang*, the Five Elements (Wood, Fire, Earth, Metal and Water) as well as to various aspects of the *I-Ching*. It is significant that many of these ideas can be found in Zeami's treatises.
66. Zeami's 'Rinzai' connection is important because it was a saying of a Rinzai priest, Gettan Sôkô, who inspired his formulation of a seminal section in his treatise – *Kakyô* – which is based on a string puppet analogy.
67. See Yasuo Nakamura, *Noh: The Classical Theater*, New York and Tokyo: Walker and Weatherhill, 1971, p. 81.
68. For more details of Zeami's Zen leanings and of Omote Akira's discovery of the 15th century documents from the Fugan or Hogan temple, see Kosai Tsutomu, *Zeami Shinko* ('New Theories on Zeami'), Tokyo: Wanya, 1962, pp. 56–58. See also Kato Shuiichi *Chosakushû Zeami no Senjutsu matawa Nogakuron (Zeami's strategy in treatises on the Noh)*, Tokyo: Heibonsha, 1978, pp. 215–216.
69. This quotation can be found in Tsuchiga Keichiro, *Noh,* Tokyo: Shinyusha 1989, p. 7.
70. Kanze Hisao, *Kanze Hisao Chosakushû* ('Collected Writings of Kanze Hisao'), Vol.2, Tokyo:Heibonsha, 1981, p. 241.
71. Ibid., p. 271.
72. Ibid., p. 55.
73. Ibid., p. 150.
74. Ibid., p. 162.
75. Ibid., vol.1, 1980, p. 85.
76. Ibid., vol.11, 1981, p. 44.
77. Ibid., p. 150.
78. Ibid., p. 23.
79. Ibid., vol.1,1980, p. 60.
80. Ibid., vol.11, 1981, p. 79.
81. Ibid., p. 225.
82. See Poh Sim Plowright, *The Classical Nô Theatre of Japan,* op.cit., p. 111.
83. In this connection it is interesting to have the comments of the famous contemporary Canadian puppeteer, Ronnie Burkett, who staged a successful season of his latest production entitled *Happy* at the Barbican Theatre in London from 20th June to 7th July 2001. He said *'What's made me a better actor with puppets is the knowledge that these things that I'm controlling and speaking for don't breathe. I know that. But what the audience doesn't know, and they don't need to know, is that they, by believing in these characters – if I can make them focus on that little realm, and if I can control their breath – they will breathe for the character. So the life the puppet has is coming from all sides of the theatre.'*

84. Compare the Indian puppeteer's attitude towards his puppet which he calls *puttalika* meaning 'son'.
85. See Derek Bruce (tr.) *Wisdom of the Daoist Masters* (from Léon Wieger, *Les Pères du Système Taoiste)*, Lampeter: Llanerch Enterprise, 1984, pp. 85–86. This is taken from Chapter 5 in the *Writings of Lie Zie* (Lieh Tzu).
86. See Roberta Helmer Stalberg, *China's Puppets,* San Francisco: China Books, 1984, p. 18.
87. Sergei Obratsov, *The Chinese Puppet Theatre,* London: Faber and Faber, 1961, p. 27.
88. See J.J.M. De Groot, 1910, p. 1250.
89. Ibid., p. 1276.
90. Stalberg, 1984, p. 19.
91. In 1951 all the three troupes belonging to the Pear Garden Theatre disbanded and in 1953 the 'Experimental Li Yuan Company' of Fujian province was established to take its place.
92. See Helga Werle-Burger *Chinesische Oper*. Zürich, Würzburg and Paris: U. Bar Verlag, 1982, p. 16. The thinking behind this is that since a puppet only has as many feelings as can be demonstrated on the outside, movements and appearances are of paramount importance.

Chapter Six: Western Attitudes to Puppets – Their Allies and Adversaries

> *The puppet is the actor in his primitive form. Its symbolic costume, from which all realistic and historically correct impertinences are banished, its unchanging star, petrified (or rather lignified) in a grimace expressive to the highest degree attainable by the carver's art, the mimicry by which it suggests human gesture in unearthly caricature – these give to its performance an intensity to which few actors can pretend, an intensity that imposes on our imagination...*[1] G.B.Shaw

Not everyone in the West has been as enthusiastic about puppets as George Bernard Shaw and although, particularly from the 18th century onwards, there have been other supporters of their power and dignity, western attitudes, unlike eastern, have been ambivalent to say the least towards this form of theatre. Whereas in India, as we have seen, a Brahmin priest belonging to the highest caste might take the word *gombe*, meaning 'puppet' as a surname, western comments have ranged from abuse of puppets for their counterfeit nature (see, for example, Shakespeare's *A Midsummer Night's Dream*, Act 3, Sc.1) to wholehearted attempts, first by the Catholic Church and later by Protestant reformers to suppress them. Even in the early 20th century, Edward Gordon Craig, himself a great champion of puppets, cites the use of the word as a 'term of contempt'.[2]

Before I examine the central difference in attitude between East and West, a word about the distinction between 'puppet' and 'marionette': according to their definitions in the Oxford dictionary, the former refers to a figure, usually small, representing a human being or animal and moved by various means, while the latter is a figure always worked by strings. However the terms are frequently used interchangeably and 'puppet' is often used as a general term for both,[3] an approach I have adopted here, while noting that the term 'marionette' is often given a religious origin as, for example, in the claim that it began in the 10th century and was associated with the Virgin Mary – 'marionettes' meaning 'Little Marys' or little figures of the Virgin Mary. There is an irony here, since it was 'religion' that became the agent of their abolition in the 16th century and though they were later reinstated in the chronicles of theatrical history, the status of the puppet in the West has perhaps never fully recovered from its battle with the Church. In any case, though this connection has been, and is, disputed, it remains an important area of research and needs to be discussed more fully.

The Origin of the Term 'Marionette'

The year is 944 in the Church of Santa Maria della Salute in Venice. Twelve young virgins are awaiting the arrival of their bridegrooms when pirates from Trieste suddenly appear and abduct them. They are however almost immediately recovered from the hands of their would-be ravishers and their 'rescue' became the excuse for an annual ceremony called *La Festa delle Marie* in memory of the twelve betrothed virgins. For eight days, twelve lavishly dressed and beautiful young girls, chosen by the doge, were paraded through the city in pomp and splendour at the expense of the Council. But in the ensuing years, as the expenses of this lavish occasion became too heavy for the coffers of the State, the number of virgins was reduced from twelve to four and then to three, until eventually the girls were replaced by wooden figures, initially called *Maria di ligno* (Mary of wood). And hence, it is said, arose the creation of 'marionettes', deriving both from the names of the girls and from their divine model, Mary, born of immaculate conception, the 'Mother of God'.[4] The strange pattern of this transmutation or transformation is significant: in the name both of expediency and of something deeper and more symbolic – note the connection with the Biblical parable of the Wise Virgins – a real person is replaced by a wooden symbol which becomes a puppet. And here the role of the Virgin Mary, as the supreme intercessor between mortals and God, bears comparison with that of the Buddha-given child, Lady Jôruri, whose name was given to the most sophisticated form of puppetry in the East, originally called *Ningyô Jôruri* (see Chapter 4). According to both stories the origin of puppet theatre is closely connected with intercession and healing, through its association with a female intermediary, the object of pilgrimages, endowed with a similar aura of divinity. One has only to think of Lourdes and the devotion of pilgrims to the many shrines of the Virgin and compare that with the memorial sites specially marked out in the map of Yahagi and Okazaki to comprehend the deep veneration that surrounds these two women. Whatever the differences between them, both, according to powerful traditions in West and East, have given their names to a form of puppetry, have become objects of devotion and represent the same fusion of roles which determines the close connection between puppets and mediums.[5]

There is another and entirely secular claim for the derivation of the term *marionette* in the West. This associates it with *morio* meaning 'fool' or *marotte* which refers to a fool's sceptre or baton. Such sceptres were probably originally carried by simple rod puppets[6] but were later used by the stringed form as well. In his *Lexicon* of 1741 Frisch referred to the connection of the word with medieval fool names like *morio, morione* but already, by the end of the 16th century and the beginning of the 17th, the term 'marionette' was being used in both senses.[7] Again there has been much scholarly dispute about these derivations: how can words like 'buffoon' or 'foolery' be yoked to the definition of *marionette*, otherwise so linked with the figure of the Virgin Mary as an object of devotion? One answer might be to reject the religious connection entirely, as some scholars have done. But there is a more intriguing answer which relates the Western medieval world-view to the traditional Eastern attitude towards the puppet. Neither saw any incompatibility in marrying high and low, reverent and obscene, religious and secular in their drama and festivals. When I was researching the role of string puppets in Quanzhou in Fujian Province (see Chapter 2) in 1994 and speaking and understanding the Min-nan dialect which was used in 'sacred' exorcistic performances, I was initially disconcerted by the scatological puns and innuendoes which were flying across the auditorium and only gradually appreciated that bad taste, bawdy jokes and overall vulgarity were indispensable elements in puppet performances intended to exorcise and cleanse the community of evil forces. Marshal Tian, the 'Puppet King' who presided over every performance was both an 'Exorcist' and the 'Drunken Jester' but it was also clear that he was a deity to be worshipped. The great Tang Emperor Ming Huang who was responsible for setting up Marshal Tian as the 'Puppet King' in the 8th century, and who then encouraged an exchange of techniques between the human and puppet theatres, saw himself as clown, buffoon, emperor and puppet, all rolled into one, but the diversity of contradictory roles did not rule out the element of divinity included in his mandate to rule as the Son of Heaven. Indeed the puppet theatre in China in the 6th century was initially called the 'Jesters' Theatre', in which starred a comic figure referred to jokingly as 'Baldy Guo'. So even before Emperor Ming Huang came on the scene, the pre-eminent role of foolery in puppet theatre was recognized, going back to 'Jester Meng' who was considered to be the first actor in Chinese theatre (see Chapter 2).[8]

Early on, this ambivalence was also true of Western puppet theatre. In Germany, for instance, at the end of the 15th and beginning of 16th century, the expression *Himmelreich* ('kingdom of heaven') was introduced for a puppet show or perhaps the box of the puppet showman.[9] So far there has been no satisfactory explanation for this except that perhaps this religious appellation referred to the repertoire of plays which were mainly drawn from Biblical sources. But significantly there has been no attempt by scholars to attach any importance to the identification of the German puppet play with the 'kingdom of heaven' and this has very much to do with the general debased or ambivalent attitude towards puppets in the West. Unlike the Eastern attitude which regards the puppet as at once profane and divine, the early Western attitude shifted uneasily between dislike and regard.

To cite a few examples of dislike: We can read Sophocles own antipathy towards puppets through his character Athenaeos in *Deipnosophists* who reproached the citizens of Athens because they preferred puppets to the human staged characters of Euripides' plays and accused them of handing over the theatre of Dionysos to the marionettes of the *neuropastes* ('string-puller') Potheimos.[10] Until the 12th century there were hardly any clear records of puppet plays but after that more records were evident which suggested that they were beginning to be popular. In 1253 the minnesinger Meister Sigeher compared the way in which Pope Innocent IV behaved toward the German princes with a puppet play.[11] Martin Luther called the papacy "a public puppet show" and also referred to the "holy puppets" in a way that was clearly intended to be derogatory and reflected his own attitude towards puppets.[12] There were in fact very few references in illustrative form or text to puppets because itinerant jugglers with their puppet shows were not considered respectable and scholars felt that they would be demeaned to take notice of them. So the few scanty documentary records of actual puppet performances testify to the low esteem in which puppets were held. For example it is recorded that in 1363 Count Jan von Blois ordered a puppet show to be given in Dordrecht; in 1395 a man was paid for a puppet play he had presented before the Count of Holland and that in 1451 a ban was imposed on puppet-shows during Easter.[13] It is interesting that considering the antipathy the Fathers of the Church felt towards all manifestations of heathen culture including theatre, Clement of Alexandria, Tertullian and Synesius did not include puppets in their declamations.[14] Opinion is divided whether it was because puppet entertainments were considered utterly innocuous or that they were beneath contempt.[15]

Savonarola and 'The Burning of the Vanities'

The Catholic Church's strong condemnation of puppets came through the zealous figure of the Dominican monk and martyr Savonarola Giralamo (1452–1498) who rose to become the most influential man in Florence. In 1497, determined to transform the city into a 'Puritan' place, and impelled by voices and visions, he instituted a mammoth cleansing – 'Burning of the vanities' – in which masks, pictures, playbooks, play props and puppets, all regarded as works of the devil, were summarily burnt in a conflagration which eventually extended to include himself in 1498. But the heaviest condemnation of puppets was to be left to the Council of Trent (1550–64) which felt that their ribaldry and growing popularity with the common people were getting out of the Church's control[16] and attempts were made to ban, or at least secularize, the art to which the Church had originally given a name and function. Reform implied a distinction between the sacred and the profane and nowhere was this more ambiguous than in the ingenious use of 'moving statues'.

Moving Statues and the 'Boxley Rood of Grace'
A 7th century Church Council authorised the placing of a carved figure of Christ on the cross and distinguished between his representation as a symbolic figure – Sacrificial Lamb or Good Shepherd – and as an incarnation of the human.[17] From the carving of such figures developed the idea of 'moving roods' – the figure of Christ could be manipulated to move his eyes or mouth – and then to the rise of moving statuary in general. From the 8th century 'moving statues' were harnessed to the liturgy and used to make the Gospel accessible at particular yearly festivals inside and outside churches. This practice continued, despite canonical prescriptions against it, almost to the end of the 16th century. For example, there is an account of an elaborate ceremony referred to as 'The Mysteries of Mid August' which occurred in 1443 at the Church of St James at Dieppe, in which puppets, automata, and live actors combined to present a religious drama[18] which included God the Father, a figure of the Virgin, a host of large and small angels whose wings were animated in mid air, and a clown called *Grimpe-Sur-l'Ais*. The figures not only ascended and descended through the air, but were capable of an impressive range of movement. Similarly impressive were the Polish puppet nativity plays called *szupka* with their stages built to resemble churches, which have, astonishingly, been performed in an unbroken line in Poland since the thirteenth century.[19] Elsewhere though, the Catholic reformers were making it increasingly difficult for such performances to take place.

The Reformation extended and deepened these attacks with all the vigour of a new beginning as is rather delightfully shown by the episode of 'The Boxley

Rood of Grace',[20] a piece of moving statuary, originally installed in the English Cistercian Church at Boxley near Maidstone in 1144, by William de Ipres, Earl of Kent, and later burnt by the 16th century reformers after the dissolution of the monasteries. The story goes as follows: an English carpenter who was taken prisoner in the wars between England and France carved an ingenious crucifix for the purpose of using it as a means of his ransom. It was so excellently constructed that the figure of Christ was able *to bow down and lifte up it selfe, to shake and stirre the handes and feete, to nod the head, to rolle the eies, to wag the chaps, to bende the browes, and finally to represent to the eie, both the proper motion of each member of the body... With the intention of handing over this figure to a craftie College of Monkes, to deifie and make it passe for a verie God*, the carpenter placed the image on the back of a donkey and returned to England, coming as far as Rochester where he stopped at an alehouse for refreshment while allowing the donkey to go forward alone into the city. The donkey, as soon as it was out of its master's sight, lost its way, and, as though driven by some divine fury, arrived at the door of the Cistercian Abbey and kicked and bounced with its heels till the monks opened the door. The story went that the donkey ran hastily to a pillar where it stopped and would not be moved until the image was removed from its back and installed in that very place. The carpenter, following close behind, was unsuccessful in reclaiming his crucifix but for a sum of money left the Rood with the monks. According to the account – in *Foxe's Book of Martyres*, and therefore unlikely to be objective – the monks were thought to have exploited the lucrative uses to which the image could be put, encouraging superstitious worshippers, through its hidden mechanism, to give generously. Accordingly, *a piece of silver was received with frowning lip,* but a piece of gold caused the *jaws to wag merrily.* Many other picturesque details grew up around this wonderful figure which could *foam at the mouth, weep from the eys, and raise its hands in blessing.* One can imagine the utter delight of the Reformers to have discovered such a perfect justification for their wrath and *the miraculous rood which had bowed its head, and stirred its eys, was paraded through the roads from market town to market town, exposed to ridicule at Maidstone and St Paul's Cross, and eventually publicly burnt together with many images of the Virgin and saints.* What can be gleaned from this strange and semi-comic episode is that the more life-like moveable figures became and the greater their ability to enchant or bewitch audiences, the more they fell into disfavour and disrepute and their manipulators were branded as wizards or magicians who possessed 'little devils called marionettes'.[21] For example in the second half of the seventeenth century there is a record of one of the members of the famous Brioche family, renowned for their skill in puppetry, who barely escaped with his life while staging a show at Solothurn in Switzerland, because the inhabitants of the town suspected him of being a wizard.[22]

Inevitably too, as the skill of puppeteers improved and their popularity increased in a more secular age, both puppets and their manipulators attracted less the wrath of the Church (though in France in the seventeenth century, Bishop Bossuet was a fearsome adversary) and more the vituperation and envy of stage-actors who saw their takings reduced by competition from the puppet theatre. From 1676 the director La Grille produced his operas with string marionettes in the Marais district in Paris which attracted vast crowds because of the richness of the costumes, and the elaborateness of their stage settings. La Grille's puppet machinery enabled him to present fairy operas with ballets and complicated scene changes. There was no doubt that puppet popularity in the French capital was on the increase to such an extent that during the last years of the 17th century the actors forced the puppet stages out to the Parisian suburbs.[23] By this time any hostility towards puppets in Europe was largely secular and professional; as a popular art form they were an undoubted success. Not surprisingly, since the development of puppets outside the church also has a long, difficult and tortuous history.

Puppets and Their Secular Popularity

So far no written records of puppets in Western Europe between AD 400 to 1200 have been recovered and our knowledge of them has to be gathered from scattered references. A Bishop of Alexandria in the sixth century, for example, refers to little wooden figures seen dancing at weddings and moved by remote control.[24] It is assumed that many entertainers including puppeteers, though unrecorded, must have remained in Constantinople even after its fall to the Turks in 1453. According to some theories, Karagoz, the Turkish shadow puppet, is derived from a common original with Pulcinella[25] and many puppeteers must have continued with their trade in the provinces of the old Roman Empire though unchronicled by contemporaries. By the 10th century every court in Europe and every baron seemed to have a troupe of minstrels, jongleurs, troubadours and puppeteers representing as it were a powerful renaissance of old forms of entertainment. There is on record a description in the early 13th century Provencal romance *Flamenca* of a great aristocratic feast in honour of the King and Queen of France, given on St John's day at Bourbon, in the Auvergne. The entertainment which followed the feast included tumblers, dancers and 'puppet players'.[26] It seems to have been a magnificent celebration reminiscent of the 5th century BC Athenian banquet given by Callias, a wealthy dilettante, to a brilliant company of guests which included Socrates. Though no puppet entertainment was given at this banquet, the Syracusan, who had been hired to be the master of ceremonies, in response to a question put to him by Socrates about his activities and interests, unmistakably referred to his use of puppets at other celebrations.[27] Such entertainment in Ancient Greece was clearly for the privileged few but in the Middle Ages puppet entertainment had a far wider appeal. There is a recorded reference in 1408 of a puppeteer going to a French village along with his wife and children, a bear, a horse, a nanny goat and a trumpet, to entertain an audience of peasants.[28]

There is no doubt that in medieval Europe, religious and secular puppetry developed side-by-side, though by the early sixteenth century the shift from religious instruction to entertainment within the former and the inevitable addition of ribaldry and bawdiness had sufficiently alarmed the Church to withdraw its patronage. By then puppetry was sufficiently strong in its own right to survive and flourish as a popular form. It had also become a theatrical form that appealed to the highest levels of society, partly as entertainment and partly as relaxation after the cares of state. The difficulties of controlling human subjects certainly made the control of inanimate puppets a relief.[29]

The Battle of the Puppets
The popularity of actors in the wider social world was not easily maintained nor the hostility of actors easily avoided. The victory of the Puritans in 17th century England gave the puppet theatre a new lease of life, since it was the only form of theatre not forbidden by them, creating further indignation among the actors of Drury Lane who demanded unsuccessfully that all puppet plays should also be banned. In France, in the 18th century, actors and actor-managers did their utmost to make life difficult for puppeteers who were not allowed to give their puppets interactive dialogue, only stylized monologues being permitted.[30] In Germany the attacks on puppeteers were even more virulent: an 18th century Director of the Court theatre at Munich, Count Seeau, refused to permit the puppet theatre to play at the annual fairs while the historian of the Hamburg theatre, Schutz, called the puppets 'miseries', dangerous and demoralizing and attacked with special hatred the Kasperle theatre as 'pitiful trick puppets worked by vagabonds with thumb and forefinger.'[31] But despite all attacks the puppet theatre remained popular. In England, France and Germany, it managed to give voice to everything the regular theatres excluded and, for example, the German character *Hans Wurst*, much treasured by popular audiences and famous for his vulgarity, was given absolute freedom to satirize and attack well-known figures of the time with his large head, grotesque arms and hands, rolling eyes and sticking-out tongue. As a class, puppet showmen had become so numerous by the end of the 17th century that they formed a kind of guild with their own regulations and customs including a rule

that none of their play texts was to be written out but had to be learned by heart. By the first quarter of the 18th century marionettes were the rage all over Europe. But decline followed, in France at least, where, after the Revolution in 1789, scenes were presented on the puppet stage in which Polichinelle ended his life under the guillotine.[32]

As is now well known Polichinelle instead of coming to England directly from Italy, took a roundabout way and is variously known as Polichinelle, Punchinello or Mr Punch. Opinions differ as to whether the Stuarts brought him back with them from France or William of Orange introduced him from Holland but he appeared in England after the Revolution of 1688 with his wife Judy and his dog Toby, to become a great favourite.[33] But marionettes in general had never gone away and were particularly popular after the Reformation. There is an entry in the diary of Samuel Pepys on October 8 1662 that marionettes performed at Whitehall marking their entry to Court under Charles the Second. When Pepys visited a fair on August 30th 1667, to his astonishment he met Lady Castlemaine, the King's mistress, in a puppet theatre where the presentation was *Patient Grizell*.[34] And throughout the whole of the next century puppet popularity in England remained high, their themes not being confined to legend or the Bible and their performances involving jigs, sarabandes, and quadrilles. Addison and Steele popularized Mr Powell, one of the most eminent puppet-showmen in England, in their weekly papers.[35] The puppet stage also adopted the plays of Shakespeare and the general respect for puppets was increased by the endorsement of that arbiter of quality, Samuel Johnson. The great man settled the rivalry between the puppet stage and the regular theatre by declaring that marionettes performed much better than living actors. He even declared that *Macbeth* was more impressive in the puppet theatre than on the human stage.[36]

Puppets and their Advocates

From the 18th century onwards there is an impressive list of puppet lovers in Europe like the French novelist George Sand,[37] Moliere, Rousseau, Charles

Dickens,[38] Maurice Maeterlinck,[39] Goldoni, Goethe,[40] and Stanislavsky. George Bernard Shaw places his emphasis on the ability of the puppet to impose on the imagination and this has certainly found an echo in the recommendations of twentieth century pedagogues that puppets should be used 'in the interests of the artistic education of our children.' This is because of the special rules on which the marionette stage is based and the fact that 'the possibilities of expression confined within narrowly marked boundaries, demand of the audience a specific exercise of its imagination.'[41] The power of the imagination, shaped by dramatic economy, is the unquestioned premise of Chinese puppetry in which, in an often quoted axiom, the puppeteer declares that 'in one breath he can tell a thousand ancient tales and with two hands create the dance of a million soldiers'. The glorification of the imagination, and the swing from realism to romanticism and symbolism in the late 19th century was conducive to reviving interest in puppets whose status in the West has, as we have seen, been somewhat fluctuating. To some dramatists, puppets alone were capable of expressing poetry 'without a distracting wilfulness', since the puppet is the true expression of the artist's idea, while the living actor's personality is intrusive and tends to obstruct true expression of thought.[42] So dramatists who found regular actors too coarse and obstinate in their interpretation of their pieces, yearned for the 'purity' of the puppet theatre. The puppet represented a certain kind of stylization, 'a reaching backward from the stylelessness of naturalism to style and to powerful form'.[43] Shaw wrote in glowing terms about the puppet performance of the Italian puppet-showman Vittorio Podrecca, the founder of the famous *Teatro dei Piccoli* in Rome,[44] as did the great actress Elenora Duse, in a letter to the *maestro*: 'I envy you. I too should have liked to be the director of a puppet troupe. Your actors do not talk, but obey; mine talk and do not obey'.[45]

Puppets, the Longing for a Lost Paradise and Heinrich Von Kleist
Behind this power struggle, as it were, lies a deeper human need: the longing for innocence, childhood and a lost paradise. Max von Boehn, quoting the phrase

'homesickness for childhood', as used by the theatre scholar, Carl Niessen, makes the interesting point that the puppets and shadow plays of the Far East roused this emotion in eighteenth century western travellers and merchants who saw them.[46] But it was the 19th century German poet, Heinrich von Kleist in his essay *Über Die Marionetten Theater* ('On the Marionette Theatre') which appeared in a Berlin newspaper in 1810, who really explored the connection by recognizing the divinity in puppets. This article, though generally considered brilliant, has provoked controversy. Heinrich von Kleist's seminal point that the puppet is the first blueprint of man, having been constructed, as it were, as the perfect model of movement before the Fall, has sometimes been missed and the essay generally interpreted as a discussion of man and the loss of paradise with the only possibility of re-entry coming after 'wandering through the world' and the acquisition of 'ever broader, higher, divinely striving knowledge and self-resignation to his lost innocence'. Kleist's article is not just a camouflaged study of man using the puppet as a decoy,[47] but, as its title suggests, about marionettes and the intricacies of their functioning which serve to show up the imperfections of human movements after the Fall. The pivotal reference is to the third chapter of Genesis which equates the discovery of self-consciousness with the Fall and the ensuing sense of separation and loss of harmony.

What is valuable about Kleist's essay[48] is that rather than embarking on a general paen of praise to marionettes he focuses sharply on the special characteristics of their mechanism and so clarifies what he considers the superiority of puppet movement to that of human performers. The picture which emerges, as far as marionettes are concerned, is not that of each limb being individually moved by the operator but that of each movement having its centre of gravity which is sufficient to control that within the puppet. Once that control is established, the limbs which are only pendulums, follow mechanically of their own accord. Kleist is most illuminating when he refers to the specially subtle relationship existing between the movements of the puppeteer's fingers and the movements of the puppets attached to them, comparing it to 'the relationship between numbers and their logarithms'.[49] This comparison is extended to the idea of phantom or artificial limbs, an idea which opens up the entire inner world of movement where imagined or intentional body movements are helpful in understanding, defining, and perceiving space.[50] Referring to those who have been unfortunate enough to have lost their limbs, Kleist speaks of them dancing with their replaced artificial legs in the way a marionette operator dances with the marionettes he is manipulating on stage. It is known that those who have lost a limb still feel the pain and sense the ability to move the limb which is no longer there. This calls up for us the world of inner volition, which when applied to the control of marionettes, gives an inkling of the internal process which is translated into their external movements. The *feeling* of moving a limb seems to be even more powerful than the actual movement of one. This is where the line the centre of gravity has to follow is, in the final analysis, mysterious and Kleist compares it to 'the path taken by the soul of the dancer'.[51] In Zen thought this is put simply: 'the subject must merge with the object'; from this perspective, the marionette operator and his marionette are as indistinguishable as the swordsman and his sword in the battle for victory.

Kleist is also the first writer about marionettes to explain the effect of 'affectation' on the centre of gravity in the movements of both the marionette and the human performer. Affectation is, in Kleist's own words:

when the soul, or moving force, appears at some point other than the centre of gravity of the movement. Because the operator controls with his wire or thread only this centre, the attached limbs are just only what they should be... lifeless, pure pendulums, governed only by the law of gravity. This is an excellent quality. You'll look for it in vain in most of our dancers.[52]

In Kleist's view affectation has the power to displace the centre of gravity in movement and it is this which makes the intrusion of ego fatal to the execution of movement. But because marionettes, unlike human actors, can never be 'guilty of affectation', they become the perfect models of movement. Kleist quotes an illustration of the intrusion of the ego and the consequent loss of innocence in an incident which he himself witnessed: at the baths, a graceful young friend of his, at first unconsciously, and without awareness, replicates perfectly the action of a boy pulling a thorn out of his foot in a picture which they had seen at an exhibition in Paris, but could not repeat it when he tried self-consciously to reproduce the act. It is this which makes Kleist equate the ego-less movements of puppets, completely devoid of any sense of affectation, with prelapsarian grace:

Grace appears most purely in that human form which either has no consciousness or an infinite consciousness. That is, in the puppet or in the god.[53]

Although Kleist's essay has been called, by a fellow writer, Hugo Von Hofmannsthal, 'the most perceptive piece of philosophy since Plato', his comments on puppets belonging to a 'Paradisal' order have not been taken very seriously even though the term for puppet-show in the 15th and 16th centuries in Germany, as we have seen, was *himmelreich* ('the kingdom of heaven'). It is interesting in this connection, that the puppet in the East and particularly in China has sometimes been elevated to the status of a deity as in the case of the 8th century Marshal Tian (see Chapter 3) but there is another connection between Kleist's puppet model and 'Marshal' Tian, since soldiering was also the tradition of the Kleists and by his time the family could boast twenty generals and marshals. Kleist himself was an officer of the Prussian Guards and well acquainted with discipline and imposed form. It cannot be a coincidence that martial discipline and puppet movements seem to go hand-in-hand as has been shown in the earlier discussion of the puppet-based art of *T'ai Chi Ch'uan* which is closely connected with self defence, martial arts and the battle against evil spirits.[54] Puppet movement has, it would seem, an intrinsic, life-giving, quality, which is, in the end, even more significant than its gracefulness.

Edward Gordon Craig and the Über-Marionette

It would take another century before the arrival of Edward Gordon Craig whose famous essay on *The Actor and the Über-Marionette*,[55] written in 1906, singles out, like Kleist's article, the ego element as the central difference between pieces of wood and living actors. Referring to the absolute reliability of puppets, Craig wrote: 'The applause may thunder or dribble, their hearts beat no faster, no slower, their signals do not grow hurried or confused'.[56] While Kleist's essay was written cautiously and made little impact, Craig's passion for puppets pours out and is far more widely known, influencing William Butler Yeats (see Chapter 1) and Etienne Decroux, whose advocacy of marionettes will be discussed at the end of this chapter. Craig's essay which was incorporated in his collection *On the Art of the Theatre*, was published in December 1911 by Heinemann, and went into many editions and eight languages. Because he had quoted Eleonora Duse's famous saying at the beginning of his essay: 'To save the theatre, the Theatre must be destroyed, the actors and actresses must all die of the plague....They make art impossible', he was accused of literally wanting to replace all actors with pieces of wood. But his critics had failed to understand him and so in his new preface to the 1924 edition of *On the Art of the Theatre* he wrote:

> *I no more want to see the living actors replaced by things of wood than the great Italian actress of our day wants all the Actors to die. The Über Marionette is the actor plus fire, minus Egotism: the fire of the gods and demons, without the smoke and Steam of mortality.*[57]

What Craig was really saying was that the puppet should be the inspiration, not the replacement, of the human actor. In puppet movement he saw the key to human performance in which the actor, stripped of his ego, presents rather than impersonates. In a sense Craig is not writing about puppets at all, but using his observations on them to invest human acting with a new power. What is not in doubt is his own appreciation and knowledge of the puppet theatre. This is evident in the puppet plays he wrote initially for the amusement of his two children whom he was missing during his stay at Marina di Pisa. His plays filled three box-files and they were collectively called *The Drama for Fools,* all written by 'Tom Fool', his latest pseudonym.[58] He began to take great interest in Signor Podrecca's marionette theatre in Rome and travelled to Turin and Milan to study the permanent theatres there. In August 1918 he published his new little magazine which he called *The Marionette* but which he referred to as really a 'performance ... for Fools'. The editor was again Tom Fool, this time a court jester figure with special license to trounce everyone and yet go unpunished. The venture was in fact a kind of sublimation of his original scheme of establishing a marionette theatre in Rome. The first number of *The Marionette* was dated April 1, the second number March 15 – the last number dated August 1918, although published in July 1919, so even the dates 'fooled about'.[59] Indeed, after the disintegration of the Arena Goldoni in Florence in 1914, and the collapse of his *School for the Art of the Theatre* there, the year before – Craig had established a complex consisting of an open-air theatre, workrooms, store-rooms and offices – his vision of a new kind of theatre where the ideal actor is symbolized by the marionette, was regarded almost as an April Fool's joke. He referred to the destruction of all his models, dreams and works succinctly in *The Theatre Advancing* in 1921: 'It came in 1913; it went in 1914 ... For the war swept it away, and my supporter did not see the value of keeping the engine fires *banked*. So the fires went out.' At the end of his essay, *The Actor and the Über-Marionette*, after referring to the contempt with which puppets were regarded by many, Craig fearlessly reiterates his claim that 'they are the descendants of a great and noble family of Images, images which were made in the likeness of God.'

While Craig's ideas were slow to take root in England, he had greater success in Germany where the actor Max Reinhardt, who had been producing plays since 1902 at the Kleines Theater in Berlin, seized on them with an enthusiasm which he spread to the whole German-speaking stage so that a *Craigische Vorstellung* became an accepted expression for a performance on the lines he advocated.[60] Indeed it is generally true that Craig's ideas had a far greater impact outside England. In 1930 the King of Denmark decorated him with the Order of the Knights of the Dannebrøg for his services to the Theatre while the Danish actor Johannes Poulsen referred to him as someone who 'has written his name in ineffaceable letters on the sky of the European mind'.[61] No doubt this maverick figure with his love of puppets was a true visionary.

William Butler Yeats and Marionettes

The year 1910 marked the beginnings of Craig's fruitful relationship with the Irish poet and playwright William Butler Yeats. In Milan he made four drawings for the latter's *Plays for an Irish Theatre, Deirdre, The Hour Glass,* and *On Baile's Strand* and in 1911, the year Heinemann issued Craig's *On the Art of the Theatre,* Yeats used Craig's famous 'screens' for the first time in a play of his performed at the Abbey Theatre in Dublin. In February 1914, Yeats sailed for America where he delivered three lectures, one of them on the innovative work of Craig. So having absorbed Craig's ideas of the marionette as the ideal actor, it came as no surprise that in the publication of his Noh-inspired play *At the Hawk's Well* in 1917, Yeats' directions to his actors (in this instance aimed at the actor playing the 'Old Man' but also, in Yeats' own words, 'relevant to the other persons in the play'), stipulated that their movements must 'suggest a marionette'.[62] There is a photo showing Michio Ito, who originally danced the role of the 'Hawk Woman', playing the role of the 'Old Man', and striking an attitude strongly resembling that of a marionette.[63] Undoubtedly, Yeats, inspired by Craig, can be regarded as a strong advocate of marionettes, particularly since he recommended his actors to move like them in his first Eastern-based play, but no claim can be justifiably made that he significantly shifted the primarily indifferent Western attitude towards marionettes. Indeed, though nearly a century has elapsed since their publication, Yeats' plays are still not regarded as mainstream theatre in the West.

Etienne Decroux and his use of the Marionette Image

The final figure on my list of strong Western allies of the marionette is Etienne Decroux (1898–1991) who, in Craig's words, can be regarded as creating an 'ABC of mime' partly based on his observations of the workings of a marionette. The crucial point for him was the actor's need to 'fight against his nature', in other words his ego. After witnessing a performance of Decroux and his troupe in 1945, Craig's admiration of the French mime was unmistakable:

I have travelled far in Europe, visiting many cities in Holland, Germany, Russia, Italy, England and Scotland – but till this day I have never seen anything comparable to this attempt.... We were present at the creation of an alphabet, an ABC of mime.

Like Craig who strongly influenced his thinking, and like Yeats, Decroux's advocacy of marionettes has not hugely changed Western attitudes towards the puppet either in terms of theatrical utility or as a metaphor for movement, but it is interesting that Decroux unconsciously resembles Zeami Motokiyo (see Chapter 5) in that both have established a codified grammar of movement with reference to the marionette.[64] Decroux was a student at the Vieux-Colombier School from 1923–1925 when under the tutelage of Jacques Copeau (1879–1949) and the lead teacher Suzanne Bing, the students were working on the Noh play *Kantan* for production in 1926. Only a single performance took place because of an injury suffered by a member of the cast but Copeau referred to the Noh project as 'one of the jewels, one of the secret riches of the work of the Vieux Colombier', in terms of the lessons of restraint, economy, control and concentration it imparted to all who participated in it.[65] Although Decroux has never officially admitted to being influenced by Noh drama, he is quoted as having confided in Jacques Lecoq when they were teaching at the Piccolo Teatro in Milan that 'he hoped to make the students there move like Japanese actors.'[66]

Decroux, Zeami, the Principle of Opposition and the Marionette

Both Zeami and Decroux pinpointed the principle of opposition as a basis for effective movement in their work. In the section entitled *What is felt in the Heart is ten; What appears in Movement is seven,* included in his seminal treatise *Kakyô* ('A Mirror Held to the Flower'), Zeami revealed the duality encoded in his methodology of creating effective movement in the Noh: the full force of inner movement is checked or opposed by the restraint of outer movement. Decroux's similar reliance on the principle of opposition was couched in a more abstract way:

> *Beautiful movements are difficult. This perhaps arises from the fact that, since the beauty we have in mind is the corporeal expression of civilization, in order to achieve it, we must fight against our nature.*[67]

From this one can see why both the Noh and Decroux's theory of Corporeal Mime advocate the suppression of the ego as the starting point of all movement and, understandably, the marionette, as the supreme symbol of egolessness, features prominently in the French and Japanese grammars of movement. Broadly speaking, Decroux's training system was based on four basic character types of which the marionette is the last, while in Zeami's acting treatises on movement, the string puppet has a central position (see Chapter 5). Both masters of movement however did not put forward a reason why the marionette has been chosen as a symbol of opposition. For this we have to go back to Plato's ideas on the symbolism of puppets which has, of course, persuaded some scholars to maintain that all puppets stemmed from Greece rather than from India:[68]

> *We may imagine that each of us living creatures is a puppet made by gods, possibly as a plaything or possibly with some more serious purpose. That indeed is more than we can tell but one thing is certain:*

these interior states are, so to say, the cords or strings by which we are worked; they are opposed to one another and pull us with opposite tensions in the direction of opposite actions, and therein lies the division of virtue from vice.[69]

This is regarded to be one of the earliest available references to puppets. Without becoming embroiled in the still unresolved question of the true origin of the puppet, Plato's observation on string puppets and the way that they can be manipulated in two different directions, made in the 5th century BC, serves to illustrate the effectiveness of using the marionette as a symbol of opposition and the tensional basis of effective movement. Decroux explored the principle of opposition further by advocating that his mime should cover his face with a cloth in order to bring out in clearer relief the movements of his torso.[70] Zeami developed his opposition concept into a rule: violent body movements must be followed by gentle foot movements and vice versa[71] So, irrespective of the different attitudes towards the puppet in East and West, the marionette with its encoded two-way possibility of moving in opposite directions, has served as a universally effective model for the production of tension as the basis of eloquent movement.

The still current dispute about the puppet's origin is at least indicative of the different way it has been regarded in the West. Whereas Richard Pischel in *Der Heimat des Puppenspiels* ('The Home of the Puppet Play') puts forward a strong case for India to be regarded as its cradle, William Ridgeway in *The Dramas and Dramatic Dances of Non-European Races* challenges this claim and suggests that India rather than Europe has been the borrower. In his words:

The puppet play is not the origin of the drama, but a cheap means of placing famous historical dramas within reach of the populace... And when we come face to face with the historical fact relating to puppet entertainment, we find their dates to be comparatively recent.[72]

There is no doubt that Professor Ridgeway's view has gained support and that the puppet art is still regarded as a poor relative of human theatre, in danger of being further diminished. Even in the East, with increasing competition from television and film, this is becoming so. Whatever current attitudes, the visionary ideal of the Western theatre theorists and practitioners quoted above, remain perceptive and important. Men like Craig, Yeats and Decroux have something fundamental to say to us about the nature of acting seen through their observation of puppet and puppet-based forms and the relationship between control and freedom. What better way to end this chapter than with the words of perhaps the marionette's most eloquent advocate, Edward Gordon Craig, the visionary whose theatrical dream of 'a supremely beautiful creature – something like a Greek statue – which could be made to move and could be controlled like a marionette, but would not suffer from, or be affected by, emotions' – still haunts our imagination:

> *If you could make your body into a machine, or into a dead piece of material such as clay, and if it could obey you in every movement for the entire space of time it was before the audience... you would be able to make a work of art out of that which is in you. For you would not only have dreamt, you would have executed to perfection; and that which you had executed could be repeated time after time without so much difference as between two farthings.*[73]

Notes and References

1. Max von Boehn, *Dolls and Puppets,* tr. Josephine Nicoll, London: George G. Harrap & Co., Ltd., 1932, p. 5.
2. See 'The Actor and the Uber-Marionette' in Edward Gordon Craig, *On the Art of the Theatre,* London: Heinemann, 1911, p. 90.
3. The term 'marionette' was often applied to any kind of puppet – whether hand, string, or rod – and the word 'motion' seems at one time or another to have been used to describe every conceivable type of puppet, automaton, peep show, or *theatrum mundi.* See Malkin, 1977, p. 24.
4. See Charles Magnin, *Histoire des Marionettes en Europe del Antiquite a temps Moderne,* Paris 1862, Reprint, Paris: Slatkine-Geneve, 1981, p, 61.
5. This is also true, etymologically, of the role of the female medium and puppet in China where the same word *ang* is used to represent both 'medium' and 'puppet'. See Chapter 2.
6. Malkin, 1977, p. 18.
7. Boehn, 1932, p. 309.
8. When we look at the buffoon Vidusaka in early Sanskrit Indian drama, gluttonous, ugly, hump-backed and bald, we find nearly all his characteristics reproduced in the Western puppet 'buffoon'. In England he is called *Jack Pudding*; in France *Jean Potage*; in Holland *Pekel Haaning* ('Pickle Herring') and in Germany *Hanswurst* ('Hans the Sausage') and later *Kasper* or *Kasperle.* But whereas in the West the buffoon's lowness came to detract from the status of puppetry, in the East, as in *Wajang Purwa* (puppet show) in Java where Indian culture disseminated, the comic figure Semar is regarded as a deity. In Quanzhou, as I've shown, Marshal Tian, the puppet deity, is regarded both as the 'Divine Musician' and the 'Divine Jester'.
9. Boehn, 1932, p. 304.
10. Ibid., p. 299.
11. Ibid., p. 300.
12. Ibid., p. 301.
13. Ibid., p. 302.
14. Ibid., p. 300.
15. George Speaight, *The History of the English Puppet Theatre,* Second edition, London: Robert Hale, 1990, p. 28.
16. See Charles Magnin, 1981, p. 57.
17. Ibid., p. 53.
18. Malkin, 1977, p. 19.
19. Ibid.
20. See Chapter X1 'The Boxley Rood of Grace' in Sidney Heath, *In the Steps of the Pilgrims*, London: Rich and Cowan, 1953, p. 186. (This was originally published in 1911 as *Pilgrim Life in the Middle Ages.*)
21. Boehn, 1932, p. 312
22. Ibid.
23. Ibid.

24. Speaight, 1990, p.28.
25. Ibid., Note 15, p. 275.
26, Ibid., p. 29.
27. Ibid., p. 25.
28. Ibid., p. 28.
29. We have seen in the case of the first Chinese Emperor Qin Shi Huang Di, (see Chapter 3) that an obsession with puppets provided just such an antidote to the strain of controlling a huge empire. His counterpart in the West was Charles V, the Holy Roman Emperor of Germany, Spain and the Netherlands, who was at the centre of the struggles in Europe between reform and conservatism, Imperial and Papal power. Not surprisingly, power juggling wore him out and he turned to the solace of puppets where the control mechanism was more predictable and within human grasp. In 1557 Charles V abdicated in favour of his sons Ferdinand and Phillip and retired to the monastery of Yuste in Estremadura in Spain where he kept an eye on things behind the scenes. He was accompanied in his retirement by Giovanni Torriani from Cremona who was well known as an improver of the mechanism of puppets. It was at this time in Italy that great attempts were made to perfect the marionette and at Yuste, Charles V in retirement after struggling for years with the intricacies of controlling a huge empire, was supposed to have shot pigeons, and made puppet soldiers with Torriani, closely observing the operations and experiments of the latter to improve the mechanism of control in a puppet. He must have learned many lessons about mechanical control from this master maker of clocks and mechanical toys, which unfortunately were not wholly applicable to controlling human affairs. See Edward Armstrong's article on Charles V, Holy Roman Emperor, in *Encyclopaedia Brittanica*, Vol.5 (11th edition), London and New York: Encyclopaedia Co., Ltd., 1910–11, pp. 899–905. See also Sir W.Stirling-Maxwell, *The Cloister Life of the Emperor Charles V,* London, 1852.
30. Boehn,1932, p. 318.
31. Ibid.
32. Ibid., p. 322.
33. Ibid., p. 317.
34. Ibid., p. 323.
35. Ibid.
36. Ibid., p. 324.
37. Ibid., p. 345.
38. Ibid., 341.
39. Ibid., p. 348.
40. Ibid., p.320.
41. Ibid., pp. 396–7.
42. Ibid., p. 393.
43. Ibid., p. 395.
44. Ibid., p. 426.
45. Ibid., p. 395.
46. Ibid.

47. This seems to be the view of Boehn. See ibid., pp. 326–8.
48. See the entire essay in Idris Parry, 1981, op. cit., pp. 9–18.
49. Ibid., p.14.
50. See Merleau Ponty, *Phenomenology of Perception*, tr. Colin Smith, London: Routledge, 1989, pp. 80–82.
51. Idris Parry, 1981, p. 14.
52. Ibid., p. 15.
53. Ibid., p. 18.
54. Compare the puppet-like art of Kathakali in Kerala which was originally military-based. The puppet-loving Dravidians were the original inhabitants of Kerala. When the Aryans penetrated Kerala this started a productive synthesis of two cultures and Kathakali was born. In 400 AD, the Nayar militia, led by warlords, became prominent and at one time only the Nayars could participate in Kathakali performances, and next to the Brahmins, they were the most powerful group. See Beryl de Zoete, *The Other Mind: A Study of Dance in South India*, London: Gollancz 1953, p.94.
55. At first Craig referred to his ideal figure as a 'being' and then later used a word compounded from French and German.
56. Craig, 1911, p. 82.
57. Janet Leeper, *Edward Gordon Craig*, Harmondsworth, Middlesex: Penguin Books Ltd., 1948, p. 22.
58. It is interesting that as in the East, Craig identified puppetry with foolery. See Edward Craig, *Gordon Craig: The Story of his Life*, New York: Alfred A. Knopf, 1968, p. 302.
59. Ibid., p. 306.
60. Leeper, 1948, p. 15.
61. Ibid., p. 30.
62. See W. B. Yeats, *The Collected Plays of W.B. Yeats*, London: Macmillan & Co. Ltd., 1934, p. 210.
63. See Shataro Oshima,*W.B. Yeats and Japan*, Tokyo: Hokuseido Press, 1965, plate 27. Michio Ito's brother, Kisaku Ito, who made the masks for a production of Yeats' earlier play *The Hour Glass*, had for a long time been involved in the making and manipulation of marionettes. The Ito family must have contributed to Yeats' love of marionettes.
64. See Wylie-Marques' article entitled 'Zeami Motokiyo and Etienne Decroux: Twin Reformers of the Art of Mime' in Benito Ortolani and Samuel Leiter, eds., *Zeami and the Nô Theatre in the World*, New York: Casta Publication, 1998, pp. 109–126.
65. Jacques Copeau, *Souvenirs du Vieux Colombier*, Paris: Nouvelle Editiones Latines, 1931, p. 11.
66. Thomas Leabhart, *Modern and Post-Modern Mime*, New York: St Martin's Press, 1989, pp. 31–32.
67. Etienne Decroux, *Words on Mime*, Claremont,California: Mime Journal 1985, p. 128.

68. See Henryk Jurkowski, *A History of European Puppets from its origins to the end of the 19th century,* Lewiston, Queenston, Lampeter: Edwin Mellen Press Ltd., 1996. He notes that Pischel's conclusions about India as the cradle of puppetry have been challenged particularly by Fritz Echler (author of *Das Wesendes Handpupen und Marionettenspiele,* (1937) who thought that puppets follow dance and Hermann Reich who believed that all puppets stem from Greece
69. See A.E. Taylor, (tr.) *Plato, The Laws,* (Book 1), London: J.M.Dent & Sons Ltd, 1969, p. 22.
70. Ortolani, 1998, p. 114.
71. Rimer, 1984, p. 7.
72. See Speaight, 1990, p. 27.
73. Craig, 1911, pp. 70–71.

Postscript

> *As emotions were the first motives which induced men to speak, his first utterances were tropes. Figurative language was the first to be born, proper meanings were the last to be found. Things were called by their true name only when they were seen in their true form. The first speech was all in poetry; reasoning was thought of long afterwards.*
> J.J. Rousseau, 1783. 'Essai sur l'origine des langues'.

This study has not come to any clear conclusions about the origin of the Asian Birdwoman or solved long-standing controversies about the true home of the string puppet. Neat conclusions or solutions to such subjects are probably impossible and certainly outside the scope of this book. My purpose has been to explore relationships and make connections across a range of puppet and human theatres in a number of Asian countries in order to account for their similarities of movement. On this journey, the presiding image, as it were, has been that of the 'Birdwoman', whether in myth, history, or that borderland between the two which is far better understood in the East than in the West. Indeed, running beneath all my research, which has been largely performance and story based, is a deeper and older debate about the validity of oral versus textual evidence, a debate which again I believe to be more complex in an Eastern context. Western scholars like John Miles Foley have already pointed out that the so-called dichotomy between these two kinds of evidence is a huge oversimplification and my experience in watching, and exploring the background to, a number of Eastern theatrical performances amply bears this out.

Take, for example, the performance I witnessed in the summer of 1994 given by the Quanzhou Municipal Marionette Troupe of the famous play *Mu Lien Saves His Mother*. It was performed, as I have described, in August, the month of *pu du*, when it is customary to placate the spirits of wandering ghosts, and therefore was seen to have a propitiatory, exorcistic, function, though there was perhaps a more down-to-earth reason for the performance in the shape of an attractive fee provided by a visiting group of wealthy Japanese patrons. Whatever the motives, the show itself – a lively, often scatological, affair laced with doggerel and word-play – served as an uproarious purging of communal tensions. It also had the feel of something totally improvised and playful, drawing on a tradition of story-telling and vaudeville passed down orally over many generations. In fact, if you look up at the puppeteers, during the show, you find them turning the pages of a text: every word of the play has been written down and pinned to the back of the stage, a fact which was a source of pride for its performers who cherished and honoured a piece of writing that had been compiled from an oral tradition or traditions but at some point committed to paper and adhered to. No separation between the literary and oral tradition here and it is not perhaps surprising that puppeteers, who, unlike actors, had never been banned in China from sitting for the civil examinations, should hold the written word in high respect.

If this 'moment of truth' in Quanzhou illustrates the thin divide between the oral and the written in Chinese theatrical tradition, the story of Marshal Tian – and by extension, that of other important figures in this book, including Lady Jôruri – is a warning against drawing similarly clear-cut conclusions about their 'historicity'. There is no primary evidence for the birth of Marshal Tian in Quanzhou but its inhabitants have no doubt that he was born there and continue to revere his life and memory. He has become for the Fukienese, as I have shown, the 'patron saint' of their string puppet theatre with a temple dedicated to him and his image widely available in shops. He is credited with the transfer of puppet-like movements to the human stage and even today, Chinese actors – still referred to as 'Children of the Pear Garden' – are told to think of themselves as puppets moved by an invisible puppeteer. Many Western scholars remain sceptical of this kind of connection, distrusting the hyperbole and symbolism of the 'evidence', but as Wu Jie Chiu, the leading Chinese scholar on Marshal Tian pointed out to me in Quanzhou, within the context of Chinese thought and conventions of expression, the confrontation between Emperor Ming Huang and his new young protegé, the story of a jade flute brought from the moon and the subsequent development of Tian's influence and 'canonisation', represent an acceptable way of describing an important theatrical phenomenon. Tian's 'historicity', for the Chinese, lies in the theatre that survives him and the work of its practitioners.

The same is true of Lady Jôruri. Here too the attitudes of local people together with the living evidence of an ancient but still thriving theatrical form that originally bore her name, overrule doubts about her historicity. The French ethno-psychologist, George Devereux, has written eloquently about the connection between fantasy and reality, showing how one may buttress the other and for the people of Yahagi there is little doubt that the 'fantasy' of Lady Jôruri has become a vital part of the town's self-confidence. As for the 'truth' of her life and death, an anecdote concerning my last visit to one of her memorial sites is revealing. It is said that the site in question, the Takisanji Temple, holds Lady Jôruri's *kôtô*, her favourite instrument and a mark of her musical skill. I arrived at the temple towards evening, shortly before the temple keeper was due to lock up. However she allowed me to go round the site, watching with an enigmatic smile, as I examined and checked dates and descriptions on my map and in my notebook. When I asked to see the *kôtô*, she said that it was locked, kept behind closed doors and not available to visitors. Had she seen it herself? A smile. Did she believe in the reality of Lady Jôruri? Another smile. This temple-keeper, like the town of Yahagi itself, knew the truth of what Devereux and indeed Sigmund Freud have claimed: what is significant to people and institutions is not the evidence of an actual historical event so much as the account and memory of the past through a powerful story.

I began this book with the image of the twenty-four flying Birdwomen in the Kai Yuan Temple, Quanzhou, connecting them with other Birdwomen in Japan, Thailand and Malaysia and citing the fictional Lady Jôruri and the historical Yang Kuei Fei as examples of heroines whose sacrifice and death linked them with the Birdwoman myth and with the controlling symbolism of string puppetry. I would like to end with a story about another Birdwoman, whose picture serves as frontispiece to this book and whom I have discussed in the context both of Japanese Noh Drama and the plays of W.B. Yeats: the heroine of Zeami Motokiyo's *Hagoromo* ('The Feather Robe'). It is believed that after recovering her feather robe from the Fisherman, she flew back to Heaven from the pinewoods of Mio Bay in Suruga (Shizuoka Prefecture). This was the location which Zeami had chosen for the setting of his play and the original material he drew on – mainly local history legends – mentioned the descent of some heavenly maidens to bathe in a lake or the sea nearby. Hundreds of miles away from this legendary site, in the city of Osaka, there is a train station called Hagoromo with a nearby stretch of pinewood, said to resemble a similar stretch at Mio Bay. The day before I returned to London from Japan in the spring of 2000, I was taken by taxi from the station to the pinewood. On the way, the driver was adamant that for the people of the area the story of *Hagoromo* was a precious one, and that the myth, in defiance of geography, belonged to them. Once again, the line from legend to drama to 'memorial site' had been preserved and given physical expression. Fiction had once more become reality.

My exploration of the Birdwoman story and its connection with the theatres of the East and the movements of its actors has taken me seven years and three long journeys to complete. Perhaps, as I have indicated, 'complete' is not the right word, since the territory I have chosen to explore is hard to define and even harder to map. What I hope I have been able to show is that this image of the power of women, trapped and free, in the legends and theatres of Japan, China, Malaysia and Thailand – an image which can be found mirrored in other parts of the world – has affected the functions and forms of these theatres and the lives of their communities and continues to resonate in their performances today.

Poh Sim Plowright, August 2001

Bibliography

Aldington, Richard & Delano Ames. trs. *New Larousse Encyclopedia of Mythology*. Twickenham, Middlesex: The Hamlyn Publishing Group Ltd., 1959.
Amin, P.L. Sweeney. *The Ramayana and the Malay Shadow Play*. Kuala Lumpur: The National University of Malaysia Press, 1972.
Araki, James T. *The Ballad Drama of Medieval Japan*. Berkeley and Los Angeles: University of California Press, 1964.
Baird, Bill. *The Art of the Puppet Theater*. New York: Macmillan, 1965.
Berry, Mary Elizabeth. *Hideyoshi*. Cambridge, Massachusetts, London: Harvard University Press, 1982.
Blacker, Carmen. *The Catalpa Bow: A Study of Shamanistic Practices in Japan*. London: George Allen & Unwin, 1975.
Bordahl, Vibeke. *The Eternal Storyteller: Oral Literature in Modern China*. Richmond, Surrey: Curzon Press, 1999.
Brazell, Karen. tr. *The Confessions of Lady Nijo*. New York: Anchor Press and Doubleday, 1973.
Bruce, Derek. tr. *Wisdom of the Daoist Masters*. (from Leon Wieger, *Les Pères du Système Taoiste*). Lampeter: Llanerch Enterprise, 1984.
Campbell, Joseph. *Primitive Mythology: the Masks of God*. Harmondsworth: Penguin Books, 1976.
----------. *The Hero with a Thousand Faces*. Princeton: Princeton University Press, 1949.
----------. *The Myth of the Eternal Return*. London, New York: Arkana Press, 1989.
Carter, Angela. *Fireworks*. London: Virago Press, 1988.
Chan, Wing-tsit. tr. *A Source Book in Chinese Philosophy*. Princeton: Princeton University Press, 1963.
Cheng, Man-ch'ing & Robert Smith. *T'ai Chi: The "Supreme Ultimate" Exercise for Health, Sport and Self-Defense*. Rutland, Vermont: Charles Tuttle Co., 1967.
Collicut, Martin, et al. *Cultural Atlas of Japan*. Oxford: Maidon Press Ltd., 1988.
Cooper, Michael. tr. and ed. *This Island of Japan*. Tokyo & New York: Kodansha International, 1973.
Craig, Edward. *Gordon Craig: The Story of His Life*. New York: Alfred A. Knopf, 1968.
Craig, Edward Gordon. *On the Art of the Theatre*. London: Heinemann, 1911.
Creel, H.G. *Chinese Thought*. New York: New American Library of World Literature, 1953.
----------. *Confucius: The Man and the Myth*. London: Routledge & Kegan Paul, 1951.
Decroux, Etienne. *Words on Mime*. tr. Mark Piper. Claremont, CA: Mime Journal, 1985.

de Groot, J.J.M. *The Religious System of China*. Vols. 1-6, Leyden: E.J. Brill, 1892–1910.

de Silva, Anil. *Chinese Landscape Painting in the Caves of Dun Huang*. London: Methuen, 1964.

de Zoete, Beryl. *The Other Mind: A Study of Dance in South India*. London: Gollancz, 1953.

Delza, Sophie. *Body and Mind in Harmony. T'ai Chi Ch'uan: An Ancient Chinese Way of Exercise to Achieve Mental Health and Tranquillity*. New York: Cornerstone Library, 1973.

Dolby, William. *A History of Chinese Drama*. London: Paul Elek, 1976.

Douglas, Mary. *Purity and Danger: An Analysis of Concepts of Pollution and Taboo*. London: Routledge & Kegan Paul, 1966.

----------. 'The Social Control of Cognition: Some Factors in Joke Perception' in *Man, Journal of the Royal Anthropological Institute*, III, No. 3. London: Royal Anthropological Institute, 1968.

Dunn, Charles J. *The Early Japanese Puppet Drama*. London: Luzac, 1966.

----------. & Torigoe, Bunzô. trs. and eds. *The Actors' Analects* (Yakusha Rongo). New York: Columbia University Press, 1969.

Eliade, Mircea. *Shamanism*. New York: Arkana Press, 1989.

Feldman, Eric A. *The Ritual of Rights in Japan*. Cambridge: Cambridge University Press, 2000.

Feng, Gia-fu. *Tai Chi – A Way of Centering and I Ching*. London: Collier-Macmillan, 1970.

Foster, Roy. *W.B. Yeats: A Life. The Apprentice Mage, 1865–1914*. Oxford: Oxford University Press, 1997.

Gerstle, C. Andrew. *Circles of Fantasy: Convention in the Plays of Chikamatsu*. Cambridge, Massachusetts: Harvard University Press, 1986.

----------. *18th Century Japan: Culture and Society*. First Published in 1989 by Allen & Unwin Australia Pty Ltd, Richmond, Surrey: Curzon Press, 2000.

----------. 'Heroic Honor: Chikamatsu and the Samurai Ideal' in *Harvard Journal of Asiatic Studies*, Vol 57: No. 2 (December 1997).

----------. 'The Tragic Hero in Japanese Traditional Popular Drama' in *Paolo Beonio – Brocchieri Memorial Lectures in Japanese Studies*, Venice: Università da Foscari di Venezia, 1996.

Ginsburg, Henry. 'The Manora Dance Drama: An Introduction' in *Journal of the Siam Society*, LX, Part 2 (July, 1972).

Graham, Masako. *The Yang Kuei Fei Legend in Japanese Literature*. New York: Edwin Mellen Press Ltd., 1998.

Granet, Marcel. *The Religion of the Chinese People*. tr. Maurice Freedman. Oxford: Oxford University Press, 1975.

Haindan, H. *Tun Kudu*. Kuala Lumpur: Pusta Antara, 1967.

----------. *Tun Fatimah: Sri Kandi, Melaka*. Kuala Lumpur: Syarikat Buku Uni-Text, 1977.

Halifax, Joan. *Shaman: The Wounded Healer*. London: Thames & Hudson, 1982.

Hall, Edwin. *The Arnolfini Betrothal*. California: University of California Press, 1994.
Hall, John et al. *The Cambridge History of Japan*. Vols. 3 & 4. *Medieval Japan and Early Modern Japan*. Cambridge: Cambridge University Press, 1990 & 1991.
Hanawa, Hokinoichi. ed. *Munenaga Shuki* ("The Handbook of Munenaga") in 2 vols. In *Gunsho ruijû* ("Complete Collection of Japanese Literary Works"), Vol. 326, Nikki-bu 7. Tokyo: Ono Gakkai, 1986.
----------. *Karaishi-ki* ("Account of Karaishi"). In *Gunsho ruijû* ("Complete Collection of Japanese Literary Works"). Vol. 9, 1928.
Harper, Donald. 'The Sexual Arts of Ancient China' in *Harvard Journal of Asiatic Studies*. Vol. 47, No. 2. Cambridge, Massachusetts, (December 1987).
Harris, Victor. tr. *The Book of Five Rings* by Musashi Miyamoto. London: Allison & Busby, 1974.
Hatto, A.T. 'The Swan Maiden: a Folk-Tale of North Eurasian Origin?' in *Bulletin of the School of Oriental and African Studies*. London: Luzac, 1961.
Heath, Sidney. *In the Steps of the Pilgrims*. London: Rich & Crown, 1953. (Originally published in 1911 as *Pilgrim Life in the Middle Ages*.)
Herbert, Jean. *Shinto: The Fountainhead of Japan*. New York: Stein & Day, 1967.
Hook, R.H. *Fantasy and Symbol: Studies in Anthropological Interpretation*. London, New York, San Francisco: Academic Press Inc. (London) Ltd., 1979.
Howard, Roger. *Contemporary Chinese Theatre*. London: Heinemann, 1978.
Hsu, Tao-ching. *The Chinese Conception of Theatre*. Seattle: University of Washington Press, 1985.
Hughes, E.R. ed.and tr. *Chinese Philosophy in Classical Times*. London, Melbourne and Toronto: Dent, 1982.
Hung, Sheng. *The Palace of Eternal Youth*. trs. Yang Hsien-yi and Gladys Yang. Peking: Foreign Language Press, 1955.
Hurlimann & Francis King. *Japan*. London: Thames & Hudson, 1970.
Ishida, Mosaku. *Jôrurihime no Koseki to densetu* ("The Memorials and Legends of Lady Jôruri"). Okazaki: Shibundo, September 1969.
Iyer, K. Baratha. *Kathakali: The Sacred Dance Drama of Malabar*. London: Luzac, 1935.
Jaini, Padmanabh S. 'The Story of Sudhana and Manohara: an Analysis of the Texts of the Borobudur Reliefs' in *Bulletin of the School of Oriental and African Studies*. London: Luzac, 1966.
Jeffrey, Ian et al. eds. *La France: Images of Woman and Ideas of A Nation, 1789–1989*. Uxbridge: Hillingdon Press, 1986.
Jurkowski, Henry K. *A History of European Puppets from its Origins to the End of the 19th Century*. Lewiston, Queenstown, Lampeter: Edwin Mellen Press Ltd., 1966.

Karim, Wazir Jahan. *Women and Culture: Between Malay Adat and Islam*. San Francisco, Oxford: Westview Press, 1992.
Kao, Ming. *The Lute*. (P'i-p'a chi). tr. Jean Mulligan. New York: Columbia University Press, 1980.
Keene, Donald. tr. *Major Plays of Chikamatsu*. New York: Columbia University Press, 1961.
----------. *The Battles of Coxinga*. London: Taylor's Foreign Press, 1951.
----------. tr. *Four Major Plays of Chikamatsu*. New York: Columbia University Press, 1998.
----------. *Nô and Bunraku: Two Forms of Japanese Theatre*. New York: Columbia University Press Morningside Edition, 1990.
----------. 'Fujimoto Kizan and the Great Mirror of Love' in *Appreciations of Japanese Culture*. Tokyo: Kodansha, 1971.
----------. *World Within Walls: Japanese Literature of the Pre-Modern Era, 1600–1867*. New York: Holt, Reinehart & Winston, 1976.
----------. ed. *Twenty Plays of the Nô Theatre*. New York: Columbia University Press, 1971.
Khokar, Mohan. *Traditions of Indian Classical Dance*. New Delhi: Clarion Books, 1979.
Kirby, E.T. *Ur-Drama: The Origins of Theatre*. New York: New York University Press, 1975.
Kitagawa, Hiroshi, & Bruce Tsuchida. trs. *The Tale of the Heike*. Tokyo: University of Tokyo Press, 1975.
Kitagawa, Joseph. *Religion in Japanese History*. New York and London: Columbia University Press, 1966.
Kiyota, Minoru. *Kendô: Its Philososphy, History and Means to Personal Growth*. London, New York: Kegan Paul International, 1995.
Kuroda, Toshio. 'Gukanshô and Jinno Shôtôki: Observations on Medieval Historiography' in *New Light on Early and Medieval Historiography*. Gainesville: University of Florida Monographs, Social Sciences. No. 4. Fall (1959).
Law, Jane Marie. *Puppets of Nostalgia: the Life, Death and Rebirth of the Japanese Awaji Ningyô Tradition*. Princeton, New Jersey: Princeton University Press, 1977.
Leeper, Janet. *Edward Gordon Craig*. Harmondsworth, Middlesex: Penguin Books Ltd., 1948.
Legge, James. *The Chinese Classics, vol. 1.: Confucian Analects, The Great Learning, The Doctrine of the Mean*. First edition, 1861. Hong Kong: Hong Kong University Press, 1960.
Levy, Howard S. *The Complete History of the Curious Erotic Custom of Footbinding in China*. New York: Prometheus Books, 1991.
Lévy, Jean. *The Emperor*. tr. Barbara Bray. London: Viking Press, 1988.
Li, Yu-ming. ed. *Chinese Women Through Chinese Eyes*. London: M.E. Sharpe, Inc., 1992.
Lindqvist, Cecilia. *China: Empire of the Written Symbol*. London: Harvill, 1991.

Liu, Da. *T'ai Chi Ch'uan and I Ching: A Choreography of Body and Mind.* London: Routledge and Kegan Paul, 1974.
Liu, Ruixiang. tr. *The Classic of Filial Piety.* (From *The Complete Works of Confucian Culture*). Shandong Friendship Press, 1991.
Mackenzie, Donald. ed. *China and Japan: Myths and Legends.* New York: Avenal Books, 1985.
Mackerras, Colin. *The Rise of the Peking Opera 1770–1870.* Oxford: Oxford University Press, 1972.
----------. *The Chinese Theatre in Modern Times: From 1840 to the Present Day.* London: Thames & Hudson, 1975.
----------. ed. *Chinese Theater: From its Origins to the Present Day.* Honolulu: University of Hawaii Press, 1983.
Mackintyre, Michael. *The Shogun Inheritance: Japan and the Legacy of the Samurai.* London: William Collins, Sons & Co., Ltd., 1981.
Magnin, Charles. *Histoire des Marionettes en Europe de l'antiquité a temps Moderne.* ("The History of European Marionettes from Ancient to Modern Times"). Paris 1862. Reprint Paris: Slatkine-Geneve, 1981.
Maisel, Edward. *Tai Chi for Health.* New York, Chicago, San Francisco: Holt, Reinehart and Winston, 1972.
Malkin, Michael, R. *Traditional and Folk Puppets of the World.* Cranbury, New Jersey: A.S. Barnes and Co., Inc., 1977.
Mass, Jeffrey P. *Court and Bakufu in Japan: Essays in Kamakura History.* New Haven & London: Yale University Press, 1982.
Matisoff, Susan. *The Legend of Semimaru: Blind Musician of Japan.* New York: Columbia University Press, 1978.
McClain, James L. *Kanazawa: A Seventeenth Century Japanese Castle Town.* New Haven & London: Yale University Press, 1982.
McCullough, Helen Craig. tr. *Yoshitsune: A Fifteenth Century Japanese Chronicle.* California: Stanford University Press, 1965.
Mills, Winnifred H. & Louise Dunn. *Marionettes, Masks and Shadows.* New York: Doubleday & Co., Inc., 1947.
Nakamura, Yasuo. *Noh: The Classical Theater.* New York & Tokyo: Walker & Weatherhill, 1971.
Nasrudin, Mohammad Ghouse. *Malay Dance.* Kuala Lumpur: Dewan Bahasa dan Tustaka, Kementerian Pendidikan Malaysia, 1995.
Nobori, Asaji. tr. *Kadensho: A Secret Book of Noh Art* by Zeami Motokiyo. Osaka: Union Services Co., 1975.
Obratsov, Sergei. *The Chinese Theatre.* London: Faber and Faber, 1961.
O'Neill, Patrick G. *Early Nô Drama: Its Background, Character and Development 1300–1450.* London: Lund Humphries, 1958.
Ortolani, Benito. *The Japanese Theatre: From Shamanistic Ritual to Contemporary Pluralism.* Princeton, New Jersey: Princeton University Press, 1995.
----------. and Samuel L. Leiter. eds. *Zeami and the Nô Theatre in the World.* New York: Castra Publication, 1998.

Pani, Jiwan. *Living Dolls: Story of Indian Puppets*. New Delhi: Publications Division, Ministry of Information and Broadcasting, Government of India, 1986.
Pischel, Richard. *The Home of the Puppet Play*. Hereford: Stephen Austin & Sons, 1900.
Plowright, Poh Sim. *The Classical Nô Theatre of Japan*. Cambridge: Chadwyck and Healey, 1991.
Po, Chui I. 'The Song of the Everlasting Sorrow' in Alan Ayling & Duncan Mackintosh, *A Further Collection of Chinese Lyrics*. London: Routledge, 1969.
Ponty, Merleau. *Phenomenology of Perception*. tr. Colin Smith. London: Routledge, 1989.
Pound, Erza. *The Classic Noh Theatre of Japan*. New York: New Directions, 1959.
Rangacharya, Adya. *The Indian Theatre*. New Delhi: National Book Trust, 1971.
Rimer, J. Thomas and Yamazki Masakazu. trs. *On the Art of the Nô Drama: The Major Treatises of Zeami*. Princeton, New Jersey: Princeton University Press, 1984.
Rosenberger, Nancy R. *Japanese Sense of Self*. Cambridge: Cambridge University Press, 1992.
Schechner, Richard. *Between Theater and Anthropology*. Pennsylvania: University of Pennsylvania Press, 1990.
Schipper, K.M. 'The Divine Jester, Some Remarks on the Gods of the Chinese Marionette Theater' in *Bulletin of the Institute of Ethnology*, 1966.
Scott, A.C. *The Puppet Theatre of Japan*. Tokyo: Charles Tuttle Co., 1963.
----------. tr. *Mei Lan Fang. The Life and Times of a Peking Actor*. Hong Kong: Hong Kong University Press, 1971.
----------. *The Theatre in Asia*. London: Weidenfeld & Nicolson, 1972.
Shingyo, Norikazu. *Jôruri Gozen Monogatari to Yahagi no han-mei* ("The Tales of Lady Jôruri and the Prosperity of Yahagi") in Chapter 2: 'Muromachi Feudal Government and Yahagi Area' in *The History of Okazaki City: Medieval Age*. Vol. 2. Okazaki: Okazaki City, March 1989.
Shivalingappa, Savitry. *Marionettes and their Role in Society*. Teheran: Asian Cultural Documentation Centre for UNESCO, 1975.
Shively, Donald, H. *The Love Suicide at Amijima (Shinju Ten no Amijima): A Study of a Japanese Domestic Tragedy by Chikamatsu Monzaemon*. Cambridge: Cambridge University Press, 1953.
----------. 'Tokugawa Plays on Forbidden Topics' in James Brandon, ed. *Chushingura: Studies in Kabuki and the Puppet Theatre*. Honolulu: University of Hawaii Press, 1982.
----------. & William H. McCullough. eds. *Cambridge History of Japan*. Heian Japan. Vol. 2. Cambridge: Cambridge University Press, 1999.
Sima, Qian. *Historical Records*. tr. Raymond Dawson. Oxford, New York: Oxford University Press, 1994.

Speaight, George. *The History of the English Puppet Theatre*. Second Edition. London: Robert Hale, 1990.
Stalberg, Roberta, Helmer. *China's Puppets*. San Francisco: China Books, 1984.
Storry, Richard. *The Way of the Samurai*. London: Orbis Books, 1978.
Sumiko, Iwao. *The Japanese Woman: Traditional Image and Changing Reality*. New York: The Free Press, A Division of Macmillan Inc., 1993.
Sunoo, Harold Hakwon. *China of Confucius: A Critical Interpretation*. Virginia Beach, VA: Heritage Research House, 1985.
Suzuki, D.T. *Essays in Zen Buddhism*. First, Second, Third Series. London: Rider & Co., 1950, 1953 and 1958.
---------. *Zen and Japanese Culture*. New York: Princeton University Press, 1959.
Suzuki, Jiro. *Talking about the Legend of Lady Jôruri*. Okazaki, Aichi, Mikawa Koron Ltd., 1968.
Takahashi, Shinji and Penny Tosui. trs. *Yakushiji: Head Temple of the Hosso Sect in Nara*. Tokyo: Asukaen Co., Ltd., 2000.
Takeda, Isamu. *Jôrurihime no kenkyû* ("A Study of Lady Jôruri") in *Bulletin of the Society for the Study of Okazaki Local History*. Vol. 3. Okazaki: Society for the Study of Okazaki Local History, 1974.
Takuan, Sôhô. *The Unfettered Mind*. tr. William Scott Wilson. Tokyo, New York & San Francisco, Kodansha International, 1986.
Tanizaki, Jun'ichirô. *Some Prefer Nettles*. tr. Edward G. Seidensticker. New York: G.P. Putnam's Sons, 1929.
Taylor, A.E. tr. *Plato, The Laws*. Book 1. London: J.M. Dent & Sons Ltd., 1969.
Thornbury, Barbara. *Folk Performing Arts: Traditional Culture in Contemporary Japan*. New York: State University of New York Press, 1997.
Tillkasiri, J. *The Puppet Theatre of Asia*. Ceylon: Department of Cultural Affairs, 1969.
Totman, Conrad. *Tokugawa Ieyasu Shogun*. California: Heian International Inc., 1983.
Tsuneyoshi, Matsuno. *Wives of the Samurai. Their Eventful Lives Under the Period of Civil Wars*. New York, Los Angeles, Chicago: Vantage Press, 1989.
Tsuruo, Ando. *Bunraku: The Puppet Theatre*. New York & Tokyo: Walker & Weatherhill, 1970.
Turner, Victor. *Dramas, Fields and Metaphysics: Symbolic Action in Human Society*. Ithaca: Cornell University Press, 1974.
Umewaka, Naohiko. 'The Inner World of the Nô: The Influence of Ritual and Metaphysics on the Choreography of the Nô Theatre' in *Contemporary Theatre Review*, vol.1. London: Harwood Academic Publishers 1992.
van der Loon, Piet. *The Classical Theatre and Art Song of South Fukien*. Taipei: SMC Publishing, 1992.
----------. 'Les origines rituelles du théâtre chinois' in *Journal Asiatique*. Paris: Asiatique Societé, 1997.
Varadpande, M.L. *Invitation to Indian Theatre*. New Delhi: Arnold Heinemann Publishers India Ltd., 1987.

von Boehn, Max. *Dolls and Puppets*. tr. Josephine Nicoll. London: George G. Harrap & Co., Ltd., 1932.
von Kleist, Heinrich. 'On the Marionette Theatre' in Idris Parry, ed. *Hand to Mouth and Other Essays*. Manchester: Carcanet New Press, 1981.
Waley, Arthur. tr. *The Nine Songs: A Study of Shamanism in Ancient China*. London: George Allen & Unwin Ltd., 1955.
----------. tr. *The Nô Plays of Japan*. London: George Allen & Unwin Ltd., 1921.
----------. tr. *The Analects of Confucius*. London: George Allen & Unwin Ltd., 1938.
----------. *The Way and its Power: The Tao Te Ching and its place in Chinese Thought*. London: Unwin Hyman Ltd., 1987.
----------. tr. *Ballads and Stories from Tun-huang*. London: George Allen & Unwin Ltd., 1960.
----------. tr. *The Tale of Genji* by Lady Murasaki. London: George Allen & Unwin Ltd., 1973.
Wang, C.H. *From Ritual to Allegory: Seven Essays in Early Chinese Poetry*. Hong Kong: Chinese University Press, 1988.
Wilhelm, Richard. tr. *The I Ching: or "Book of Changes"*. Series XIX. Princeton, New Jersey: Princeton University Press 1951.
Willet, John. ed.& tr 'Alienation Effects in Chinese Acting' in *Brecht on Theatre*. London: Metheun, 1964.
Willis, Roy. ed. *World Mythology*. London: Simon and Schuster, 1993.
Wilson, William Scott. tr. *The Unfettered Mind, Takuan Sôhô. Writings of the Zen Master to the Sword Master*. Tokyo, New York and San Francisco: Kodansha International, 1986.
Winstedt, Richard. 'Indian Influence in the Malay World' in *Journal of the Royal Asiatic Society*, Parts 3–4, 1944.
Wu, Jie Chiu. *Li-yuan yu li-yuan hsi hsi-lun ("The Origin of the Pear Garden: An Examination of the Pear Garden Theatre")*. Fuzhou: Fujian Theatrical Research Institute, 1985.
Yang, Hsien-yi & Gladys Yang. trs. *Love Under Willows* or *Liang Shan Po and Chu Ying Tai*. Peking: Foreign Language Press, 1956.
Yasuda, Kenneth K. 'The Structure of "Hagoromo" a Nô Play' in *Harvard Journal of Asiatic Studies*, 33:5–89 (1973).
Yousof, Ghulam, Sawar. *Panggung Semar: Aspects of Traditional Malay Theatre*. Petaling Jaya: Tempo Publishing, 1992.
----------. *Dictionary of Traditional South-East Asian Theatre*. Kuala Lumpur: Oxford University Press, 1994.
Zucker, A.E. *The Chinese Theatre*. Boston: Little, Brown, 1925.

Index

Adat 19
Aichi 88, 91
akusho (bad places) 114
Amateratsu 134
Amida no munekiri 125
Amida no munewari 125
ang 47, *ang i* 67
Ankia Nat 170
Arjuna 17
Aryans 163
ashi-tsukai 133
asobi 111, *asobime* 112
Asuras ('unfriendly gods') 32
At the Hawk's Well 6, 35–6
Awaji Island 138
Awashima Jinja shrine 129
Ayuthaya 9

Babylonians 163–4
Baika Mujinzô 124
bai noi (mask) 30
bakufu 114
'Baldy Guo' 47, 210
balian 26
Banri Shûku 124
Bendahara 17–19
Brecht, Bertolt 55–7
Bharata 161
bhats 161
Bhudapati 164
biwa hôshi 87
bodaiji 96
Bodidharma 171, 201
bomoh 22–3
brothels 114
Buddhism 105–108
Bunraku-ken, Uemura 85

Callias 215
Chalawan ('crocodile') 31

Charles V (Holy Roman Emperor) 230
Ch'en San Wu Niang 54
Chih Chi Liang 130
Chirikuburo ('Bag of Dust') 100
chôja ('manager of a prostitute establishment') 93
chôja no musume ('daughter of a chôja') 99
chônin 112
Chu Mu Wang 191
Church of St. James at Dieppe 212
Circe-like 99
citta 172–3
Coghill, George 79
Confucius 76
Copeau, Jacques 225
Council of Trent (1550–64) 212
Craig, Edward Gordon 222–4
Craigische Vorstellung 223
cukur rambut ('shaving the hair') 29

Daimon ('Big Gate') 94
dalang ('shadow puppet master') 170
Dao ('Way') 115
daomadan ('woman warrior') 44
Daughter of Ki-no-Aritsune 186
Decroux, Etienne 225–6
Deipnosophists 210
Devas ('friendly gods') 32
Devereux, George 235
Dhanvantari ('Divine Physician') 32
Dickens, Charles 218
Dôjôji 178
Dokumbo 139
Dotombori 121
Dravidians 163–4
'Dual Powers' 72
Duke of Chou 63

Dunn, Charles 91, 124 et passim
Duse, Elenora 218, 222

Ebisu 139
ebisu-kaki 100
Eisai (Rinzai Zen Priest) 171
'elixir of life' 32
Emperor Nintoku 118
Emperor Ojin 118
Emperor Temmu 108
Empress Jingo 129
Empress Jito 108
Empress Suiko 106
empu 'magical power' 11
Erh Ji ('The Two Breaths') 72

Fangxiangshi 193
Fathers of the Church 211
Fenollosa, Ernest 138
Flamenca 215
Freud, Sigmund 235
Frisch (Lexicographer) 209
'front seat' 34
Fugan (Hogan) temple 184
Fujimoto, Kizan 110, 112–15
Fu Mu Lan 44
furyû 135

Gakkô 86
Ganlujie 43
Gelangang Seni 23, 24
Genji Monogatari ('The Tale of Genji') 33
Gettan Sôkô 171
Giô 88, 104
Gion 120
giri 85, 132
Goethe 218
Gokuraku 119
Goldoni 218
gombe 166
Goô no hime 125, 127
Grand Buddha Hall 1, 43

Hachiman 90
Hagoromo 2, 33, 35, 236
Hans Wurst 216
Harappa 161
Hayashi, Razan 120
he he shen ('god of union') 53
'Heart sûtra' 180
'Heavenly Cowherd and the Weaving Maiden' 45
Heike Monogatari ('The Tale of Heike') 87, 99
Hekigan-shu ('Blue rock collection') 171
Herodotus 164
hidarite-tsukai 133
Hideyori 122
Hideyoshi, Toyotomi 113, 120
Hiei (Mt.) 96
Higurashi Kodayu 128
Hikayat 13, 18
Hime Kuyôtô 92
Himmelreich ('Kingdom of Heaven') 210, 221
Hitta 125
Hôgan-dono 88
hôgan biiki 123
Hokekyô ('Lotus Sûtra') 93
Hôraiji 88
Hotoke Gozen 104
hotoke-mawashi 100
Hsu Hsuan-ping 83
Hung Sheng 5, 47

Ichimura, Rokunojo 138
I-ching (definition) 63
Ikkyû (Rinzai Zen monk) 180, 203 (note 54)
Indus Valley 162–3
Ishimpô 111, 115

Jacob and the Angel 2
'jade flute' 53
'jade girl' 53

Index

Jakô Dsuka 92
Jakô Ike 92
jamu and *majun* 21
jataka (definition) 39
Johnson, Samuel 217
Jô 86
Jôjuin 92
jôruri (meaning) 86, 124
Jôruri ga Fuchi 92
Jôruri-ji Temple (Kamo-cho, Kyoto) 103
Jûgoya 89
Jûgoya no haka 93

Kada, Wakayama 129
kaimami 147
kairaishi 100
Kai Yuan 1, 43
ka le hi 45
Kamo (River) 119
kampongs 19
Kanetaka Chôja 93, 97–8
Kanze Hisao 187–91
Kao Ming Kuan 78
karana 167
Karagoz 215
Karim, Wahir Jahan 20
Kasperle 216
katazuke 181, 182
Kathakali 166
kawamono (river bed people) 130
Kenreimon-in 88
kenshenteki (self sacrifice) 119, 127, 156 (note 120)
Kerala 165
khlong hong 30
Kinnari 11, 40
Kiyomori 88
Kobori Enshu 137
kokoro 182
Kômyôin 93
Konkomyôkyô ('Sûtra of the Golden Light') 106
Konparu Zenho 183
Koya (Mt.) 96

ko-zatô (a blind performer) 125
Kraithong ('The hero who slays the crocodile') 31
k'uang (basket) 102
Kuchipudi 170
kuei lei hsi 45
kugu 102
kugutsu 100, 102
kuro-honzon (formerly *krosonbutsu*) 95
kutilaka 170
Kyûi 180

La Barre, Weston 2
La Grille (French theatre director) 214
lawan 21
Lecoq, Jacques 225
Legong (Balinese) 7
li ('propriety') 118
Li Yuan Hsi ('Pear Garden Theatre') 53, 197–8
lotus 28
Love Suicides at Sonezaki 132
Luo diagram 74
Luther, Martin 211

Mahabharata 50, 165
Mahashivarati (Festival) 165
Mahayana ('Buddhism of the Greater Vehicle') 107
marabito 107
Maria di Ligno 208
marionette (definition) 207–209
marotte (associated with *morio*) 209
Marshal Tian 51–4
Matsuwaka 126
Matsukaze 179
'Medicine Master' 86
Mei Lan Fang 55–7, 78
Melaka (Malacca) 16
melawan 21
Meng (Jester) 210
Menukiya Chôzaburô 125
Mesi Mala 11

Mesopotamia 163
'middle seat' 34
Midsummer Night's Dream, A 162, 207
Mikawa 88
military strategy 76
Minamoto 88
Minamoto, Yoshitsune 88
Misokasu Iwa 94
Misuji-machi 113
Miyamoto, Musashi 183
mizushobai ('water trade') 130
muga 173
Murasaki Iwa Ishi ('Purple Rock Stone') 93
myô, myôkafu 180
'Mysteries of Mid August' 212

Nagasamu, Asai 122
Nakhon Sri Thammarat 3
Nang Talung 16
Nataraja (Temple of) 167
Natyashastra 166, 168
Ngadju Dyaks 26
Niessen, Carl 219
Nihonshoki 105
Nikkô 86
ningyô jôruri or *jôruri ningyô* 85–145 passim
ninjô 132
Ninnôkyô ('Benevolent King's Sûtra') 106
Nishinomiya 119
Nobunaga, Oda 108–10
Nôgô village 136
Nora Toem, Nora Wan 13
Nuensamli (princess) 11

Ôe Masafusa 101
Oichi, no Kata 122
Okazaki castle 94, 144
Okiku 122
Okuni 85, 119
omo-tsukai 133
On-zôshi 88

Onna Daigaku ('The Great Learning for Women') 134
Ono, no Komachi 104
Ono, no O-Tsû 108–10, 143
Origu Shinobu 101
Osiris 164
Otogawa (River) 94, 129
o-togi-zôshi 144
Otozuru 85
Oyudono no ue 100

Panggung 38
Parvati 161, 165
Peeping Tom 88
Pejabat Agama Islam 20
Peng Lai Shan 3
Pepys, Samuel 217
perempuan 11
Phran Bun (clown) 12
Pischel, Richard 227
Plato 226
Podrecca, Vittorio (puppeteer) 218
Polichinelle, Punchinello, Mr. Punch 217
Potheimos 211
Pound, Ezra 138
Powell, Charles (puppeteer) 217
Prince Genji 89
prostitute 113
puja 161
Pulchinella 215
puppet (*pupa*) 170, 207
'Purification Doll Festival' 86
puttalika 170

Quanzhou 1, 43, 52, 194
Qu'ranic (Koranic) Verses 22

Rahu 32
Raja Iskanda Shah 38 (note 9)
Rajasthan 161–2
Rama 165
Ramayana 165
Rashômon (Nô play) 137
Ravana 165

Reinhardt, Max 233
Reisei-ji 92
Ridgeway, William 227–8
Riken no ken ('Detached Eye') 179
ruri 86
Rurikô 86
Ryûkyû islands 99

Sacrifice 116, 118
Sadafusa (father of Emperor Go-Hanazono) 100
sai hu (puppet master) 51
Sand, George 217
Sanemori 182
Sanko kikagi 125
Santa Maria della Salute 208
sarugaku 151 (note 42)
Sarugaku Dangi ('Reflections on Art') 184
Savonarola, Giralomo 211
Sattva, Rajas, Tamas ('The three divine control strings') 169
scapegoat 68
Seeau, Count 216
Seiganji 93
sekkyôbushi 127–8
Senbon Toba 93
Senyumaru (son of Lady Jôruri and Yoshitsune) 149 (note 30)
Senhime 122
seppuku ('ritual suicide') 129
Seri Kandi 17
Settsu Nishinomiya 139
Sevakram 159
shamaness 15
Shaw, George Bernard 207, 218
Shibata Katsuie 122
Shimbara 113, 120
Shingyo Norikazu 97
Shin sarugaku-ki ('New account of *sarugaku*') 99
Shintoism 106
shite (main actor) 33 et passim
Shiva 16, 164–7, 179

Shao-lin 83 (note 34)
Shih Ching ('Book of Odes') 102
Shikidô Ôkagami 110, 114–15
Shizuka, Lady 111
Sho Kannon ('Goddess of Mercy') 94
shosaki (front of stage) 182
Shôtoku (Prince) 106
silat 18, 23
Sima, Qian 63
Sleeping Beauty 89
Sôchô 111, 124–5
Soga clan 105
Sô-kokubunji ('The Chief Temple') 106
Sonezaki Shinjû 132
'Son of Heaven' 64
soota ('measuring string') 167–8
Sophocles 210
Stanislavsky 218
sunyata ('emptiness') 173
Suthon 10
szupka 212

T'ai Chi Ch'uan 69–81
Taira (Family) 88
Takano, Shigeyoshi 175
Takasago 136
Takayama Matsuri 135
Takeda Isamu 95
Takisanji 94, 235
Takuan, Soho 174
Tale of Genji 89
Tanabe, Hisao 98
tandava 166
Tanizaki, Jun'ichiro 177
tayû 112, 120
tekugutsu ('puppet manipulators') 100
tengu ('goblins') 90
Tenju, Lady 126
Tethered Steed and the Eight Provinces of Kantô 131
thaeng khe ('stabbing the crocodile') 31

'Third Eye' 179
t'ien kang ('celestial evil influences') 194
Tien Kun Lun 3
Tokugawa, Ieyasu 95–6, 144
Tom Fool 223
Torriani, Giovanni 230
Tozai 85, 141
trimurti 162
Tung Yai 29
Tzu (River) 130

Uemura, Bunraku-ken 85
Umewaka, Minoru 138
Umewaka, Naohiko 203
Ushiwaka 125
Ushiwaka-marû-junidan 125
Usuzume (Yoshitsune's flute) 93

Vajrachedika ('The Diamond Sûtra') 172
Valkyries 2, 39
Verfremdungseffekte 55, 56
Vieux-Colombier 225
Virgin Mary 208
Vishnu 32
Von Boehn, Max 218 et passim
Von Hofmannsthal, Hugo 221
Von Kleist, Heinrich 1, 7, 219–21

Wang (puppets, mediums) (see also *ang*) 47, 68

Wen, King 63
wu-hsin 172
Wu, Jie Chiu 234

Xian (current name for Chang-an) 63
Xianggong yeh (Reverend Lord Minister) 69, 71, 194, 197

Yagyû Tajima no Kami 174–5
Yahagi 88, 94, 95
Yakushiji 1
Yakushi-rurikô-nyorai 86
Yamashina Tokitsugu 125
Yanagimachi 113
yang 45
yang sheng ('nurturing life') 111
Yang Shih 65, 67, 191
Yeats, William Butler 35–6, 224
yin 45
Yodo 117
Yoritomo 94
Yoroboshi 182
Yoshinoe (daughter of Lady Jôruri and Yoshitsune) 149 (note 30)
Yûgao (Lady) 89
yujô ('bath girl') 112

Zatô 125
Zenchiku (Zeami's son-in-law) 184
Zhuang Zi 81, 176
Zôjôji 95

MELLEN STUDIES IN PUPPETRY

1. Grace Greenleaf Ransome (compiler), **Puppets and Shadows: A Bibliography**
2. Paul McPharlin, **A Repertory of Marionette Plays**
3. Keith Owen Tribble (ed.), **Marionette Theater of Symbolist Era**
4. Poh Sim Plowright, **Mediums, Puppets, and the Human Actor in the Theatres of the East**